THE CAVENDISH Q & A SERIES

JURISPRUDENCE

L B Curzon
Barrister

Cavendish
Publishing
Limited

First published in Great Britain 1992 by Cavendish Publishing Limited, 23A Countess Road, London NW5 2XH.

Telephone: 071-485 0303   Facsimile: 071-485 0304

British Library Cataloguing in Publication Data

Curzon, L B
Jurisprudence - (Q & A Series)
I Title II Series
340.1

ISBN 1-874241-23-6

Printed and bound in Great Britain

Contents

Introduction

This collection of Questions and Answers has as its objective the provision of structured material designed to assist students preparing for first examinations in Jurisprudence. The mode of presentation adopted involves the setting of a question of the type usually asked in examinations of this nature, and the providing of an appropriate answer. The answers are not to be considered as 'model answers'; they are intended specifically as illustrations of the type of answer required, with particular reference to content and structure.

The format is as follows:

Introduction to chapter. This indicates the subject-matter to be covered by the questions.

Checklist. The relevant jurisprudential concepts to be tested are noted. They should be learned or revised carefully before the answer presented is considered.

Question. The rubric and its specific demands should be studied carefully. 'Comment', 'Critically examine', 'Outline', are not interchangeable terms; each requires its own pattern of answering.

Answer plan. This indicates the approach which is taken to the question and suggests a skeleton plan which is followed. Students should consider the advisability of planning an answer in this form; the production of a skeleton plan is a useful method of arranging content.

Answer. Content and structure are of major significance and ought to be noted carefully.

Notes. Details of suggested reading are given under this heading. Students who require some guidance in the choice of reading material might consider the following texts: Harris' *Legal Philosophies*; Lloyd's *Introduction to Jurisprudence*; Hart's *The Concept of Law*; Dworkin's *Law's Empire*; Davies and Holdcroft's *Jurisprudence - Texts and Commentary*. Useful adjunctive material may be found in Kelly's *A Short History of Western Legal Theory*; *The Western Idea of Law*, edited by Smith and Weisstrub; *Philosophy of Law*, edited by Feinberg and Gross.

L B Curzon
November 1992

Table of Cases

Table of Cases

Table of Statutes

Chapter 1

General Aspects of Jurisprudence

Introduction

Questions in this chapter deal with some typical introductory topics which are related to the general framework of jurisprudence. The nature of the subject-area, problems of classification of the 'schools' of thought, are of particular significance. Questions of verbal analysis - prominent in a subject of this nature - and the place of logic in our law are touched on. The 'open-ended' type of question is appropriate to this area of the syllabus.

Checklist

Ensure that you are acquainted with the following topics:

- definitions of jurisprudence
- general scope of the study
- the problem of 'definition'
- essence of classification
- 'movements' in jurisprudence
- essence of verbal analysis
- meaning of 'communication'
- logical positivism
- induction and deduction
- definition of 'logic'
- the syllogism

Question 1

'For those who study jurisprudence today, it is nothing but a troubling mass of conflicting ideas': Arnold.

Why, then, study the subject?

Answer plan

The question is an invitation to argue on the positive features of jurisprudence in reply to Arnold's dismissive comment. A discussion of those features is required, together with comment on reasons for the undoubted (but not unwelcome) conflict of ideas. A skeleton plan might take the following form:

Introduction - acknowledgement of conflict of ideas in jurisprudence - positive features of a study of the subject - why criticisms have arisen - conclusion on the role jurisprudence has to play.

Answer

It is necessary, initially, to comment briefly on Arnold's statement by noting what seems to be a highly-subjective reaction to the undoubted ferment of opinions, principles and ideologies characterising contemporary jurisprudence. It may be that the emergence of a jurisprudential tradition of questioning everything, of accepting no 'self-evident' principles, of 'debunking' ideas which have held sway for decades, creates an impression of a nihilism triumphant. Arnold's use of pejorative terms, such as 'troubling', 'conflicting', may indicate a lack of awareness of the value of a continuous probing of 'received knowledge'. So it is in physics (in which the recent appearance of 'chaos theory' demands a rethinking of traditional concepts), in economics (in which not only traditional theories but the very reasoning processes that produced them are under attack), and in linguistics (in which the works of the 'founding fathers', such as Chomsky, are under intensive criticism). And so it is in jurisprudence where, for example, the American Critical Legal Studies movement is engaged in a radical reappraisal of the objectives and methodology of legal studies. The continuous flux in the evolution and enunciation of legal theories must, by its nature, give rise to conflict, which observers, such as Arnold, find 'troubling'. The alternative to a conflict of ideas can be a lack of vitality or a sterility which vitiates intellectual progress in jurisprudence.

One must be aware, however, that a study of jurisprudence has not been considered an essential component of the education and training programmes of large numbers of lawyers. Concentration by some jurists on the highly-abstract, to the exclusion of the severely practical concerns of the law, may have contributed to a dislike of the subject and a rejection of its pretensions. Posner's condemnation of much recent jurisprudence as 'much too solemn and self-important' and of its votaries as writing 'too marmoreal, hieratic, and censorious a prose' is worthy of note.

Much of the true value of jurisprudence resides elsewhere than in the practical applications of the law. It is claimed that its study provides a discipline of thought which seeks not to ignore the realities of legal practice, but rather to give added dimension to an understanding of that practice. Jurisprudence offers an overall view of the law, a unified picture, in which the nature of legal institutions and theories becomes more comprehensible. Austin viewed jurisprudence as providing a 'map' of the law which presents it as 'a system or organic whole'.

Some legal scholars and students have found a major attraction of jurisprudence to be its intrinsic interest, which emerges from the importance of the questions with which it deals. 'What are human rights?' 'Are there any absolute values in the law?' 'What is justice?' These problems exemplify matters which have been raised over the centuries by philosophers and jurists. Not only the content of the law and the administration of legal institutions, but the basis of society itself, have been affected by attempts to answer questions of this nature. They are of abiding human interest.

The intellectual discipline required for a study of this area of thought must be of a high order. Intensive, systematic analysis, the ability to exercise one's critical faculties, and to engage in a questioning of one's own basic assumptions - all can be heightened by a study of jurisprudence. The intellectual skills required to see into the essence of current arguments which turn on 'the right to silence', 'the value of the jury', 'the presumption of innocence', can be sharpened by a consideration of legal theorising.

The study of jurisprudence should enlarge one's perception of the patterns of fact and thought from which today's legal structures have emerged. Specifically, awareness of the evolution of legal thought provides a key to an understanding of *change* as a basic phenomenon of the law. It is the continuous shifting of views and the transformation of social institutions which tend to be reflected in jurisprudence - and which give rise to the deep conflicts which trouble observers such as Arnold. The ability to perceive a process of change beneath the apparently static processes of the law should be intensified by jurisprudential analysis. It is of interest to note the recognition of change which emerged in the decision of the House of Lords in *Alcock and Others v Chief Constable of S Yorks Police* (1991) and in which could be discerned a modification of views concerning nervous shock and tort - an area in which there has been much jurisprudential speculation and debate. The War Crimes Act 1991 was preceded by debates which turned on important aspects of legal theory, such as changing social attitudes towards crime, punishment, and retribution. A shift of emphasis in the role of forseeability and intent in assault, which has formed the basis of much recent jurisprudential debate was evident in the decision of the House of Lords in *R v Savage* (1991). Perception of the law as an aspect of a changing social environment characterises much contemporary juristic thinking.

Additionally, awareness of change and its reflection in legal theory, may enable jurists to note, and perhaps warn against, the invisible, unacknowledged, yet extremely potent influence of 'defunct scribblers' who continue to affect the thoughts and the activities of those 'practical persons' who have 'no time for theorising'. Jurists and philosophers have pointed out the significance of the paradox that those who affect to reject theory are, effectively, embracing it. The statement, 'I don't need any theory to tell me that violence can be met only by a law which sanctions counter-violence', is, in fact, the expression of a basic, complex theory. The belief, 'You haven't to be a theoretician to know that the law has no place in family relationships', implies acceptance of a profound analysis of functions of law. A study of the growth and social context of legal theory makes clear the relationship of theory and practice, the one modifying the other.

The very wide range of contemporary jurisprudence has enlarged its relevance and interest. The days when legal theory was equated with an implied rejection of the significance of 'problems of the real world' have gone. The figure of the jurist as a recluse, uninterested in law in action, is seen as a caricature. Modern jurists include many who demonstrate a profound concern for social justice and communal harmony - this is obvious in the writings of contemporary American legal theoreticians. Dworkin, for example, argues cogently that the real purpose of the law can be found in the aim of ensuring that a community acts towards *all* its members in a 'coherent, principled fashion'. Rawls proposes a public conception of justice which must constitute the fundamental character of any well-ordered human association.

Nozick lays stress on the importance of using principles of justice so as to clarify problems inherent in the holding and transferring of society's resources. It may be that a pattern of concern is emerging in which the responsibilities of the law, its theoreticians and practitioners, are clearly emphasised, a pattern which is in clear contrast to the implications of Arnold's perception of a 'chaotic' jurisprudence.

Where jurists survey the established socio-legal order, the result is often of significance for students of the law who are a part of that order, and whose perceptions of law as an instrument of social policy are thereby challenged. One type of perception relates generally to the relationship between jurisprudence and other disciplines. Because modern jurisprudence ranges very widely over society and because it builds some of its theoretical framework on material derived from contact with other disciplines, students are brought to an awareness of the interdependence of *all* social studies and to acceptance of the complex nature of their own place within the social framework - a positive achievement which belies the negative nature of Arnold's comment.

The role of the lawyer within our society - and it is that to which many law students aspire - is the subject of continuing analysis by jurists, with the result that the very rationale of the legal profession in the Western world has become a matter of debate and can no longer be taken for granted - a valuable event in itself. Thus, Luban has investigated facets of the role of the lawyer as 'partisan advocate' - a creature of the common law adversarial system. He believes that the standard view of the role of the lawyer, based on principles of 'partnership and non-accountability' in some respects, may no longer be acceptable to society save in a highly-qualified form. He calls for a more intensive debate on professional ethics as they relate to the individual conscience and socio-legal institutions. D'Amato, in a novel analysis of the law and its institutions, suggests that the lawyer acts as a 'broker of the conspiracy at the centre of the legal system' - a conspiracy between citizens and legal institutions, each acting within defined areas so as to maximise power. Jurisprudential analysis of this nature is thought-provoking and valuable.

Perhaps the most important product of a study of jurisprudence could be an enhanced ability to discern the shape of legal things to come, albeit in shadowy and inchoate form. The attitudes of today's legal theoreticians in relation to matters such as *mens rea*, causation, the concept of economic loss in tort, the basis of property rights, and the nature of parental responsibility, might mark tomorrow's ideologies and legal structures. A study of the modes of thought of contemporary jurists cannot but be advantageous to those who have an interest in the future of society and the law.

None of these comments should be taken as denying the existence of trivial, often worthless, theorising in the name of jurisprudence. Feinberg's objections to 'portentous and hoary figures from the past' being paraded, each with an odd vocabulary, and a host of dogmatic assertions, to the confusion of students, are not to be ignored. These objections add weight to Arnold's complaint. But interest in the past for its own sake has little appeal to lawyers or students. *'Jurisprudence for its own sake'* is now a meaningless slogan. Jurisprudence has changed its objectives and its methodology. The search for justice in human relationships, the search for certainty in the law and the continuous probing of the role of the state in the recognition and promulgation of human rights are rarely absent from legal theorising. The result is a challenging of entrenched positions and a questioning of the hitherto unquestionable. This is, indeed, a sign of 'conflict'; but it is also a sign of vitality.

When Stone wrote of the science of jurisprudence as 'the lawyer's extraversion ... the light derived from present knowledge in disciplines other than the law', he acknowledged the structure of legal theory as being linked totally with knowledge in general, thus proclaiming the relevance of jurisprudence to life in general and law in particular.

In that sense a study of jurisprudence can be valuable in that it ensures perceptions of the law in the setting of a comprehensible, changing world. At times these perceptions will appear, in Arnold's words, as 'a troubling mass of conflicting ideas', chaotic and often contradictory. But this is not necessarily a negative state of affairs, for it is in the attempted resolution of apparent contradictions that the study of jurisprudence is advanced.

Notes

Valuable material concerning this question may be found in
Lloyd, *Introduction to Jurisprudence*, ch 1; Dias, *Jurisprudence*, ch 1,
and Posner, *The Problems of Jurisprudence*. Luban's *Lawyers and
Justice* is stimulating; D'Amato's *Jurisprudence, a Descriptive and
Normative Analysis of Law* contains introductory chapters of
unusual interest. Lord Goff's 'The Search for Principle' in
Proceedings of the British Academy (1983) contains critical
observations concerning jurisprudence.

Question 2

Is there any value to be derived from attempts to define 'jurisprudence'?

Answer plan

The general difficulties involved in definition, as outlined by
Popper, should be mentioned. The specific problem, related to
jurisprudence, arises from the difficulty of attempting a formal
definition. The process of defining a term should be mentioned
and attention drawn to the advantages emerging from the effort
to define. It is of importance to refer to some of the many
'authoritative' definitions. A skeleton plan on the following lines
is suggested.

Introduction - note the essence of the problem and indicate
the value of a search for a definition - basic difficulty of
defining 'by characteristics' - consideration of some
definitions - advantages of pursuing a search - objections to
the process - conclusion on the positive nature of
attempting to define.

Answer

Attempts to define jurisprudence are made by jurists for whom
the delineation of its proper subject matter is seen as a
fundamental task, and by teachers and students anxious to
recognise, even in imprecise terms, the range and boundaries of
their subject area. Jurists are aware of the problems inherent in

the technique of defining terms; students may be confronted, at an early stage of their quest, by warnings as to the 'misguided and misleading' nature of the search for definitions. Our comments concerning the value of attempts to define will note the difficulties of the process, but will stress the arguments of those who assume that the nature of jurisprudence is knowable and amenable to precise description, or definition. It will emphasise the value to be derived from exploring those paths which might lead to an acceptable definition.

By 'definition' we have in mind a precise enunciation of the principal characteristics of the defined object which will allow it to be distinguished from other objects. It will mark out boundaries, or other limits, thus enabling us to state with a high degree of accuracy that, for example, 'a tort is ...', 'possession means ...', 'a contract comes into existence when ...'. There are, however, basic problems involved in the process of defining 'by characteristics'. Popper, the philosopher of scientific method, rejects in their entirety arguments for the 'value' of definitions; he sees these arguments as involving no more than 'infinite regressions', so that controversies concerning the 'correctness' of a definition can lead only to empty discussions about words. Consider, for example, the definition of 'alienation' as 'an exercise of the power of disposing of or transferring property'. Popper would dismiss this as, at best, mere tautology, or, at worst, a collection of words which demand further elucidation. What is the meaning of 'exercise', 'power', 'transferring'? Consider, next, Holland's apparently simple definition of 'jurisprudence' as 'the formal science of positive law'. The terms which make up the defining formula ('formal', 'positive', etc) require, according to Popper, further specific definition, with the result that an infinite regression seems likely to follow on any definition based on a collection of terms. Hart, in that section of *The Concept of Law*, entitled 'Definition', raises the question of the predicament facing those who seek to define terms such as 'right', or 'law'. His conclusions stress the type of difficulty noted by Popper.

Other problems must be taken into account by those seeking to define legal terms. The shifting nature of words, changes in their meanings and in perception of their 'significance', make verbal analysis a difficult matter. Hence, it is argued, the precision required in order to define becomes virtually impossible. Thus, attempts to define 'dishonesty', following the decision in *R v Ghosh* (1982) have become very difficult. Doubts as to the meaning of the word 'natural' in expressions such as 'natural justice' remain even after attempts at definition. Further, given advances in epistemology - the theory of knowledge and its methods and validation - how ought we to interpret the vital word 'knowledge' in Wortley's definition of jurisprudence as 'the knowledge of law in its various forms and manifestations'? When Cross defines jurisprudence as 'the study of a lawyer's fundamental assumptions', what weight is to be placed on the ambiguous adjective, 'fundamental'?

Notwithstanding these and other problems arising from verbal analysis and an expanding subject area, 'useful' definitions are plentiful. Their usefulness rests, for the student, in their power to point an enquirer in certain directions, and to adumbrate, even in a rough manner only, the essential features of the field of study. Such definitions range from the prosaic ('the skill or knowledge of law': Cotgrave) to the lapidary ('the knowledge of things divine and human, the knowledge of the just and unjust': Ulpian); from the terse ('the scientific analysis of the law's essential principles': Allen) to the verbose ('any careful and sustained thinking about any phase of things legal, if the thinking seeks to reach beyond the practical solution of an immediate problem in hand': Llewellyn). Definitions of this type represent the continuing, valuable attempts of jurists to determine the essential qualities and characteristics of a subject area.

An attempt to define jurisprudence may be of particular value if the processes involved are *systematic*, ie, if they are related to an identifiable objective and necessitate a search for unique and characteristic qualities. This demands awareness of the vast area of knowledge subsumed under the general heading of 'jurisprudence'. There is no other area of legal studies which is so extensive. Indeed, with the possible exception of 'philosophy' itself, there can be few divisions of knowledge with such a wide-ranging content as that of jurisprudence. A glance at a bibliography of jurisprudence can be a sobering experience, for no aspect of knowledge seems at first sight to be outside the scope of the jurist's studies. Politics, sociology, ethics, semantics, psychology - all impinge on the literature of jurisprudential thought. The search for a definition of jurisprudence must, therefore, take into account a wide variety of human experience and must attempt to exclude the totally irrelevant. The search for relevant characteristics and qualities cannot but be valuable in itself for those seeking to comprehend the basis of the subject.

The search for a basis upon which a definition might be constructed ought to produce a growing awareness of disciplinary inter-relationships. At first sight, it would seem, for example, that the connections between recent advances in the study of the neuronic basis of motor activity in the human body, and the concepts of 'motivation' and 'intention' in the criminal law, are very slight. Research has suggested, however, the existence of connecting links between our physical nature and our subjective goals - the very stuff of some areas of jurisprudential speculation. The changing concepts of the nature of property, in relation to issues of social responsibility, as reflected in the work of Reich, Glendon and Gray, the mounting dissatisfaction with the M'Naghten Rules when considered in the context of current research into mental trauma, exemplify the bonds between seemingly disparate disciplines, the significance of which will emerge swiftly in any methodical attempt to study the dimensions of the 'concept field' of today's jurisprudence prior to attempting a definition. The essential unity of all knowledge is mirrored in the contributory sources of legal theory, so that those who seek for a comprehensive definition would reject as facile a definition of jurisprudence as 'a study of the workings of a legal system'.

The attempt at constructing an adequate definition of jurisprudence will necessitate an examination of some of the better-known examples. This activity can provide a valuable insight into the significance of historical context for an understanding of some aspects of legal theory. Consider the celebrated definition attributed to Ulpian ('the knowledge of things divine and human ...'). Here is language used in a fashion which represents clearly the manner in which a third-century Roman jurist and imperial official conceptualised his world. Pound, writing in twentieth-century America, and defining jurisprudence as 'a consideration of the ethical and social merits of legal rules', reflects the mores and aspirations of an important social and intellectual group within that country. Legal theories and definitions are not produced *in vacuo*: hence the search for a definition can lead to a valuable consideration of the historical circumstances which have attended the growth of those theories.

A further valuable product of the quest for definition may be a deepened understanding of the long *pattern of development* which has produced modern jurisprudence. Each generation of legal thinkers stands on the shoulders of its predecessors. The definitions favoured by one generation do not appear spontaneously but are rooted in the complexities of previous eras. Thus, attempts by the American positivists of the early twentieth century to define jurisprudence indicate the *evolution* of legal thought as part of a continuing line of theoretical analysis. Awareness of this aspect of legal thought is deepened by an examination of comparative definitions.

Reference was made above to objections raised against the very process of definition as applied to jurisprudence, in particular to the difficulties held to be insuperable in relation to 'infinite regressions'. Allied to these objections, and arising from the difficulties of the process, is the condemnation of the search for definition as a *diversion* from the more important task of discovering 'the rational interdependence and ultimate significance' of legal thought. This task is said to involve a study of law as part of a 'coherent body of jurisprudential theory'. Definitions of jurisprudence, it is suggested, can be no more than highly-subjective reactions to phenomena which add little, if anything, to our understanding of the 'true' objective nature of those phenomena. Concentration upon description or definition is seen as removing attention from the coherence of theory. It is not made clear, however, in what sense description vitiates coherence of thought.

In 1913, Vinogradoff, who was then Professor of Jurisprudence at Oxford, voiced his objections to the use - or place - of definition in the process of studying jurisprudence. His arguments continue in use today. Vinogradoff argues that definitions given at the outset of a course of study may impose on students, who have only vague ideas at this stage, patterns of thought which they tend to accept passively, largely because of the dogmatic mode of assertion common to definitions. Definitions ought to emerge towards the *end* of a course of study as a natural reaction to the conflict of ideas which characterises jurisprudence. In our own time, Olivecrona has stated that it is impossible to start from a definition since that would involve a *petitio principii* (the logical fallacy of 'begging the question'). Before a definition can be reached, he states, the facts must be analysed.

One may reply in terms which, in themselves, constitute arguments for the value to be derived from attempting to define jurisprudence. Vinogradoff's argument seems to be directed essentially against the manner in which definitions are utilised in the teaching of the subject. The point at which definitions ought to be introduced into a course of study depends on pedagogical principles - it cannot be determined by the nature of the object of study. It has been found possible to attempt a preliminary definition at a very early stage of one's studies and to modify it repeatedly, where that is necessary, so as to reflect one's increasing awareness of the complexities of the subject area. This will involve attention to content, links between concepts and the unique nature of some of those concepts - an important activity in juristic investigation.

We summarise the value of a methodical attempt to define jurisprudence in the following terms: it involves a useful examination of the wide area of the subject matter; it necessitates investigations of the interconnections of content; it reinforces the significance of the historical context of legal theories; it deepens appreciation of the continuing, evolutionary pattern of legal thought; it necessitates a rigorous testing and amendment of formulations. If the search for a definition of jurisprudence be considered as a 'journey' for the legal student, it may be better, perhaps, to 'travel rather than to arrive'. If the ultimate destination be comprehension of the major areas of jurisprudence, then the journey towards a definition can be considered not as leading to a terminus, but rather to a milestone marking a point from which further travel will be necessary. It is the *continuing processes* involved in definition which are valuable as tools for analytical investigation.

Notes

Popper's classic essay, 'Two Kinds of Definitions', is reprinted in Miller's selection, *A Pocket Popper*. Dias, ch 1, deals with definition in jurisprudence, as does Hart's essay 'Definition and Theory in Jurisprudence'. Moles comments on Hart's analysis in *Definition and Rule in Legal Theory: A Reassessment of HLA Hart*. Vinogradoff's arguments are set out in his *Common Sense in Law*, ch 1. An interesting exposition of problems related to the analysis of legal terminology is given by Shuman in *Jurisprudence and the Analysis of Fundamental Legal Terms*.

Question 3

'Arrangement is not classification, although classification is arrangement; the difference being that while arrangement may be empirical, classification must be in accordance with some principle': De Witt Andrews.

Give a critical account of some of the attempts to classify systematically 'schools' of jurisprudence.

Answer plan

The value of a classification of the various 'schools' of jurisprudence has been questioned repeatedly. The process has been held responsible for a pigeon-holing approach to patterns of thought which are not always easily dealt with in this manner. Compartmentalisation of jurisprudence, given its nature, has its dangers. The extract from Andrews' essay draws attention to the need to classify on the basis of some *principle*. An answer should seek to provide examples of classifications and should point out the difficulties inherent in this type of arrangement. The following skeleton plan will be used:

Introduction - outline of the approach to be taken - De Witt Andrews' suggestions - Keeton's classification - Stone's classification - problems arising from attempts to classify patterns of thought - difficulties of attempting classification based upon Andrews' standards.

Answer

By 'classification' we have in mind the construction of a system of categories which will express and delineate relationships. As applied to jurisprudence the term is used to refer to the process of arranging aspects of the subject area and cataloguing them under a variety of systematic headings so that 'schools of thought' might emerge. The schools, eg, 'natural law jurists', 'Marxist school of jurisprudence', tend to be separated on the basis of content, approach to the phenomena of law, or, occasionally, methodology of enquiry. We shall refer to examples of attempted classification of juristic thought, noting that none is truly 'systematic', and shall comment on the problems arising from attempts to classify. The advantages said to result from classification will be mentioned.

In Kocourek's seminal work, *Classification of Law*, he distinguishes 'a collection', 'an arrangement', and 'a classification'. The first is based on chance or non-systematic choice; the second involves some 'mechanical plan'; the third recognises a logical relationship of parts. A satisfactory classification of aspects of legal thought may presuppose axioms of arrangement based upon logical schemata. In similar vein, De Witt Andrews, in his *The Classification of Law*, rejects a catalogue based upon mere empiricism (ie, speculation based solely upon experience) and stresses the importance of using fundamental *principles* in the procedures of arranging jurisprudential ideas in categories. It is, however, in the application of such basic principles to the wide and complex content of jurisprudence that severe difficulties arise, as will be evident in the classifications mentioned below.

Keeton's classification, published in 1930, results from a belief that a precise arrangement is necessary because of the growing number of different methods of approach to jurisprudence. Four major classifications are presented: those based on the 'standpoint of time', those based on the 'standpoint of the orbit of the legal system', those taking into account the 'standpoint of the number of legal systems examined', and those based on the 'standpoint of the science by virtue of which the law is examined'. Each classification involves sub-sets, most of which take their names from titles used by jurists to describe significant and separate 'schools' or 'movements' within jurisprudence.

The first classification involves historical, analytical, and critical, jurisprudence. Historical jurisprudence is based on the interpretation of processes of change within legal systems; its general method has been characterised as 'evolutionary doctrine' applied to the investigation of societies and their institutions. Analytical jurisprudence examines 'the operation of logic upon legal materials' and aims at the discovery of fundamental propositions upon which an actual legal system is based. Critical jurisprudence necessitates an estimation of the 'real value' of existing legal institutions and an exposition of desirable changes in the law. (Salmond has classified the 'functions' of critical jurisprudence as involving consideration of the concepts of justice, the relationship of law and justice, the manner in which the law is able to fulfil its role of maintaining justice, and the ethical significance of basic legal concepts in general.)

A second limb of Keeton's classification scheme, based on content of legal systems, involves two areas: municipal and international jurisprudence. The first arises from the investigation and analysis of any single system of law; the second concerns the principles upon which inter-state law rests. The third section of Keeton's arrangement refers to particular, comparative and general jurisprudence. Particular jurisprudence has as its field the study of legal relationships within the context of a geographical area. Comparative jurisprudence studies, compares and contrasts two or more systems of law. General jurisprudence, in this scheme, is held to refer to a study of those legal rules to be found in most known systems of law.

The final section of Keeton's scheme contains reference to 'schools' of jurisprudence. An initial sub-set of the classification relates to the 'sociological school' (which considers the interaction of social forces and the law), the 'realist school' (which investigates the official actions of the courts), and the 'functional school' (which examines the effects of judicial decisions). A second sub-set is 'economic jurisprudence' (which studies the influence of economic phenomena on the law and its institutions). A third sub-set is 'psychological jurisprudence' (based on an analysis of the minds and behaviour of those involved in the operations of the law). The fourth and fifth sub-sets comprise the schools of ethnological and ethical jurisprudence: the former concentrates on the legal institutions of groups of persons at an early stage of their social development; the latter school examines the ends which the law desires to achieve.

Keeton's classification scheme is, in his own words, 'neither exclusive nor exhaustive'. It omits, perforce, some very important schools, such as that described by Shapiro as 'political jurisprudence'. It is not always easy to discern the principles underlying Keeton's argument, nor is there evidence of any type of systematic approach from which a structure could be fashioned.

Another classification scheme is that constructed by the American jurist, Stone. Its framework is less complex than that used by Keeton, and its content reflects the singular view of the purpose of jurisprudence taken by Stone. He sees jurisprudence as concerned fundamentally with the formulation of theories which will be of assistance in understanding the very nature of law, its place in society, and the sources of its apparent authority. The classification necessitates three major sub-divisions described by Stone as 'analytical jurisprudence', 'sociological jurisprudence' and 'the theory of justice'.

Analytical jurisprudence (Kocourek's proposed 'logic of the law') has for its area of study a detailed analysis related to the articulation of legal axioms, the definition of legal terms, and the prescribing of methods allowing one to perceive a 'legal order' within society, considered as a 'self-consistent system with its own coherent, logical structure'. (Stone refers to Kelsen's work as exemplifying the approach of jurists of the school of analytical jurisprudence.) The second sub-division - 'sociological jurisprudence' - is concerned essentially with *what is*, rather than with *what ought to be*. Its data are derived from investigations of the effects of social phenomena on the legal order. Because its focus is descriptive rather than normative, jurists of this school are interested particularly in the validation and interpretation of data. The third sub-division - 'the theory of justice' - involves jurists who are concerned to articulate the values a given legal order desires to realise.

This classification appears to be more methodical, more logical, than that of Keeton: it abstracts three basic areas (but not in systematic manner) from a wide range of jurisprudential thought. But in spite of Stone's intentions it does not avoid the problem of overlap (Kelsen, for example, is claimed by schools other than those associated with analytical jurisprudence), nor does it embrace important movements in other fields of jurisprudence which had achieved prominence at the time the classification was made.

It is necessary at this stage to enumerate the more important of the problems attached to any attempt at classifying *systematically* categories other than objects or phenomena, in the scientific sense of that term (which suggests an objective existence). First, the categories of jurisprudential thought, the approaches to knowledge which characterise the various schools, are neither 'objects' nor 'phenomena' in the usual sense accepted by scientific classifiers. It is very difficult to identify, inspect, and argue over, categories of thought as one can examine, say, the botanical specimens referred to in the classification by Linnaeus. It is one thing to classify buttercups as belonging to the order *Ranales*; it is quite another to place Dworkin's theory of rights in one school rather than another. Secondly, it must be emphasised that classification of theories and theoreticians on the basis of the characteristics of 'schools' is essentially the result of human processes of thought applied to defining properties of classes before naming them. Keeton, Stone and other legal classifiers are reacting to theories *subjectively*; their assumptions and reactions may reflect highly-personal values, so that the results of their reactions do not necessarily reflect any objective reality. A third difficulty arises from the 'fuzzy', indistinct boundaries within jurisprudence. The result is often overlap, allowing one jurist to be classified as a member of more than one school. How shall a classifier deal with, say, Llewellyn? Is he to be associated with the school of realism or the anthropological school? What of classifiers who see Marxist jurisprudence as reflecting a doctrine of natural law?

Further problems emerge from the *methods* involved in placing a jurist within a particular school. Is the deciding factor to be one specific text, or his approach as evidenced by his writings over a long period of time? Upon which of his many writings does one place emphasis? What of the 'inarticulate premises' which make a jurist's position difficult to evaluate? These are some of the problems of classification which make the principled approach suggested by Andrews almost impossible to achieve.

Is there anything to be gained from an attempt to classify the contents of jurisprudence? The sketching of very general lines of demarcation, separating, say, the advocates of natural law from the positivists, the anthropological school from the historical school, might be of some value in indicating differences in approach. The sub-division of areas of juristic thought, if only in mechanical fashion, might assist a student in the recognition of patterns of analysis. But there is always a danger for the student in expecting one jurist to share the approach of another jurist in its entirety because both have been categorised as members of the same school. There is also the risk that, because a jurist has been placed in one school, he is perceived as remaining there permanently. This is to ignore the changed positions taken by some jurists as their thought evolves. Radbruch is an interesting example of a scholar who changed his position (from support of relativism to hostility to its main principles). Classification can induce a reliance on 'labels' rather than an examination of patterns of thought.

It would seem, therefore, that the type of classification envisaged by Andrews is unlikely to be attained in relation to jurisprudence and its 'schools'. There are no agreed principles and no generally accepted systems of classification as there are in, say, modern biological taxonomies. Empiricism is likely to continue to dominate the cataloguing of schools of jurisprudential thought, at least for some time to come. The catalogue itself will remain of limited significance for those attempting to comprehend the fundamentals of legal theory.

Notes

The principles of classification theory are explained in Korner's article in the *Encyclopaedia Britannica (15th edition)*. Kocourek's essay on 'Classification of the Law' appeared in 1934 in NY Univ LQR, vol 11. Keeton's classification is set out in his *Elementary Principles of Jurisprudence*, ch 1. Stone's classification appears in 'The Province of Jurisprudence Redetermined', (1944) 8 MLR 178. Andrews' essay on 'The Classification of Law' is a section of *Readings in Jurisprudence*, ed Hall.

Question 4

In what ways has linguistic theory clarified our general understanding of the significance of 'the language of the law'?

Answer plan

An interesting question which indicates the growing significance for jurisprudence of disciplines related directly to an analysis of language itself. The works of Hart, for example, illustrate ways in which this type of analysis may be used so as to elucidate problems of jurisprudence. A detailed knowledge of linguistic theory is not required: the phrase 'general understanding' suggests an answer in wide terms. A skeleton plan is suggested as follows:

> Introduction - the essence of linguistic theory - problems related to words - logical positivism - Hart's views on word 'usage' - communication and the legal process - Danet's analysis of legal discourse - semiotics and law - conclusions for legal theory.

Answer

Linguistic theory has arisen from attempts to apply scientific method to a study of the background, nature and use of language. The study has engendered specialist types of enquiry, such as communication analysis, semantics, semiotics and discourse analysis, some of which are touched on below. Fundamental to the significance of the theory for law is the obvious fact that 'the currency of the law is words', and that, in the phrase used by the legal historian, Pollock, 'Language is no mere instrument which we can control at will; it controls us'. Hart pays particular attention in *The Concept of Law* to the necessity for 'a sharpened awareness of words'. Danet, in an analysis of legal discourse, which is outlined below, reminds lawyers that, while language is central to all human affairs, it is particularly critical in the law, so that, '... in a basic sense, law would not exist without language'. An investigation of language is, therefore, of direct interest to the jurist.

An important problem for the jurist and lawyer in relation to the language of the law rests in the changing nature of words.

Pound has noted: 'Jurisprudence suffers from having to do with so many words of so many meanings'. The poet, Eliot, tells how words 'decay with imprecision, will not stay in place, will not lay still'. The shifting, often-ambiguous nature of legal terminology can result in changes in meaning, often because of context. In *A-G v Prince Ernest Augustus of Hanover* (1957), Viscount Simonds stated: 'Words, and particularly general words, cannot be read in isolation; their colour and content are derived from their context'. This is no mere truism: much work in linguistic theory illustrates the important effect of context upon precision of meaning. Terms such as 'fiduciary', 'honesty', 'fraud', are invariably coloured by their setting. Linguistic analysis has sought to identify and understand the constituents of the phenomenon of 'colour from context', with obvious advantage for a study of the ideas and workings of the law.

The 'meaning' of words and propositions is of particular interest to the 'logical positivists', who emerged from the 'Vienna Circle' of the 1930s. Theoreticians such as Carnap and Schlick, and the English philosopher, Ayer, produced a mode of investigating meaning which called, initially, for a total rejection of metaphysics. They claimed that the 'propositions' advanced by metaphysics cannot be verified directly or indirectly. The logical analysis of propositions must be related to the *method* of their verification. Ayer emphasised that we can say that a sentence is factually significant to a person if, and only if, he knows how to verify the proposition it purports to express - that is, if he knows what observations would lead him under certain conditions to accept the proposition as being true or reject it as being false. Hence, according to this analysis, the pretensions of natural law would be dismissed. Statements by the advocates of the doctrines of natural law, eg, that it mirrors a divine plan for mankind, would be condemned as nothing but a series of empty words. Propositions of this nature are 'neither true nor false, because they assert nothing ... they lie outside the discussion of truth or falsehood'. Carnap states, in terms which have been approved by some legal positivists: 'The danger lies in the deceptive character of metaphysics: it gives the illusion of knowledge without actually giving any knowledge'. Hence, jurists who accept Carnap's view demand that statements concerning law be presented in terms which are devoid of normative ethics and value judgments.

Carnap applied his analysis of propositions to a specific consideration of the statement, 'Killing is evil'. He pointed out that this was a 'value statement' with the grammatical *form* of an assertive proposition (eg, 'X is Y'). But value judgments are, for Carnap, nothing else than 'commands in a misleading grammatical form'. Such statements may have effects on our actions, and these effects may or may not be in accordance with our wishes. But an assertion of this type is neither true nor false; it asserts 'nothing' and can neither be proved nor disproved. It is of interest to note that the philosopher, Schweitzer, saw Carnap's comments as representing a view 'likely to lead to the self-destruction of civilisation'. The reply of the logical positivists is to state that emotive utterances are cognitively worthless.

Other linguists suggest that the problem of words and definitions in law might be clarified by concentrating on the logical interrelations of legal propositions and on the *use* of words. Wittgenstein states that 'the meaning of a word is its *use* in the language'. Hence, the 'meanings' of, say, 'property', 'nuisance', 'motive', are determined by the ways in which these terms are *put to use* in the language of the law. Descriptions of terms rather than definitions, analysis of usage rather than examination of semantic origins, may clarify some perennial problems in jurisprudence.

Hart has suggested that legal words can be clarified only by considering the very conditions under which statements in which those words have their 'characteristic use' are true. Consider, for example, the word 'duty' - defined by some writers as 'an obligation under the law, related to recognition of another's rights'. Hart would ask us to examine its *usage*, ie, the circumstances which characterise its use, in statements, such as: 'We have a duty to pay income tax'; 'Society has a duty to help those who cannot help themselves'; 'A pregnant woman has a duty to her unborn child'. Little would be gained by examining a dictionary definition of 'duty'. Hart suggests, rather, a study of 'the standard uses of the relevant expressions and of the way in which these depend on a social context, itself often left unstated'. The resolution of some controversies in jurisprudence might be hastened, therefore, by examining terminology, not on the basis of simple verbal definitions, but by reference to the wider circumstances in which particular words are used and which give colour to their acceptance.

The theory of communication which emerged in the 1950s from the work of Shannon and Weaver has become the centre of an attempt to examine 'communication' as a process whereby people attempt to share meaning *via* the transmission of symbolic messages. Thus, 'I plead not guilty' is a *message*, using verbal symbols, from defendant to the court. It involves a 'system' whereby a 'source' (defendant) uses a 'channel of communication' (his voice) to transmit that message to a 'receiver' (the court). The effectiveness of that communication is said to be determined by the 'clarity' of the message, ie, by its being understood on a level shared by source and receiver. Interference with clarity ('noise' in the technical language of communication theoreticians) may arise from a variety of events, eg, imprecision in the use of terms, ambiguity, and the existence of 'overtones'. Linguists stress the importance of the subsidiary 'tones' carried by words, eg, 'prisoner', 'accused', 'defendant', which may convey pejorative overtones to listeners. Hence the insistence of communication analysts on the need for lawyers to use, as far as possible, terms free from such overtones, and for jurists to make use of a vocabulary which is precise and unambiguous. It has been suggested that the law can become more comprehensible only when its practitioners and scholars accept the implications of Richards' description of communication as taking place when 'one mind so acts upon its environment that another mind is influenced, and in that other mind, an experience occurs which is like the experience in the first mind, and is caused in part by that experience'.

Danet, in an unusual investigation of 'legal discourse', analyses the vocabulary of the law in relation to 'the nature, functions and consequences of language used in the negotiation of social order'. The term 'discourse' is used in linguistic analysis to refer to 'sets of utterances which constitute recognisable speech events', eg, an interview between lawyer and client, speeches delivered during legal proceedings. Because modern legal language has become so highly-differentiated, it has turned, according to Danet, into a separate dialect, a sub-language, or, in the terms of linguistic analysis, a 'register'. That register includes a variety of styles, such as 'casual' (eg, lawyer-to-lawyer conversations out of the hearing of their clients) or 'frozen and formal' (eg, drafting of pleadings, questioning of witnesses). Use of the latter style is indicative, in Danet's view, of 'an authoritarian approach'. Further, the formal style is never the speaker's 'native language' - it has been acquired only as the result of a formal education. Hence, the very nature of much legal discourse may prevent effective communication during legal proceedings because of its restricted capacity for transferring messages at appropriate, shared levels.

In order to illustrate the difficulties of communication inherent in the legal register, Danet analyses in detail the 'lexical features' of a deed of assignment. The analysis reveals - not unexpectedly - the use of a large number of obscure 'terms of art', eg, 'forfeiture', 'free simple', common terms with uncommon meanings, eg, 'beneficial owner', archaic expressions, eg, 'hereinafter', 'aforesaid', and a proclivity for 'high formality', eg, 'unto the trustee'. Deeper analysis reveals features such as a large number of unusual prepositional phrases, eg, 'in the event of', and word pairs, eg, 'cease and desist'. The result is an opaque document, almost incomprehensible to the non-lawyer who is a party to the agreement embodied in its complex clauses. For Danet this is an inexcusable obfuscation of communication in the legal process.

Danet suggests that the 'thickening' of the legal register, ie, the adding of language to 'give it body', has the effect of creating an illusion of certainty in an uncertain world. Convoluted legal language may derive, in part, from early preliterate periods when complex legal formulas acted as a kind of 'word-magic'. Other linguists, following Danet's analysis, argue that professions, including the law, tend to use language in a deliberate fashion so as to mystify the public and keep them dependent, or to mask 'the irrationalities in human decision-making'. Danet's analysis has been used to give weight to a general call for the use of 'plain language' in the legal process.

Another aspect of linguistic theory - semiotics - has extended the very concept of 'language'. Semiotics is the study of the properties of 'signalling systems', natural or artificial. It embraces patterned human communication in all its sensory modes - hearing, seeing, etc. As applied to the legal process it would take in a study of the 'vocal-auditory mode' (speeches in court), and the appearance (costume, etc) of the participants. The 'real language' of the legal process, in semiotic terms, would emerge from a study of the 'register' used by participants, the dress and general appearance of the judge, jury, defendant, the physical positioning of the participants. In sum, semiotics seeks to determine the nature of the 'messages' conveyed among participants by the *entire range* of experiences arising from legal procedure.

The conclusions for jurisprudence would seem to range from the obvious (avoid ambiguity in language, use terms with precision), through the novel (examine the usage of words and do not be over-concerned with formal definitions), to the highly controversial (consider the validity of the so-called 'non-verifiable assertions', and give appropriate attention to the overall significance of the legal process viewed as a 'mode of communication'). It may be that some of the fundamental disputes which have formed the core of much jurisprudence - the 'relationship of law and morality', the 'inviolability of human rights', lend themselves to reappraisal in the light of linguistic analysis; and it might be valuable to consider enquiry into the use of words as an enquiry into the facts they describe. Analysis of this type may contribute to the state of affairs which J S Mill considered essential to the solution of a problem: 'Insist upon having the meaning of a word clearly understood before using it, and the meaning of a proposition before assenting to it'.

Notes

Hart's *The Concept of Law* embodies his views on the significance of language in the law. Mellinkoff's *'The Language of the Law'* is a survey of the growth of legal language. Glanville Williams' important survey, 'Language and the Law' appears in 61 LQR (1945). Ayer's *Language, Truth and Logic* explains the outlook of Logical Positivism. Bodenheimer considers linguistic analysis in relation to jurisprudence in *Jurisprudence*, ch 6. Danet's surveys are contained in 'Legal Discourse', in *Handbook of Discourse Analysis, Vol I*, and in 'Language in the Legal Process', *Law and Society Review for 1980*. *Semiotics and Legal Theory* by Jackson is a technical account of semiotics in relation to aspects of jurisprudence.

Question 5

Comment on the role of formal logic in English law.

Answer plan

It is important to differentiate 'formal logic' and 'legal reasoning'. The former involves a scientific approach to problems of induction and deduction; the latter is an imprecise description of a common attitude to the determination of a legal dispute. The answer ought to show how far formal logic is used in a judgment, and attention should be directed to some of the problems involved in attempts to apply a rigid system of rules to legal procedure. The following skeleton plan is used as a framework for the answer:

Introduction - definition of logic - its restricted use in law - the Aristotelian *syllogism* - inflexibility of formal logic - reasoning in adjudication - references in judgments to logic - argument by analogy - logic and prevention of inconsistency - arguments concerning logic and control - Dewey's warning on logic and law - conclusion, stressing danger of abandoning logic in the law.

Answer

We define logic, for the purposes of this answer, as a science that is concerned with the canons and criteria of validity in thought and demonstration. It is a methodology, a technique, enabling conclusions to be drawn from information presented in a specific, prescribed manner. In English law it plays a restricted role and is never used as the sole rationale of a legal decision, so that it is unlikely for a judgment to rest on the belief that 'plaintiff has demonstrated the logical superiority of his case'. Almost invariably its use is qualified, as will be illustrated below. Reference will be made to those who believe that an extended use of logic, as the basis of a scientific approach to the law, is desirable.

There are several different types of logic; in Europe, Aristotelian logic is dominant. Aristotle taught that logic was 'the science of sciences', ie, a methodological introduction to the other

sciences. It necessitated 'thinking about thinking' and involved a
system of rules by which deductive thought might be represented
and analysed. The essence of deduction involves the derivation of
a conclusion from a set of statements ('premises'). Aristotle
advocated the use of the syllogism - a formal scheme of
demonstration. A simple example is as follows: (1) All A is B; (2)
Some C is A; (3) Therefore some C is B. There are here three
'categorical propositions', containing only three terms (A, B and
C), with each of the terms appearing in two statements. (By
comparison, 'inductive logic' involves reasoning from particular
statements to a general truth.)

The rules of logic are precise, inflexible and systematic. They
are, therefore, incapable of modification to suit particular
circumstances. 'Logic with a changing content' is a contradiction
in terms. To seek to modify the rigid rules of logic is as
unproductive as an attempt to solve a problem in Euclidean
geometry by 'changing' Euclid's fundamental propositions.
Hence, syllogistic reasoning is not always adequate for the
representation or solution of a problem in English law, and, save
for some trivial matters, it is rarely possible to compress the
essence of a complex legal problem within the unyielding
framework of a syllogism. Indeed, if the schemes of formal logic
were applicable to the analysis and resolution of disputes, then
settlement would be possible without the intervention of legal
procedures. X's dispute with Y arising from Y's alleged invasion
of X's property rights might be resolved swiftly and correctly by
reference to an exact, immutable system of logical propositions. It
is precisely because this *cannot* be done that the process of
adjudication becomes necessary.

This is not to say that the use of 'reasoning' has merely a
minor role in the legal process. But 'reasoning' and the
application of formal logic must be differentiated. Thus, a
judicial decision which was clearly 'unreasonable', ie, irrational,
would not stand - a principle enunciated in *Associated Provincial
Picture Houses Ltd v Wednesbury Corporation* (1948); a finding
which 'flies in the face of the facts' would be difficult to sustain.
This is far removed, however, from situations in which purely
formal logic is used in the solution of a problem. Strict logical
rules cannot 'make' decisions in English law, if only because the

disputed facts are often 'untidy' and cannot be presented in the exact form required for the exercise of those rules. Thus, in a recent decision of the House of Lords (*Hammersmith and Fulham LBC v Monk* (1991)), the question was whether a periodic tenancy held by two or more joint tenants was determinable by a valid notice to quit given by one joint tenant without the knowledge or consent of the other(s). The facts were not always precise and the House did attempt to reason from ordinary contractual principles. But the train of logic which had led from consideration of one precedent to another and which did suggest that one joint tenant *could* validly end a tenancy, was halted when reference was made to a statement to the contrary in *Howson v Buxton* (1928). This was considered and rejected as having 'insufficient weight'. Other matters than logical principles have to be taken into account.

References are made occasionally within a judgment to the significance of logic, but generally within a wider context, eg public policy, social concerns. In *R v Gotts* (1992), the House of Lords decided that duress was *not* available as a defence to a charge of attempted murder. Lord Jauncey asked: 'Is there logic in affording the defence of duress to one who intends to kill but fails, and denying it to one who mistakenly kills intending only to injure? ... I can see no justification in logic, morality or law in affording to an attempted murderer the defence which is withheld from a murderer'. It is of significance, however, that these remarks were preceded by reference to 'the pervading climate of violence and terrorism'. Lord Jauncey was placing his reference to logic within a setting of social facts and desirable policies. Similarly, in *R v R* (1991), in which the House of Lords decided that a husband could be criminally liable for raping his wife, the matter was approached by means of a logical interpretation of the word 'unlawful' as used in the Sexual Offences Act 1956, s1, and the Sexual Offences (Amendment) Act 1974, s1. But it was preceded by an important observation on historical and social change: the status of women had changed in recent years out of all recognition, so that marriage is to be regarded now as a partnership of equals. Again, purely logical reasoning is taken into account *together with* interpretations of social realities.

The use of 'reasoning by analogy' which is prevalent in English law and which, if it is to be in accord with the rules of formal logic, demands the application of rules in exact style, illustrates a general departure from the strictness of those rules. Analogy arises from a process of arguing from similarity in known respects to similarity in other respects. 'Running a country is like running a ship - the crew must obey the captain' - here is an analogy involving perceived similarities. Cast in formal terms, argument by analogy may be stated thus: 'X has certain elements, P, Q and R. Y also has elements P, Q and R. But X has S. Therefore Y has S'. Argument by analogy has been used in English law to support, for example, the concept of the right of the State to interfere so as to prevent breaks in 'the seamless web of the law' in relation to breaches of conventional morality. The statement of Lord Simonds in *Shaw v DPP* (1962), suggesting the existence of a residual power in the courts of law which can be used to guard the State against attacks 'which may be the more insidious because they are novel and unprepared for', stems from an analogy between the defence of the state by its 'guardians' and the defence of morality by the 'guardians of the law'. Specific criteria of formal rules relating to analogy (eg, 'the greater the number of elements shared by X and Y, the stronger the conclusion', or 'as the dissimilar elements between X and Y increase, so the conclusion is weakened') tend to be neglected in legal arguments based on analogy. Critics have pointed to some of the decisions in 'causation cases' (in particular, *R v Jordan* (1956) and *R v Blaue* (1975)) as having resulted from false analogies between the laws of physical causation and the type of causation perceived in the facts of these cases.

Some jurists have suggested that the unwillingness of English lawyers to follow rigidly the principles of formal logic may be a sure guarantee of continuing inconsistencies in the law. They point, for example, to the continuous 'lease or licence' saga in land law, exemplified by *Facchini v Bryson* (1952), *Somma v Hazelhurst* (1978), and *Street v Mountford* (1985), and argue that, had the concept of a lease been applied in logical fashion to a consideration of the facts in these and similar cases, uncertainty and inconsistency might have been avoided. Holmes' comments on the question of consistency in law are pertinent: the law, he declares, is always approaching and never reaching, consistency.

'It will become consistent only when it ceases to grow'. Pound reminds jurists that so-called 'scientific legal systems', dominated by strictly logical reasoning, will result in the 'petrifaction' of law and the stifling of independent consideration of new problems and of 'new phases of old problems'. Jurists who support the stance of Holmes and Pound have noted that the principles of formal logic were *not* responsible for the vital change in the law of torts effected by the enunciation of the 'neighbour principle' in *Donoghue v Stevenson* (1932), or the important development of the 'proximity test' in *Alcock and Others v Chief Constable of S Yorks Police* (1991).

Others argue that law based on systematic logical principles will enlarge control over the increasing diversity of legal situations. 'It is like fishing with large nets rather than single lines'. Cohen, in an examination of the place of logic in the law, suggests that this argument ignores the important differences between the natural sciences, in which logic is essential, and the legal order, which involves matters which are neither as definite nor as rigid as those of the physical order. The facts of the physical order allow highly exact description (eg, in quantitative terms); the facts of the legal order can almost always be disputed and disregarded as wrong in principle. 'The specific gravity of mercury is 13.6' is a statement which, in terms of its logical derivation, is on a different level from that occupied by the statement, 'The court finds for defendant'. Cohen warns that, like other useful instruments, logic is 'very dangerous and it requires great wisdom to use it properly ... A logical science of law can help us digest our legal material, but we must get good food before we can digest it'.

Dewey, jurist and logician, urges caution in the face of arguments advocating a more intensive application of syllogistic logic to legal questions. He notes that the syllogism implies that thought or reason has fixed forms of its own, 'anterior to and independent of concrete subject-matters and to which the latter have to be adapted whether or no'. This is to put the activity of rigid demonstration *before* that of search and discovery and to fall into the trap of accepting that for every possible case which might arise in the legal system, there is a fixed antecedent rule 'already at hand'. The result is to produce what Pound terms 'a mechanical jurisprudence'; it flatters the human longing for certainty. Thinking derived from a consideration of premises is, in itself, not to be condemned; the problem for the jurist is to *find* statements of general principle and particular fact which are worthy to serve as premises. Hence, Dewey concludes, *either* logic in legal thinking must be abandoned, or it must be a logic relative to consequences rather than to antecedents - 'a logic of prediction of probabilities rather than one of deduction of certainties'.

The difficulties of relying *solely* on formal logic in a search for solutions to problems of jurisprudence and to cases arising within the legal system are obvious. The danger may be, however, in the *total rejection* of logic as a tool in legal reasoning. In Cohen's phrase, law without concepts or rational ideas, law that is not logical, is like pre-scientific medicine. Lord Devlin, too, warns: 'The Common Law is tolerant of much illogicality especially on the surface; but no system of law can be workable if it has not got logic at the root of it' (*Hedley Byrne v Heller* (1964)).

Notes

The rules of formal logic may be found in *Fundamentals of Logic*, by Carney and Scheer. Bodenheimer considers law and scientific method in ch 17. Dewey examines the problem in 'Logical Method and Law' 10 Cornell LQR 1924. Cohen's article, 'The Place of Logic in the Law' appears in *Law and the Social Order*. A lucid account of basic problems related to logic and the law is given by Levi in his essay, 'The Nature of Judicial Reasoning', in *Law and Philosophy*, ed Hook.

Precursors of Modern Jurisprudence

Introduction

The precursors of modern jurisprudence selected as the basis of the questions in this chapter are Plato (c 427 - c 347 BC), Aristotle (384 - 312 BC), Hobbes (1588 - 1679), and Locke (1632 - 1704). Plato and Aristotle were concerned with fundamental problems such as the nature of justice and the functions of law. Hobbes and Locke sought, through their theories of 'the social contract', to explain the place of government and law within society. The theories produced by these philosophers formed the basis of many problems which continue to be posed in modern jurisprudence. Questions of the type forming this chapter call for an understanding of the *basic* teachings related to justice, law, State and government. Answers must concentrate on *fundamentals*.

Checklist

The following topics should be revised carefully:

- Plato's theory of the State
- Plato's view of justice
- Plato's 'ideal State'
- the 'good' according to Aristotle
- man as a 'political animal'
- distributive and corrective justice
- Aristotle's view of the State

- the social contract viewed by Hobbes
- Hobbes' 'natural laws'
- Hobbes' 'sovereign'
- Locke's 'state of nature'
- the social contract viewed by Locke
- 'property' according to Locke
- 'natural rights' according to Locke

Question 6

Give an account of Plato's theory of justice.

Answer plan

The problem here is how to compress the fundamentals of this complicated theory into a relatively small space. It is possible to deal with the theory in *outline only*. Particular attention should be given to Plato's views on 'harmony' and the State, and reference should be made to his ideal State. A skeleton plan is suggested as follows:

Introduction - emergence of the State from the nature of man - justice as a 'general virtue' - justice and the degeneration of the State - the ideal state of Magnesia - necessity for a code of laws - the modern approach to Plato's theory of justice.

Answer

Plato, together with Socrates and Aristotle, laid and shaped a large part of the foundations of the entire intellectual and cultural traditions of the West. His theory of justice was expounded in *The Republic* (c 370 BC); a development of that theory and its application to an ideal State are embodied in *The Laws* (c 340 BC). Neither the theory nor its application is found attractive to modern jurists, save for a group who favour an authoritarian approach to the law and who claim to find support for their views in *The Republic*. Critical studies of *The Republic* and *The Laws* (which, in a sense, are complementary) have been responsible for much of the theorising which burgeoned into early European jurisprudence.

The Republic is, in a number of respects, the crowning work of Plato's philosophical writings: it brings into sharp focus many of his basic beliefs regarding the nature of man and the essence of good government and law. It takes the form of a dialogue between Socrates and his friends and is, essentially, an application of Plato's ethical theory to the delineation of the features of an ideal State. Socrates is used as a mouthpiece for Plato's own thoughts. The dialogue moves swiftly towards the central question of *the nature of justice*. Socrates' friends attempt definitions which collapse under his scrutiny. He suggests that, because it is easier to perceive things in the large than in the small, it might be better to look for justice 'writ large' in the State. Hence it would be valuable to seek to establish what makes a 'just State' rather than to concentrate on a 'just individual'.

Because justice will figure large in the attributes of an ideal State, it is necessary to outline such a State with particular reference to its constitution and its attitudes to justice.

The State must be considered as emerging from the very nature of man and as reflecting the structure of human nature. Individuals are not self-sufficing, hence a division of labour is essential, allowing each person to perform, at the right time, 'the one thing for which he is naturally fitted'. A multitude of crafts and craftsmen will emerge. Exhaustion of the community's resources may result and wars with other communities will take place, necessitating the creation of an army of warriors. From the ranks of the warriors will emerge the guardians of the State, and from the most highly-trained guardians will come an elite which will rule the State. The three classes - craftsmen, guardians, and rulers - epitomise, according to Plato, the 'three parts of the soul', ie, the appetitive, the spirited and the rational. The virtues associated with the three classes are temperance (among the craftsmen), courage (characterising the guardians), and wisdom (to be found among the rulers). Members of the three classes would have to be taught (on the basis of what Plato refers to as 'a convenient fiction ... a single bold flight of invention') that nature approves a perfectly stratified society and that it had mixed gold in the composition of those who were to be the rulers, silver in the guardians, and brass and iron in the craftsmen.

The achievement of justice in a State depends on whether the elements of wisdom and philosophy could achieve dominance. Evils within society will continue until the philosophers acquire political authority, or until those in authority become philosophers.

Justice is a general virtue; it necessitates all parts of the State fulfilling their special functions and thereby achieving their respective virtues. It will be attained within the State only when and if each class fulfils its functions. When every individual stays in his place, does the special task for which his aptitudes equip him, then will justice emerge. *Justice is, indeed, harmony.* It involves a harmony of the fundamental virtues of temperance, courage and wisdom. Therefore each person within the State must attain his own individual harmony based upon these virtues. Hence, in the 'just State' the craftsman must pursue the appropriate virtues which will teach him to accept his position within society and to obey the rules made by the elite.

'Balanced uniformity' within the State, which mirrors the desirable healthy, harmonious unity within individuals, will produce the settled community within which justice will flourish. Plato recognises, however, that not all States can achieve and maintain an appropriate degree of harmony, nor can individuals attain their own internal harmony because of variations in human character. Even the State in which justice predominates may contain the seeds of its eventual decline. Plato notes five forms of government, each one of which reflects appropriate kinds of 'mental constitutions' within individuals. The ideal State, characterised by a high degree of justice in its constitution, and in which the philosopher-rulers are supreme and each person's appetites are controlled by individual reason, is termed by Plato an *aristocracy*. The essence of the aristocratic State is the proper subordination of classes. Justice emerges naturally from this arrangement. But this type of State tends to degenerate into a *timocracy*, epitomising ambition and love of honour, and mirroring the individual in whom irrational characteristics are assuming a significant role. Further degeneration takes place and culminates in the rise of a *plutocracy* in which power is in the hands of those who are concerned mainly with wealth. This degenerate form of State is a reflection of those individuals whose principal characteristic is greed. Hence 'the rich rise and the virtuous sink'; self-gratification produces antagonistic groups of rich and poor, and justice is weakened.

The legitimising of all appetites under a plutocracy produces an insatiable craving for wealth, equality and unrestricted freedom. The stage is set for *democracy* - a further degeneration. Modern jurists emphasise that Plato probably could not have had in mind a style of democracy other than that which he had experienced in the small city state of Athens. Direct popular government, as practised in Athens, seemed to him a total violation of the concept of a State ruled by those with special, trained aptitudes. Within a democracy, justice will be incomplete and inadequate. The final degeneration takes the form of *despotism*, a reflection of the 'enlargement of the unjust soul'. The absolute despot who enslaves a community mirrors the single 'master-passion' which has enslaved the individual soul. The harmony which is necessary if justice is to prevail has been shattered totally, so that justice disappears completely under despotism.

Some years after *The Republic* was written, Plato produced a detailed, practical plan for his ideal 'just State'. *The Laws* is an account of the structure and organisation appropriate for this 'Utopia'. The significance of law is emphasised: law is viewed by Plato in this work as essential for the moral salvation of the community and the maintenance of an appropriate standard of justice. The ideal State involves government based on a minutely-detailed code of laws which points the way to achievement of 'the true good'. The resulting picture of an ideal State has few attractions for contemporary jurists who find its picture of a regimented community to be repulsive. The ideal State emerges as an authoritarian regime based on laws which are almost unalterable and which seek to control every aspect of individual life.

The State will be named 'Magnesia'. Its guiding principles are: the existence of certain absolute standards of morality and their embodiment in a code of laws; the total obedience of the population to the rules and regulations made for them. Magnesia will be ten miles from the sea, with a population of 5,040 citizens, plus some resident aliens. Justice will necessitate the encouragement of modest living standards, so that 'excess', which can destroy harmony, is discouraged. Each family will own a farm and most of the manual labour will be performed by slaves (who enjoy none of the rights of citizens). Trade will be carried out by the resident aliens. All persons will be educated in a manner which will prevent their subversion by undesirable ideas, which will fit them for their destined occupations and allow them to defend the State. In the interests of the social harmony upon which justice will rest there will be a State religion and adherence will be enforced rigidly.

The government of Magnesia will include officials elected by the citizens. It will, however, observe the general policies laid down by the 'Guardians of the Laws'. The imposition of standards so that harmony and justice might prevail is the direct responsibility of this governing elite. Members of the elite will pursue a programme of philosophical studies, designed to enable them to comprehend the 'true reasons' behind the laws of the State and their significance for the maintenance of justice.

Justice will reflect harmony, and that harmony will require an all-embracing, detailed and systematically-arranged code of laws.

It is the criminal code of Magnesia which has attracted considerable attention from generations of political scientists and jurists. Its range of penalties is very wide; the nature of the penalties is often, in our eyes, bizarre. Apart from basic crimes, such as theft, assault and homicide, there is a long list of offences, trivial and serious, attracting severe penalties. Thus, it is an offence under this code to attend weddings when forbidden to do so, to fail to marry, or to arrange for extravagant wedding feasts. There are penalties for the pursuit of an unsuitable occupation, for the carrying on of retailing (except in the case of resident aliens or temporary visitors), or for the staging of unauthorised comic plays. Meddling in law or education, the inconsiderate planting of trees, and truancy from school, also attract penalties. The code of laws will assist in the establishment and maintenance of that *unity of purpose* from which justice will flow.

Some aspects of Plato's penology are based on his belief in reform rather than vengeance - in the interests of justice for all citizens. He perceives crime as involuntary, in the sense that the 'true nature' of the offender has been conquered against his own fundamental wishes. Hence he should be 'cured' rather than punished. Yet, in contrast, Plato's code prescribed the death penalty for the 'incurable' criminal in a large number of cases, particularly where the security of the State is endangered. The punishment to be meted out to slaves is often of an abhorrent nature.

The modern approach to Plato's theory of justice acknowledges that he was a remarkable 'child of his time', that his attitudes were conditioned by beliefs which are not easily comprehended in our day, and that to condemn him, say, for his acceptance of slavery, is to condemn an entire era. His lasting contribution to legal theory is in the basis of early jurisprudential thought founded on concepts of harmony, virtue and balance as desirable ends to be reflected in the law. Our own society, its laws and institutions, have changed since Plato's time, and our conceptions of justice are often far-removed from his. But, in Friedmann's words, the fundamental issues for jurisprudence have *not* changed, nor has their solution greatly advanced beyond the problems and conflicts as stated by Plato.

Notes

The Republic has been translated by Lee, Jowett, and many other scholars; a large number of editions exists. *The Laws* has been translated by Saunders. Friedmann's *Legal Theory*, ch 2, contains an account of the essence of Plato's theory of justice. The theory is analysed in Calhoun's *Introduction to Greek Legal Science*, and in Jones' *The Law and Legal Theory of the Greeks*.

Question 7

'Man when perfected is the best of animals, but if he be isolated from law and justice he is the worst of all': Aristotle (*The Politics*).

Discuss.

Answer plan

The question calls for comment on Aristotle's view of man as achieving 'the good' and fulfiling his role within society. Aristotle's legacy to jurisprudence was his concept of law as a means to an end. His classification of justice as 'distributive' and 'corrective' is of particular significance. No more than an outline should be attempted. The following skeleton plan is used for this answer:

> Introduction - concept of 'the good life' - man's dual aspect - law as the community's sovereign guide - educational element in law - essence of equity - distributive and corrective justice - social framework for the just society - conclusion, noting the significance of Aristotle's theories in relation to modern jurisprudence.

Answer

One of the most celebrated polymaths of all time, Aristotle was educated at Plato's Academy in Athens and was influenced deeply by Platonic rationalism. In his writings on law and justice he seems to advance well beyond Plato's general idealism. Aristotle was concerned, in particular, with how man might achieve 'the good'; indeed, for him the 'science of the good' was politics. The 'good life' involved the exercise of reason, so that it became an activity of the soul aimed at perfect virtue. The highest of the moral virtues was justice. Man must be involved closely with law and justice if he is to perform his 'true functions'; to separate him from the exercise of those functions is to separate him from law and justice, thus taking from him the possibility of self-development and the attainment of ultimate happiness.

Aristotle views the world as a unity, a 'totality of nature'. Man is a part of nature, but in a 'dual sense': he is a constituent element of the natural order, but his active reason, which differentiates him from everything else, allows him to *control* nature. He has a will which, when it acts on the basis of an insight into reason, gives him a power denied to all other animals - the power to distinguish good from evil so that he is able to dominate nature by his spirit. Man's nature requires the powers and qualities separating him from other creatures to be developed to the full. Man is essentially moral, social and rational, and the natural law will embody the obligations which will be apparent to him if his reason is 'perfected'. Man's laws may be judged by the extent to which they assist in that perfection. Laws are to be considered 'just' only if they permit the full development of human innate powers.

Laws that are 'rightly constituted' should be the community's 'sovereign guide' Their sovereignty should embrace *all* issues, with the exception that rules formulated by the community's executive should prevail in those areas in which general pronouncements are impossible. The rule of law is preferable to that of a single citizen, even though he is of outstanding quality. Aristotle sees clearly the disadvantages inherent in personal rule and personal promulgation of laws. One who commands that *law* should rule is commanding, in effect, that 'God and reason' alone ought to rule; but he who commands that *one man* should rule 'adds the character of the beast'. 'Appetite and high spirit' pervert those who hold high office, even when they are the best of men. Law must be seen, therefore, as 'reason free from passion'. Aristotle stresses that it is the office of the law to direct the magistrate in the 'execution of his office and the punishment of offenders'. Friedmann points out that it is to this statement that some modern jurists turn in their opposition to unfettered administrative discretion.

The law has an educational element, too. Because its aim is the attainment of the good life, the life characterised by the exercise of those faculties separating man from beast, the lawgiver must assist the citizen to become 'good' by habituating him, through the law, to an understanding of 'the good'. Indeed, law will derive its validity among the citizens from the very *habits* upon which obedience is founded. Where citizens understand that the law is to be viewed as a pledge that members of the community will do justice to one another, and where they understand that 'good law' means 'good order', they will respond appropriately with good behaviour. Because of the educational nature of the law, and because of the habits it inculcates over long periods, Aristotle warned of the evils arising from changes in the law made without careful consideration. Law has no power to command obedience except through habit, which can result *in time*; readiness to change from old to new laws, without full preparation, may enfeeble the power of the law.

Circumstances may arise, as Aristotle noted, when the application of universal, rigid rules will result in hardship in some individual cases. It is not always possible, he said, to make universal statements about some things. When a lawmaker promulgates a universal rule and a case emerges which is not covered by it, there arises a necessity to 'correct' that rule. 'It is the nature of the equitable to correct the law where, because of its universality, it is defective'. In his *Rhetoric*, he expresses a fundamental notion of equity in Western law: 'It is equity to pardon the human failing, to look to the lawgiver and not to the law, to the spirit and not the letter, to the intention and not to the action ... to prefer the arbitrator to the judge, for the arbitrator observes what is equitable, whereas the judge sees only the law'. Aristotle suggests that a defect arising from the absoluteness of the law be rectified by the judge deciding as the lawgiver would *himself* have decided had he been present on the occasion in question and would have enacted if he had been cognisant of the case in question.

Aristotle makes a clear distinction between 'positive law' and 'natural law'. Natural law must be seen as having everywhere the same force; it 'does not exist by people thinking this or that'. Its force resides in its derivation from human nature everywhere and at all times. Positive law derives its special force from the fact that it is set down as law, whether it be considered just or unjust. Both types of law make a contribution to the good of the community.

One of the best-known contributions of Aristotle to jurisprudence is his perception of 'distributive' and 'corrective' (or 'remedial') justice. An essential feature of justice is its concern with *relationships among individuals*. 'Justice alone is the good of others because it does what is for the advantage of others'. The unjust man is the man who breaks the law and the man who takes more than his due. Hence justice involves 'some sort of equality' among individuals. It demands the equitable distribution or allotment to members of the community of 'the things of this world' in accordance with the principle of *proportionate equality*, which necessitates a measuring standard of 'merit and civil excellence'. Equal things should be distributed to equal persons; unequal things should be given to unequal persons. Should A be 'twice as deserving' as B, A's share will be twice as large as B's.

Corrective justice relates to the administration of the law within a community. The importance of redressing the undesirable consequences of encroachment upon the property and other rights of an individual stands high in the tasks of those who administer the law. The violation of a norm of distributive justice, which leads to X depriving Y of his rights so that X makes an unjustified gain, must produce the consequences of X returning Y's property to him, or compensating Y for the loss incurred. It is the task of the judge to be 'a sort of animate justice' and to repair the situation resulting from a breach of the community's rules. Failure to achieve high standards of corrective justice results in man's isolation from those forces which make for his good.

Although laws and justice prevent the degeneration of man into a selfish, uncaring person, in that he is subjected to rules which are based on 'doing good' to others, a social framework is required so that good and justice might flourish. The definition and study of the State occupy places of much importance in Aristotle's scheme of justice and 'the good'. He classifies the main forms of government known to him under the headings of 'monarchy', 'aristocracy', and 'polity'. The aim of government is to fit the man for the good life, and the State is to be seen as a union of families enjoying a 'perfect and self-sufficing life, a happy, honourable and just existence'. Aristotle rejects monarchy as 'obsolete' and 'objectionable' because it subjects those who are equal to the rule of an equal. In an aristocracy (generally favoured by Aristotle), only the 'best' are citizens. 'Best' means for Aristotle those who are the most capable through natural endowment and education. They will comprise a small, intellectual and wise elite. 'Polity' refers to constitutional government and may involve rule by the masses under law and a system of justice protected by a constitution.

These types of government tend to degenerate, and that degeneration makes it difficult to attain and sustain the just society. Monarchy degenerates to its corrupt form, known as 'tyranny', in which the selfish ends of the ruler predominate over the need for justice and law. Aristocracy is transformed into its corrupt form of 'oligarchy', characterised by rulers who are interested in their personal advancement and not in the general good. Polity is degraded into 'democracy' in which selfishness predominates and the common good is not perceived as an important objective. Democracy, said Aristotle, arises when men think that if they are equal in any respect, they are equal in all respects. These corrupt forms of government are characterised by a lack of moderation and an absence of justice.

Friedmann argues that Aristotle's work 'anticipates all the major themes and conflicts of modern Western legal thought'. Certainly, many of the vital questions discussed in contemporary jurisprudence may be traced to his study of law and justice. The purpose of justice, its nature, the significance of distributive and corrective justice, the need for a system of equity which will temper the rigours of the law by allowing for individual cases - all appear in his writings. His emphasis on the 'dual character' of man may be found at the basis of much discussion in our own time. Because man is, by his very nature, a 'political animal', he is destined to fulfil himself only within society - 'he who is unable or unwilling to live in society is a beast or a god'. That society is established with a view to 'the good', of which justice is among its highest manifestations. It is through law and justice that man will achieve his goals; without them he degenerates, inevitably and totally. Law and justice are, therefore, means to an end. That end is the full development of man. In his 'perfected form' he is, indeed, 'the best of animals'. Justice has given him a vision of 'the good', the law has provided the means of realising the vision.

Notes

Aristotle's theories concerning law and justice may be found in his *Nichomachean Ethics*, translated by Rackham. There are interesting expositions of his contributions to jurisprudence in Bodenheimer, chs 1,3 and 11, Lloyd, ch 3, and Dias, ch 4. Friedmann analyses his theories in ch 2. An interesting background to Aristotle is given in Grene's *A Portrait of Aristotle*.

Question 8

What are the essential features of Hobbes' theory of the Social Contract?

Answer plan

The Social Contract theory can be traced back to the ancient Greeks. It enjoyed wide currency in the 17th and 18th centuries through the writings of Hobbes, Locke and Rousseau and affected theories of the law concerned with the rights and duties of governments and citizens. The theory involves the fiction of a 'state of nature', in which, according to Hobbes, there were no enforceable criteria of right and wrong; it was a state of perpetual struggle which could be ended only by the surrender of individual liberties into the hands of a sovereign. The question asks for 'essential features'. Attention should be given, therefore, to the state of nature, the 'natural laws' and Hobbes' basic remedy for social conflict. A skeleton plan is proposed along the following lines:

Introduction - Hobbes' 'laws of motion' - *Leviathan* - analysis of the state of nature - natural laws - the Social Contract - indivisibility of the sovereign power - law as command of the sovereign - problem of 'bad law' - conclusion, Hobbes' theories in our time.

Answer

Hobbes' legal and political theories are derived from his natural philosophy which is based on his 'law of motion'. All behaviour, according to this law, represents the activities of 'bodies in motion'. Just as the natural tendency of moving bodies to follow a line of their original direction will result in their colliding with other moving bodies, so the assertion by some individuals of their rights and freedoms will bring them into conflict with other individuals asserting the same type of rights and freedoms. The result is a continuous collision of wills, and perpetual struggle. In his *Leviathan* (published in 1651, the year in which the future Charles II fled to France after being defeated by Cromwell), Hobbes outlined his views on law, the individual and the State. It pleased no faction: Anglicans and Catholics resented his ideas concerning the role of the church; Royalists objected to his analysis of sovereignty; Cromwellians resented his advocacy of absolute monarchy. The doctrine embodying the fiction of a Social Contract struck a chord in legal theory which echoes even today.

The condition of men before the emergence of States or civil societies, referred to by Hobbes as 'the state of nature', is analysed closely. In such a state, all men are equal and all have a right to act so as to survive. The 'right of all to all' involves a freedom to possess, use and enjoy, all that an individual could obtain for himself. Man was driven by the will to survive and by the fear of violent death. The continuous clash of wills and 'bodies in motion' produced anarchy and a resulting 'war of all against all'. Neither 'good' nor 'evil' was recognised in this conflict: 'good' tended to be equated with 'survival', while 'evil' was associated with 'threats to survival'. In this state, individuals possess no capacity to build an ordered community.

Certain 'natural laws' emerge in the state of nature and attract some support because they are considered as involving concern for individual safety. They are essentially rules of behaviour, the observation of which might assist personal survival. Hobbes considers the first of these laws to be fundamental: 'peace is to be sought after'. This law is 'natural' because it is an obvious extension of concern for individual survival. An individual will have a better chance of survival if he assists the creation and maintenance of overall conditions of peace. A person will be impelled, naturally, to seek peace because of his desire to survive.

From the first law, Hobbes derives a second. Although men have rights to *all* things, these rights ought not to be retained to their full extent; certain rights ought to be 'relinquished or transferred'. A man should be willing, when others are similarly minded, to relinquish his rights to all things 'and be contented with so much liberty against other men as he would allow other men against himself'. To refuse to part with one's rights to all things is to act against the law of nature and 'the reason of peace'. A third law concerns the duty of a man to carry out a contract to which he is a party.

These laws are considered by Hobbes to be immutable and eternal; they have application to all societies and are supplemented by precepts, such as the need to avoid ingratitude, and the using of things in common that cannot be divided. Without observance of the laws of nature there will be continuous struggle arising from the conflict of individual judgments as to how best to survive. The result will be 'no arts, letters or society ... continual fear and danger of death, and the life of man will be solitary, poor, nasty, brutish and short'. To avoid this necessitates a Social Contract which will bring about a commonwealth or State.

Men will create a civil society only by virtue of an agreement between individuals. In Hobbes' words, it is as if men should say to one another, 'I authorise and surrender my right of governing myself to this person or this assembly of persons, but on the vital condition that you, too, will surrender your right to him and authorise all his actions in like manner'. In essence, the Social Contract is absolute and irrevocable. The parties to the Contract are individuals, making promises to transfer their rights to govern themselves to some sovereign. The Contract is *not* made between the individuals and that sovereign. Indeed, the sovereign has an absolute power to govern; there is no point at which he may be considered as subject to those who made the Contract among themselves. Further, it is important to note that Hobbes has in mind, when referring to the sovereign, a 'person' or 'an assembly of persons'. The theory of the Social Contract does not necessarily demand an absolute monarch (although that would reflect Hobbes' preference); it could have application to an elected assembly.

'Indivisibility of the sovereign power' is an important aspect of the theory. The citizens have agreed, in effect, that the totality of their individual wills and judgments will be represented henceforth by the single will and judgment of the sovereign. He acts on behalf of the citizens, and his actions are taken as an affirmation of the identity of their wills with his will. His will is their will; his actions reflect this unity. From this principle follows an extremely important political and legal concept - it is illogical and wrong, according to Hobbes, for a citizen to engage in resisting the sovereign. In doing so he would be resisting himself, and, further, resistance would be a manifestation of the type of independent judgment which characterised the 'state of nature' and is, therefore, undesirable. The sovereign's power must be total and, in effect, absolute.

Without a sovereign, civil law is not possible. For Hobbes, a law is the command of the sovereign. Law requires a legal order and a central power of enforcement. In the absence of power to enforce a law, a covenant is mere words. Hobbes suggests, too, that there can be no 'unjust law'. To the care of the sovereign belongs the making of good laws. But 'good law' does not mean 'just law', because a law made by the sovereign cannot be unjust. Justice means, in practice, obedience to the law, and this is why, according to Hobbes, justice comes into existence only *after* a law has been made by the sovereign. Justice cannot itself be the appropriate standard for the law. Further, when the sovereign makes a law he does so as though the citizens were making it collectively. That upon which they have agreed cannot be 'unjust'. Keeping the contract under which individuals have agreed to obey the sovereign is vital to justice. Because law is the command of the sovereign, and because justice involves obeying that law, an 'unjust law' is impossible.

Hobbes does make clear, however, that there can be 'bad law'. If the sovereign in making a law fails to ensure the safety of the people who have entrusted him with appropriate powers, then the law may be considered 'bad'. Yet this is not a matter for the people to judge lightly, nor should it be used as a justification for disobedience and rebellion. Given that the sovereign alone has the power to judge what has to be done in the interests of the security of the people, he must proceed on the basis of the exercise of that power. To question his judgment, to voice disagreement, is to revert to the anarchy which characterised the undesirable state of nature. This is a part of the price to be paid for the peace which is intended to flow from the surrender of one's individual will. Where a sovereign makes 'bad law' or performs acts which seem contrary to the general interests of the community, it is, says Hobbes, a matter between him and his God, not between him and the citizens. But where it is *quite clear* that the sovereign has *lost the capacity to maintain the peace* and protect the safety of the citizens, *or* where he has acted in an *obvious attempt* to destroy the individual's right of self-preservation, citizens may be absolved from their duty of loyalty. There is, therefore, always a check upon the exercise of absolute power exercised by a sovereign who opposes his own interest to the common good.

The fear of anarchy and social violence is ever-present in Hobbes' writings - a sure reflection of the conflicts of his day. Total obedience to an absolute sovereign, to the protector of the community's peace, seemed essential to Hobbes. Indeed, he insisted, in terms which offended the church deeply, on the subordination of church and religion to the State. If circumstances arose in which a Christian were to interpret the actions of his sovereign as a violation of Divine law, then he must continue to give obedience to that sovereign, failing which he may decide 'to go to Christ in martyrdom'. The church itself has the same type of legal status as that enjoyed by any other corporation. As with all corporations, the true head is, according to Hobbes, the sovereign.

Hobbes represents, in Friedmann's words, a jurist who has shaken himself free from medieval society and its ideas and, in so doing has completed the revolution of the Renaissance. He has removed the authority of Divine law from the church, and has challenged its pretensions. The protection of the individual within the community has become a matter of great importance. Law is seen as a means of preventing anarchy and assuring survival in peace. There can be no society distinct from the State. Legal authority is to be vested in a sovereign whose laws will depend upon appropriate sanctions. Hobbes insists that 'governments without the sword are mere words, and of no strength to secure a man at all'. Real law is civil law and that is constituted by the law commanded by the sovereign and enforced by his will.

Almost every aspect of Hobbes' Social Contract theory was reflected in the works of jurists and political theoreticians who were prominent in the 18th and 19th centuries. Locke built upon Hobbes' individualism, although he opposed his theory of absolutism. Hobbes' utilitarianism, which led him to view the sovereign as 'a utilitarian creature' of individuals who had empowered him to act on their behalf so as to prevent mutual destruction, was linked to Bentham's view of the law as serving the totality of individuals within a community. The concept of laws espoused by Austin - 'laws properly so-called are a species of command ... all positive law is deduced from a clearly determinable lawgiver as sovereign' - may be likened to Hobbes' view. In our century, the 'enlightened absolutism' favoured by Hobbes has been utilised by some jurists in order to buttress concepts of law at the basis of theories of the collectivist, totalitarian system of government. Others view his analysis of law as a call for the State to concern itself with ensuring the security of citizens' well-being, and for a jurisprudence which will recognise the welfare of individual members of the community as one of the supreme objectives of the law and the legal system.

Notes

Hobbes' *Leviathan*, edited by Oakeshott, contains an exposition of his views on government, society and law. Friedmann, ch 11 and Bodenheimer ch 3, outline the significance of Hobbes in legal theory. *The Logic of Leviathan*, by Gautier, is a critical account of Hobbes' theories. Peters gives a useful picture of the man and his work in *Hobbes*.

Question 9

'Locke's theory admirably expressed certain ideas which were in the ascendant at his time and about to develop continuously throughout the eighteenth century and most of the nineteenth century': Friedmann *(Legal Theory)*.

Give an account of this theory.

Answer plan

Locke's theory concerning the State and the individual differs radically from that of his predecessor, Hobbes. The 'state of nature' as envisaged by Locke is not that envisaged by Hobbes. This should be emphasised in the answer. Locke's concern for the dangers which could arise from an absolute monarchy should be noted. In particular, the essence of the Social Contract as reflecting the rights of citizens and their power to remove a government in certain extreme circumstances can be seen as a harbinger of the jurisprudential theories which emerged in Europe and America after Locke's day. The following skeleton plan is suggested:

> Introduction - the *Treatises of Government*, with an emphasis on liberty - man's 'natural state' - essence of the Social Contract - preservation of property - division of powers - right of a people to reject tyranny - continuing significance of Locke's views - conclusion, noting the importance of his awareness that tyrannies begin where law ends.

Answer

Locke's jurisprudential thought has been characterised as reflecting the doctrines underlying the 'Glorious Revolution' of 1688. His *Treatises of Civil Government* (1699) presented law as a shield against the pretensions of autocracy and despotism and as an instrument for realising and protecting the natural rights of human beings. Where Hobbes had stressed *security*, Locke placed an emphasis on *liberty*. His writings indicate a reaction against absolutism, a concern for the significance of powers delegated by a people to its government (which prepared the way for later theories of political democracy), an awareness of the importance of the concept of inalienability of individual rights and a sanctioning of the rights of property in particular. These ideas were to flower later in the doctrines which supported the Founding Fathers and the rise of democracy in America.

The 'natural state' of man, was according to Locke, in contrast to that postulated by Hobbes, a situation of total, perfect freedom. Men were able to decide on their activities and to dispose of their persons and possessions as they thought fit, 'within the bounds of the law of nature, without asking leave, or depending upon the will of any other man'. It was a state characterised by 'equality' wherein power and jurisdiction were reciprocal. The law of nature allowed men to live together according to reason 'without a common superior on earth with authority to judge between them'. Liberty, not licence, prevailed and, according to the dictates of the law of nature, no one was encouraged to harm another in his life, health, liberty or possessions.

But dangers and inconveniences arose. First, the individual's enjoyment of the natural rights of life, liberty and possessions was uncertain and was exposed to the hostile activities of others. Secondly, there was a lack of impartial judges with authority to determine disputes according to any form of established law. Each man was both judge and executioner in his own cause and each tended to avenge transgressions in intemperate fashion. Thirdly, there was a lack of a commonly-accepted power to back up and support sentences where wrongdoing had occurred. So as to end this disorder and insecurity, men found it necessary to enter into a Social Contract. Its object was the preservation of life, liberty and estate against the injuries inflicted by others. Fundamental to the Contract is a *pactum unionis*, whereby men agree 'to unite in one political society', and a *pactum subjectionis*, whereby a majority gives power to a government which will protect the individual. This is a contrast to Hobbes' advocacy of total subjection of the individual to the government. The 'law of nature' stood, for Locke, as an eternal rule made for all men, 'legislators as well as others'. An anticipation of the doctrines of popular democracy, with legislatures accountable to the people, may be discerned here.

It is the *right to enforce* the law of nature which, by virtue of the Social Contract is given into the hands of the 'body politic', thus creating a 'political, or civil society'. Nothing more is surrendered. Hence Locke rejects the concept of absolute monarchy as a desirable type of government. A government with limited powers is preferable. (This ideal was to be pursued after Locke's day by jurists and others striving for the 'rule of law' within societies.) Those who have given their 'natural power' of deciding disputes among themselves into the hands of the community are conferring upon that community the role of 'umpire', whereby government is given an authorisation to set up 'a judge on earth' with power to determine controversies and redress injuries'. Indeed, without an authorisation of this kind, without a right to enforce the law, men will remain in 'the state of nature' with all its difficulties and perils.

In words which have been echoed in a variety of forms in centuries after Locke, (as in the English case of *Entick v Carrington* (1765) and the American case of *Savings and Loan Association v Topeka* (1875)), he enunciated 'the great and chief end of men's uniting into commonwealth and putting themselves under government' as 'the preservation of their property'. The term 'property' is used in a wide sense so as to include 'life, liberty and estate'. Friedmann and other jurists have noted that Locke's views in relation to property ('a combination of noble ideals and acquisitiveness, and the protection of vested interests') underpinned later struggles within democratic societies for a sanctioning of the right to own and dispose freely of the fruits of one's labours.

Locke finds that the institution of private property existed in nature and, therefore, preceded the establishment of civil society. God gave the land to persons in common, commanding them to labour and to use the fruits of the earth. Where men remove parts of the land from the common supply and mix it with their own labour, they are entitled to the objects resulting from their toil. There is a 'natural right', therefore, to appropriate to one's own use land and its produce. Indeed, says Locke, land values arise largely from the labour expended on the land. Private ownership is enlarged, as a result of the use of money as a means of exchange, well beyond those boundaries authorised by a simple act of appropriation. The call for extended rights to private ownership of the land and other types of property became important in moves in the eighteenth and nineteenth centuries towards an extension of general political rights, when it was realised that the ownership of land conferred economic and political power. Locke's influence on this area of thought remains powerful. Gray, writing in 1991, speaks of the 'brooding omnipresence of Locke' as a pervasive influence on all philosophical thinking on property, even today.

Because of the significance of property rights in Locke's pattern of liberty, he was obliged to maintain that no part of a person's property ought to be taken from him by the government without his consent. Such an improper exercise of government power should be considered as a violation of the Social Contract by virtue of which power is exercised. The community as a whole must ensure that its governing body does not move beyond the powers bestowed on it. The legislative authority may not assume to itself any power to rule 'by extemporary arbitrary decrees; it is bound to dispense justice and decide the rights of citizens by promulgating laws'. Nor should these laws be varied so as to have 'one rule for the rich and poor, for the favourite at Court, and the countryman at plough'. Locke is enunciating an ideal which was to be advocated repeatedly in the writings of later jurists who called for equality of all before the law.

The supreme power within a community has no other end, according to Locke, but 'preservation'; it can never have a right to 'destroy, enslave or designedly to impoverish subjects'. This necessitates a 'division of powers' within the State: a legislative power to create rules, an executive power to enforce them, and a 'federative power' to control the State's external relations. Where the legislative and executive powers are concentrated in the same hands, a breach of the desired ends of the Social Contract is likely. But this danger was not viewed by Locke as an argument for removing the prerogative of the executive to use its general discretion for the good of the community. Where appropriate laws have not been promulgated by the legislature, where no general directions have been given to the executive, where unusual stress and emergency demand swift action, the executive may act for the public advantage. But separation of powers (a concept which Montesquieu, and jurists in our day, see as essential to the rule of law) remains for Locke an important guarantee of the preservation of a commonwealth and its individual members.

Even where powers are separated, abuse and violation of individual rights may occur. There is needed, therefore, a final guarantor of the law of nature. Fundamentally, Locke rejects the 'rights' of a 'tyrant'. The people as a whole, acting in the name of the liberties which have been entrusted to the supreme power under the Social Contract, may remove a legislature which, deliberately or otherwise, forgets the purpose and nature of its trust. Locke, who had experienced the practice of absolute government under the Stuarts, urged that the power of the State must 'never be supposed to extend further than the common good', so that where a legislature moves beyond its powers, as understood by the community, the people may apply appropriate checks. The final resort by the people to an 'appeal to Heaven' which, in practice, may take the form of resistance or revolution, is seen by Locke as necessary if the law of nature is to be upheld against oppressive laws which seem to deny its validity.

Locke's appeal to 'natural rights' as the true guarantee against a regime which seems to abuse its powers, so that the community has the right to resume a trust which is in danger of betrayal, is yet another theme which came to dominate advances in the eighteenth and nineteenth centuries towards the rule of law and the extension of democracy. The American Declaration of Independence (1776) embodies the essence of Locke's doctrine relating to the fundamental right of a people to 'alter or abolish' a form of government which becomes destructive of the ends perceived by the people as constituting the very purpose of the State. The Declaration suggests the concept which Locke had stressed, but in a novel manner - the idea of a government resting upon trust, upon a *fiduciary relationship* of government and governed, rather than upon the mere duties flowing from a Social Contract. But Locke must not be considered as advocating rebellion in all cases of an abuse of governmental powers. The justification of popular resistance must be sought in a long series of abuses and a very clear threat to the 'lives, liberties and estates' of citizens. Nor does resistance imply revenge; it is an activity aimed at the restoration of an order violated by an oppressor.

The political and legal ferment within societies of the eighteenth and nineteenth centuries was often the result of the circumstances envisaged by Locke. His warnings that *whenever laws end, tyrannies will begin*, and that 'what duty is, cannot be understood without a law' were utilised by jurists who sought to express theories resting on the need for a widening of the basis of law. His cautions concerning the consequences of unbridled governmental powers were remembered in calls for the creation of popular power and an extension of the franchise. Although doubt was cast, in increasing measure, upon the veracity of Locke's 'state of nature' (thus, Hamilton, writing in this century speaks of this 'state' as being, 'a curious affair, peopled with Indians of North America and run by the scientific principles of [Locke's] friend, Sir Isaac Newton'), his contribution to political and legal theory is profound. Keeton reminds us that it is from Locke that we derive, today, 'the principle of democratic government, resting upon the consent of the governed' - an extraordinarily valuable legacy of the *Treatises of Civil Government* and the subsequent thinking which they engendered.

Notes

Locke's *Two Treatises of Civil Government* are available in an edition by Laslett. His theories are discussed in Lloyd, ch 3, Dias, ch 4, Bodenheimer, ch 3. Comments on Locke's theory of property may be found in 'Property according to Locke', by Hamilton, in 41 Yale LJ (1932) and 'Property in Thin Air', by Gray, in the Cambridge Law Journal (1991) 293. *John Locke: a Biography*, by Cranston, explains the nature of the society in which Locke lived.

Natural Law

Introduction

Natural law, which is the subject of the questions in this chapter, is an enduring concept in European jurisprudence, ranging from Aristotle, who held that there is a natural law which 'everywhere possesses the same authority and is no mere matter of opinion', through Aquinas, for whom the natural law was 'the participation of the eternal law in the rational creature', to today's neo-Scholastics, who seek to establish new values based on fundamental criteria often related directly to the social teachings of the Catholic Church. Natural law is often contrasted with the 'positive law', namely, the legal rules promulgated in formal fashion by the State and enforced through defined sanctions. A problem for students is to decide which 'type' of natural law is being referred to, since the term has been used in so many different senses. It is essential, therefore, to *check the precise historical and juristic context* of the term, particularly when answering questions on this topic.

Checklist

Ensure that you understand the following topics:

- natural and positive law contrasted
- Aquinas' divisions of law
- *lex injusta*

- neo-Scholasticism

- Duguit's 'rules of conduct'
- Radbruch's 'just law'
- natural law with a changing content
- Finnis' 'human goods'
- derivation of 'ought' from 'is'

Question 10

What is Aquinas' theory of law?

Answer plan

St Thomas Aquinas (1225-74) was concerned with systematising
knowledge, on the basis of Catholic doctrine, so that the cosmos
might be understood as a vast unit in which everything had a
place and a meaning. Within his system of knowledge, God's
plans for mankind occupied a special place, and the law was to be
comprehended as a part of those plans. Aquinas propounded a
theory of law based on his conception of 'reason'; this resulted in
a fourfold division of law in which so-called 'natural law' was of
much significance. The answer given below is based on the
following skeleton plan:

Introduction - background of Aquinas - influence of
Aristotelian thought - fourfold division of law - problem of
morality - violation of the natural law and its consequences -
conclusion, stressing the work of Aquinas as a synthesiser of
philosophy and religious thought in his interpretation of law.

Answer

Aquinas occupies an important place in the history of the
development of natural law doctrine. He had studied as a
Dominican monk under Albertus Magnus, and, in later years,
produced works of lasting significance in which he effected a
synthesis of the logic of Aristotle, the religious thought of the
early Christian Fathers, and the patterns of classical Roman law.
In his celebrated *Summa Theologica* (c 1266) he set out a fully-
systematised approach to law which, even today, dominates the
thinking of many Catholic jurists, as evidenced by the neo-
Scholastic school of jurisprudence. Law was to be understood as
part of God's plan for mankind - this is the belief which is central
to the concepts mentioned below.

It is important to remember the context within which Aquinas
worked. The authority of the Catholic Church was expanding,
and those whose task it was to explain doctrine were guided by a
strict pattern of thought. Interpretation of the Scriptures had
produced two principles which were of direct relation to attempts
at explaining the nature of law. First, the principle of *unity* (based
on 'one God, one Church') was reflected in the wish for 'one
church believing in one law'. Secondly, the principle of *supremacy*

of law, which was seen as an aspect of the unity of the world, taught that all persons, including rulers, were under the law's dominion. Aquinas' general approach to law was fashioned with these principles in mind.

In his time, the study of the works of Aristotle was not always welcomed by the church hierarchy, which viewed his 'scientific rationalism' as a potential threat to church dogma. Aquinas did not share this attitude. He was deeply impressed by Aristotle's emphasis on reason and the primacy of intelligence. He made a deep study of Aristotle's works, lectured publicly on their significance, and was affected profoundly by their elucidation of the part which could be played by reason in the understanding of phenomena such as law.

Aquinas begins his examination and interpretation of law by considering 'morality'. The very basis of moral obligation is to be discovered within man's nature. Built into his nature is a group of God-given 'inclinations'. They include self-preservation, propagation of the species and (reflecting man's rationality) an inclination towards a search for truth. Man is guided by a simple and basic moral truth - *to do good and to avoid evil*. Because man is rational he is under a natural obligation to protect himself and to live peacefully within society. A peaceful, ordered society demands human laws, fashioned for the direction of social behaviour. These human laws will arise from man's rational capacity to discern correct patterns of 'good conduct'. The rules underlying human laws will derive from a moral system which ought to be taken into account by *all* mankind - a sort of 'natural law'.

Law must be thought of, according to Aquinas, as linked essentially with reason. A law may be considered as a 'rule' and also as 'a measure' of the nature of human activities. He reminds us that the word *lex* is derived from *ligare* (to bind) and that law 'binds us' to act in particular ways. The rule and measure of human acts are to be thought of in terms of law and also in terms of our reason. Reason directs us to the fulfilment of 'our ends' (an Aristotelian concept). Man's laws should go hand in hand with reason. Indeed, man's laws may be thought of as 'ordinances of reason for the common good, made by those who have care of the community, and are promulgated'. The natural law is 'promulgated' by the very fact that God has instilled it into man's mind so that it can be known 'naturally'. The natural law is the product of God's wisdom. We can better comprehend that wisdom by studying human nature and the natural law. Theology *and* philosophy together will help in this quest for comprehension of the truth. Aquinas is suggesting that a synthetic approach to a study of the law, in which Christian dogma and Aristotelian philosophy will assist, will produce a clear understanding of the nature and power of God's law.

A *fourfold division of law* is put forward by Aquinas. The first type of law is *lex aeterna* - 'eternal law'. This is the Divine Intellect and Will of God directing *all things*. God's rational guidance is not subject to constraints of time - it is eternal. Not to know eternal law - God's plan for his creatures - is to be without direction, so that one's true ends can never be achieved. God alone knows the eternal law in its totality, but those few 'blessed persons' who have been able to know God in His essence may perceive its truth.

'Divine law' - *lex divina* - is the eternal law governing man and may be known by him through direct revelation, as in the Ten Commandments. Man requires a type of law that can direct him to his end, namely, eternal happiness. Aristotle had argued that man had a natural purpose and an end, so that natural law, known through human reason, could provide an adequate guide. Aquinas distances himself from Aristotle at this point. Because man's eternal happiness is related to God's plans, man needs direction from God's law, in addition to human law and natural law. Natural law comes from man's rational knowledge of 'the good', but that knowledge is, by its nature, limited. Divine law comes, through revelation, directly from God. Revelation is the guide for man's reason, allowing his highest nature to be perfected by Divine grace. Here is an interesting example of Aquinas giving a 'Christian gloss' to the views of the 'pagan Greeks' and achieving an imaginative synthesis.

The third type of law is 'natural law' - *lex naturalis*, which is man's participation in the eternal law governing him, as it is known through reason. Because of man's possession of God-given reason he may enjoy a share in Divine reason itself and may derive from it 'a natural inclination to such actions and ends as are fitting'. Where man exercises his reason correctly he will understand the fundamental principles of God's plan. Basic principles for human guidance will emerge, such as that 'good' ('that which all things seek after') is to be done and evil is to be shunned.

The fourth type of law is 'human law' - *lex humana*, involving the particular application of the natural law and resulting in legislation by governments. Just as men draw conclusions in the various sciences from naturally-known, but indemonstrable, principles, so, declares Aquinas, human beings must draw from the precepts of the natural law answers to problems which emerge when they live together in society. Where human law conforms to the law of reason, it conforms to the law of God.

A significant aspect of Aquinas' concept of human law, which has overtones of relevance for the present day,is the relationship he sees between human law and its moral dimensions. He repudiates the thesis that a law is a law merely because it has been decreed by a sovereign. He suggests that a rule takes on the character of 'a law' only where it has appropriate moral dimensions. Certain questions must be asked: does the rule exist in conformity to the precepts of the natural law, and does it suggest agreement with the basis of the moral law? 'That which is not just seems no law at all', he declares. Where a law diverges from the law of nature it is no longer a law, but a mere perversion of the law. *Such a law cannot bind in conscience.* This is not to say, however, that it must not, therefore, be obeyed; obedience to it might be essential so as to prevent an even greater evil, such as the spread of lawlessness.

Aquinas takes a further step forward. Laws which are opposed to the Divine plan, such as the laws of tyrants inducing to 'idolatry', must not be observed: our duty is to obey God rather than man. A violation of the natural law should *not* be obeyed.

There are many jurists, inside and outside the Catholic Church, who see Aquinas as a charismatic genius, able to synthesise a variety of approaches and capable of bringing system into an unwieldy group of theories. In moving beyond his predecessors and contemporaries he was able to produce a unified set of principles in relation to the law. Natural law was envisaged as a source of *general principles* rather than detailed jurisprudential rules. Above all, perhaps, was *the elevation of human reason* in the service of comprehension of the law. God's law was the 'reason of Divine wisdom'; Christianity was reason;

human institutions, including those related to law, required the exercise of reason if they were to be built in enduring fashion. The Thomist view of law is, fundamentally, that of Cicero, writing in *De Republica* (52 BC): 'true law is right reason in agreement with Nature ... God is the author of this law, its promulgator and its enforcing judge'. In essence: 'The proper effect of the law is to make men good ... it should lead men to their proper virtue'.

Notes

The theory of law expounded by Aquinas is discussed in Lloyd, ch 3, Harris, ch 2, Riddall, ch 5, and Davies and Holdcroft, ch 6. A classic account of the work of Aquinas is given by D'Arcy in *Thomas Aquinas*. Bloch relates the theory of Aquinas to contemporary problems in 'The Relative Natural Law of Aquinas' in his book, *Natural Law and Human Dignity*.

Question 11

Elaborate Stammler's concept of 'natural law with a variable content'.

Answer plan

Stammler (1856-1936), a German jurist and disciple of the philosopher, Kant, considered the advantages to be gained from a system of law based on fundamental principles which allowed for interpretation, and even modification, in the light of social requirements. The question necessitates an examination of this seemingly-paradoxical viewpoint. Some detailed examination of Stammler's argument is needed together with reference to the social principles he advocated in relation to the law. The following skeleton plan is used:

Introduction -the paradox within the concept - essence of Stammler's views - the 'concept' and the 'idea' of law - Stammler's views on reason - principles of 'respect' and 'participation' - the principles in practice - conclusion, summary of Stammler's views.

Answer

The concept of 'natural law with a variable content' appears somewhat paradoxical. The essence of natural law, as that term is generally understood, is its unchanging, everlasting nature. For some jurists, natural law emanates from Divine revelation and reflects the immutable, eternal aspects of God's plan for mankind. Stammler, with whom the concept is linked, believed that every era should have its own 'law of nature', its 'right-law', which would co-exist with its positive law. The rules of the positive law would have to 'justify' their existence and use by an evaluation according to standards posed by the relevant philosophical and ethical doctrines of the era. Should a law be found wanting as a result of this evaluation, it would be corrected by legislation or by the practice of the courts. Stammler was suggesting that in a progressive society, positive law needs to be tested regularly by the light of the community's prevailing *moral* ideals, in particular.

The ideal of the classical natural law which was to be found in a perfect code with an unchangeable, unconditionally valid legal content, seemed to Stammler to reflect the impossible. The jurist's task was to discover a valid formal method by means of which the changing material of 'empirically-conditioned legal rules' could be so worked out and judged that the law may have *the quality of objective justice*. For this a new approach to an understanding of the law was required.

It is essential, says Stammler, to distinguish the *concept of law* from the *idea of law*. Confusion of the two is common. The concept of law is little more than a merely formal definition. Its underlying meaning is 'the inviolable and autocratic will'. The law is an aspect of man's *social existence*; it relates to individuals living together and constituting a community. It embodies the collective will of that community and is 'autocratic' in the sense that the laws bind all members. Law is, therefore, the result of 'binding volition' (a phrase used in earlier versions of natural law) and members of the community are not free to accept or reject it as they please. The 'concept' of law is a reflection of 'inviolable volition'; it binds its adherents in a unity of purpose. 'Unity of purpose', 'will of the community', echo the classical natural law doctrines.

Stammler, having acknowledged the need for a 'binding together of the community in a unity of purpose' proceeds to discuss the 'idea of the law' - a much more complex phenomenon than the 'concept of law'. The 'idea of the law' will mirror the need for *justice within the community*. But justice is not to be viewed as a mere abstraction. For Stammler, justice arises from *necessity* - the necessity for all 'legal efforts' to be aimed at the attainment of the most perfect harmony of social life that is possible *in a given place at a given time*. Here is a meeting-point of the absolutism of the natural law ('perfect harmony') and the awareness of the need to view principle in a context of place and time.

As a disciple of Kant, Stammler accepts the Kantian principle of *man as an end in himself*. Kant's celebrated formulation of the 'categorical imperative' (ie, the principle which ought to guide human activity) was '*so act to treat humanity whether in thine own person or that of another, in every case as an end withal, never as a means only*'. The recognising of members of a community as ends in themselves, and not as mere objects of an arbitrary will, is a necessary objective of the 'right-law' which Stammler sees as the true 'idea of law'. His own social ideal, which, again, has overtones of some earlier views of classical natural law, is of a 'community of free-willing men', bound by a law which is derived from their common interests but reflecting the fundamental recognition of that community as an end in itself. Kant's 'categorical imperative' is given expression by Stammler in his advocacy of man as an end, directed by laws inspired by principles of justice, manifesting the community's 'pure will'.

In the tradition of the natural law, Stammler emphasises the role of reason in the law. One's social responsibilities may be determined by the use of reason, and the realising of the community's social ideals demands 'a rational curbing of one's own singular desires' based on respect for the community in general, and other individuals in particular. The exercise of reason is vital for the individual if the community, of which he is a part, is to move towards the standards of reciprocity which are essential where people are treated as ends in themselves. Essentially, Stammler is following the pattern of his predecessors in the natural law who elevated reason to a supreme position in the determination of the law. But Stammler does not make clear the precise meaning he attaches to 'reason'. Ginsberg, for example, has criticised Stammler's theory as based on too abstract a view of 'reason'. He pays lip-service to some remote concept of reason, says Ginsberg, but makes virtually impossible the relating of 'particular aims' of action to the 'universal'. In practice, argues Ginsberg, the actual law would be placed 'at the mercy of empiricism and the blind forces of tradition'.

Within a social framework dominated by a desire for justice, as an expression of the community's collective will (and reminiscent of many structures suggested by the earlier natural law), is a group of principles which must be kept in mind if individuals are to attain freedom under the law. The 'principles of respect' and the 'principles of participation' must be translated into practical law by the community's legislators; they should be embedded within enactments and other social rules. The community's needs will find a place in the overall framework of fundamental principle.

The 'principles of respect' demand that the content of an individual's volition be not rendered subject to the arbitrary power of another. This will mean, in practice, that no act of an individual's will is to be subjected to the caprice of another. Each member of the community is an end in himself and is to be treated accordingly. Respect for him as a person demands that he be safe from the whims of another. Further, every legal demand on an individual must be made in such a manner that the person obligated may retain his 'self-respecting personality'. A juristic claim has validity, therefore, only if this principle is respected, ie, only on the condition that the individual of whom it is made be allowed to preserve his dignity as a member of a united, free community of individuals. Stammler is calling, in effect, for the preservation of human dignity - an essential feature of the classical natural law.

The 'principles of participation' are as important as those of 'respect'. A member of the community may not be excluded from it in arbitrary fashion. This means in practice that power may not be exercised with the result that some person is deprived of his social status and reputation. The concept of 'man as an end in himself' demands from those who live by it that, because dignity involves the recognition of the right to participate in a community, that right shall not be invaded by others. Further, a power of control conferred by the community through the law may be justified only to the extent that the person affected thereby is enabled to retain his self-respect. Stammler's principles seem directed to a recognition of Kantian fundamentals concerning the 'imperatives' for social behaviour. The place accorded to man by the natural law is recognised; the rules relating to his treatment within the community are to be designed accordingly and, in practice, will recognise the needs and morals of that community.

Stammler insists on an application of the principles of respect and participation with an understanding of the specific, variable sets of circumstances arising in different types of society. Valid, basic rules are required if the 'idea of law' is to be realised - a concept acceptable to natural law doctrine. But a society in transition, in flux, will require, not a modification of the 'idea of the law', but rather an adaptation of rules to the realities of that society. Here is 'natural law with a variable content'. Tradition gives way to real needs, not at the expense of the fundamental rule, but so that the essence of the rule shall be recognised and translated according to time, place and other circumstances.

Stammler seeks to demonstrate the significance of his principles of respect of participation by applying them to a variety of actual problems derived from the German Civil Law of his day. The phenomena of the cartel and the trust received particular attention. Cartels and trusts were based on associations of firms formed so as to restrict, or exercise a monopolistic influence on, the production or sale of commodities. Prices and output are regulated, markets are divided up. Stammler argues that these economic organisations do achieve an important social purpose: they oppose 'the anarchy of production and sale' and can give some kind of protection and defence to individuals who, under conditions of unrestricted freedom in the market, will be unable to realise their 'proper activities as human beings' within the social economy. On the other hand, cartels and trusts may be viewed as representing combinations made for personal ends. They can easily become the means of abuse of the community. The principles of respect and participation must be applied to an examination of the problem. Is a cartel, by its policies and activities, invading the rights of producers outside its ranks? Are they being deprived of the right to participate in the community? Is the cartel exploiting members of the community by arbitrary demands? Is it ignoring the necessity for cooperation within the community? These questions illustrate the kinds of criteria Stammler would keep in mind in deciding a practical question, with the fundamental duties of traders and producers in mind. The reality is to be viewed in the light of principle, not merely on the basis of the desire to make a swift decision.

We may summarise Stammler's view of natural law by emphasising his concern for its traditional concepts which, he believes, assist in providing an understanding of what has to be done if man is to be treated with respect. He wishes, however, to mould some of those concepts into a structure which rests upon the axiom that it is not possible to view a principle in terms of a content which will *always* stand up to the demanding test of time. It is not the law of nature but the nature of law which is common to all countries and communities in all ages. The nature of law may be comprehended only when perceived (as through the eyes of the advocates of the classical natural law) as a harmonious whole. Rules must be 'right' for a community, and the criterion for the testing of their 'rightness' must be of a formal nature - mere relativism will not suffice. A community of free-willing individuals, each an end in himself, each contributing to a community in which he may realise his potential, is Stammler's ideal. The law, attuned to the needs of that community, and reflecting the harmony of which the natural law speaks, assists in the journey to the realisation of that ideal.

Notes

Stammler's *Theory of Justice* explains his attitude to natural law. Friedmann, ch 16, and Jones, in his *Historical Introduction to the Theory of Law*, ch 4, consider the implications of Stammler's views. Hussik analyses the theory in 'The Legal Philosophy of Stammler', 24 Col LR 373 (1924).

Question 12

'It is paradoxical that aspects of the legal philosophy of one who rejected totally any absolutist conception of state power should have been favoured by the jurists and ideologists of the authoritarian States'.

Discuss this comment on Duguit.

Answer plan

Duguit (1859-1918) illustrates the difficulty of attempting to pigeon-hole some jurists. A French legal philosopher who opposed totally the doctrines of natural law and rejected metaphysics, he produced what has been classified as a 'natural law' theory; a determined opponent of State power, his doctrines were taken up in the 1930s by supporters of totalitarian regimes. An answer will require consideration of the central themes of his doctrine, in particular those based upon 'social solidarity' and 'duty as right'. Attention should be paid to 'rules of conduct' which he formulated. A skeleton plan is used in the following form:

Introduction -paradox of Duguit's jurisprudential thought - right to do one's duty - law of social solidarity - the State - syndicalism - rules of conduct - conclusion, effect of Duguit's separation of 'right' from 'law'.

Answer

Duguit's *Law in the Modern State* (1913) has been described as 'a natural-law theory with strong sociological overtones'. The author was opposed totally to natural law and its claims; he had repudiated emphatically any suggestion of the existence of 'natural' or 'inalienable' rights of individuals, and wished to create a positivistic theory of law which would not contain any metaphysical aspects. In the event, what he did produce was a theory based on the maxim of 'a duty to maintain social solidarity' - a metaphysical brocard disguised as fact, and very suggestive of those 'abiding principles' allowing man to realise his true nature and purpose, which characterise natural law. He rejected the concept of 'the State' as meaningless. Yet some of his principles found their way into the juristic litanies of the Fascist and Falangist regimes of the 1930s and 1940s because of their emphasis on duties, solidarity and anti-revolutionary syndicalism. Some of the specific areas of overlap between Duguit's jurisprudence and authoritarian thought emerge clearly from the review of his doctrines given below.

Law, says Duguit, is an objective fact: it does not exist in any sense as a 'body of rights'. The so-called 'ethical basis' upon which law is said to rest is mere myth. 'Subjective right' in the individual or the State is a meaningless idea; indeed, the very term 'natural right' was invented, according to Duguit, as a barrier against the claims of the absolute rulers of the eighteenth century. Law has no relation to any kind of 'ideal right' and merely records an objective situation existing between individuals or between the State and individuals.

Duguit leans heavily on the theories associated with Comte, one of the founders of positivism, who enunciated the dogma that every individual has duties towards every other individual, 'but no man has any rights properly so-called'. In other words, said Comte, *the only right which any man can possess is the right to do his duty*. Duguit accepts this statement in its entirety. Its appeal to the totalitarian ethic is obvious - it stresses the obligations of the individual and, by implication, avoids analysis of right-claims to which persons, in their role as subjects of a State, or partners within an enterprise, might be entitled.

The concept of law as an 'objective situation' arising between individuals and the State, is based on a principle named by Duguit, 'the law of social interdependence (or social solidarity)'. The existence of that law may be derived from observation of the very fact of the existence of social groupings. 'Social solidarity' is a rule by which individuals must live, not because of any 'higher principle', such as 'good' or 'happiness', but because individuals can live only in some form of society. Outside of such groupings, man cannot exist. All society, proclaimed Duguit, is, essentially, a 'discipline'. Since man cannot live without society, he cannot live without discipline. 'Solidarity' is no more than a reflection of the *fact of a community and its needs*. The stress placed on discipline as an essential feature of social life, and the emphasis on solidarity as essential to social existence, were interpreted as providing intellectual support for jurists in the authoritarian States who attributed to their citizens a basic role as disciplined 'warrior - producers'.

If there is no value in the idea of 'right', it becomes all the more important, according to Duguit, to subject the role and functions of the State and its organs of authority to a basic examination. It is erroneous, he suggests to regard the State as a public power enforcing rights and duties. 'Formulated law' - the product of the State in its role as legislator - is no more than the creation of those persons who happen to have legislative power in their hands. The laws they enact may have no necessary connection with the wills of the majority. The laws they ought to enact should be an *embodiment of the concept of social interdependence* - and nothing else. 'True law' should emanate from, and represent the solidarity of, the people.

The very idea of a 'sovereign State' is, according to Duguit, a mere fiction. Hence those legal and political theories which seek to personify the State are valueless. Analysis reveals that a State, a government, should be viewed as consisting of no more than groups of individuals to whom a a variety of duties has been entrusted. Mystical concepts of the State, such as 'God's will walking on earth', are nonsense. As in the case of other individuals within society, those within a government are subject to the supreme, vital law of 'social interdependence'. Acts of agents of a government have no mystical quality - they are no more than acts of individuals. But, says Duguit, the acts of a government have a 'special legal significance' in that they are 'juristic acts'. He defines a 'juristic act' as a declaration of will emanating from a competent person, 'having as its object a thing which that person can voluntarily determine in accordance with a legal end'. The specific, actual operations of a government are to be attributed, therefore, to its individual agents, and not to any metaphysical personification of a corporate will.

In modern times, says Duguit, the State is little more than a central agency for the exercise, not of public power, but of those activities necessary to effect the performance of 'public service'. The true foundation of public law is to be found in the concept of public service. Duguit attempts to demonstrate, largely by reference to French legal development, that the responsibility of the State has changed, with the result that its essential character has changed. At one time the State guaranteed some few basic services, but today it guarantees a large number of services, and that has become its essential function. The result of this development is, according to Duguit, a replacement of the concept of 'State sovereignty' by the notion of 'public service'. Public service is to be viewed in precise terms as comprising activities, the accomplishment of which should be regulated by the authorities because they are essential to the maintenance of social solidarity. The State, comprising those individuals in whose hands is a preponderating power, has the obligation of organising, guaranteeing and controlling the operation of those services such as defence, the administration of justice. In the name of social solidarity, the State, including the apparatus of maintenance of law and order, fulfils its function of assisting the community to carry on with its activities. Here, too, was a thesis which was utilised as a justification for the establishing and operating of the economic, social and legal mechanisms of the collectivist, totalitarian regimes.

Duguit argues that the State is the central power for the maintenance of public services only. But because services of this nature increase at a vast rate as the community becomes more complex, their effective administration requires decentralisation and 'federal syndicalism'. The central power must eventually confine itself to supervision and overall control. There will grow and develop processes of direction exercised by different social classes, each of which will acquire a definite juristic structure - the legal essence of 'syndicalism'. It is important to note that Duguit was a firm opponent of the 'revolutionary syndicalism' preached by theoreticians such as Sorel, and based on the perceived 'spontaneity of the class struggle'. Duguit did not accept the Marxist concept of a 'two-class' society (a facet of his thought which found an echo in totalitarian ideology). In syndicalism, said Duguit, one may perceive a movement towards bestowing a 'juristic structure' on social classes. This would tend to reduce social conflicts and would afford powerful protection to individuals within their social group 'against the excessive claims of other classes and against arbitrary action of the central power'. Allen points out that authoritarian governments found it expedient to utilise systems based on

syndicalist group-government, and the concepts advocated by
Duguit provided intellectual support for this.

In his later writings, Duguit promulgated three 'rules of
conduct' which are framed in the imperative mode - unusually so
in the case of a 'non-natural law' theory. First, one should respect
every act of the individual will determined by an end related to
the maintenance of social solidarity. Nothing should be done to
prevent its accomplishment and one should cooperate as far as
possible in that accomplishment. Secondly, every individual
within society ought to abstain from any act that might be
interpreted as opposition to social solidarity. Thirdly, nothing
should be done to diminish the level of solidarity within the
community; indeed, everything should be done that is materially
practicable in pursuit of the aim of intensifying solidarity.

In sum, Duguit converts the 'fact' of social solidarity into a
normative principle which demands the full participation of all
members of the community. Governments and the governed have
the absolute duty to abstain from acts motivated by purposes
inimical to the realisation of solidarity. The powers of
governments are, therefore, limited, and statutes and
administrative orders are valid only when they conform with the
over-riding principle of social solidarity. Representatives of all
social classes within a community could set up 'tribunals' which
would interpret the concept of solidarity and utilise that
interpretation so as to determine the validity of legislation. Law is
to be viewed as a means to the attainment of those ends
immanent in man's nature; it may be utilised so as to achieve and
maintain social solidarity.

Friedmann suggests that Duguit was essentially a 'romantic'.
But by a strange irony of history, his 'romantic theory' was
destined to become very useful in the hands of 'the most
unromantic, cold-blooded and cynical attempt' to use the idea of
solidarity for the suppression of individual rights. Allen believes
that the result of Duguit's banishment of 'right' from the idea of
law, makes concepts of 'right', 'justice' and 'law' meaningless. To
remove 'right' from an analysis of society and law is to violate a
deep-seated instinct in human nature. Law which is deliberately
and totally dissociated from ethics lacks a vital quality. It may,
indeed, be no paradox that Duguit's jurisprudence provided

support for those who utilised his view of law in the creation of lawless regimes.

Notes

Duguit outlines his views on jurisprudence in 'Objective law' in 20 Col LR 817 (1920). Friedmann, ch 9, Allen, chs 1 and 7, Dias, ch 20, and Bodenheimer, ch 9, provide a critical analysis of his doctrines. Laski writes on 'Duguit's Concept of the State' in *Modern Theories of the Law*, ed Jennings.

Question 13

How would you account for the growth of interest in natural law doctrine since the end of the Second World War?

Answer plan

Protagonists of natural law maintain that interest in its doctrines seems to intensify in periods of crisis as if the concept of an eternal and immutable set of principles of law were an attraction to jurists and others who perceive human conflict as reflecting a failure of relativist principles. The post-war revival of interest in natural law, in countries such as France and Canada where the legal doctrines of Aquinas were re-examined with keen interest, and in Germany where the growth of tyranny was interpreted as having been assisted by legal relativism, may be viewed as a desire to establish legal barriers against the growth of lawless regimes. An answer to the question calls for an awareness of the specific manifestation of a revival of natural law jurisprudence. The following skeleton plan is suggested:

Introduction - the perceived inadequacies of legal relativism - reaction against lawless regimes - experience of France and Germany - reaction within Britain - United Nations - antagonisms within Eastern Europe - growth of religious movements - conclusion, noting restatement of natural law.

Answer

The term 'natural law' is used here to refer to the body of jurisprudential doctrine based on the acceptance of absolute value judgments said to be in accordance with 'nature' and 'reason', reflecting the 'essence of the Universe', and possessing an immutable and eternally-valid character. The growth of interest in natural law during the past half-century may be viewed as testimony to its intrinsic resilience and as reflecting particular social conditions. Attention is paid here to the effect on jurisprudence of the immediate aftermath of the Second World War and the reaction in many parts of the world to suggestions for a guarantee of basic human rights.

The years immediately following the defeat of the Axis powers witnessed attempts by jurists and others to understand how it had been possible for Germany, which was noted for a long, proud tradition of jurisprudential scholarship and a sophisticated system of legal institutions, to have declined into lawlessness. Some blamed the replacement of the natural law tradition by a value-free 'legal relativism'; others felt that the spirit of the natural law had been submerged by a wave of dogma which stressed the importance of formalistic legal structures. A return to the absolutes of natural law characterised post-war years. In particular, the teachings of Radbruch, a German jurist who had abandoned relativism in favour of 'a just law' based on absolutes, became popular. Radbruch taught that where equality 'which is the core of justice' is denied in the enactment of law, that law will be not only unjust, but will lack the true nature of law altogether. The reconstruction of Germany's legal system provided an occasion for a re-examination of the concepts of natural law - human dignity, immutable rights. Some of the events surrounding the rebuilding of the German legal system were reflected in the Hart-Fuller debate of the 1950s, which touched on the very essence of natural law doctrine in the light of Radbruch's 'conversion', and which was responsible for some intensification of interest in natural law.

The Nuremberg trial of war criminals in 1945-6 was the occasion for a restatement of human values in terms which reminded many jurists of the absolutes proclaimed by natural law. The legal indictment was based on counts which included 'crimes against humanity', and the verdicts were delivered in language which made clear the enormity of the events which had followed on the denial of human rights. At a later date, some countries enacted legislation designed to embody respect for human rights and dignity. Some teachings of natural-law jurists were referred to repeatedly during the trial, and subsequent publicity contributed directly to a revival of interest in those teachings. Belief in the relevance of natural law as a contribution to the solution of the legal and social problems of our time burgeoned.

In France, jurisprudential thought was stimulated by a consideration of the failure of the French system of law to act as a barrier to excesses during the period of occupation. The Neo-Thomists, guided by a reinterpretation of the legal doctrines of Aquinas, intensified the search for legal principles based on idealism, and stressed the need for the establishing within the law of norms transcending human will but which might be utilised in the evaluation of man-made rules of law. Maritain, for example, expounded and developed a reappraised natural law as a prerequisite for a positive law which might impose itself 'on the conscience of all mankind'.

Within Britain there was some anxiety in the face of an apparent erosion of moral values. The ground upon which the law was based - respect for fundamental values and a shared attitude to right and wrong - was shifting. In the face of obvious public concern a Royal Commission was set up to report on aspects of sexual behaviour in relation to the criminal law. This led to wide public debate on the nature of morality and the place of the law in its enforcement. Catholic jurists, upholding the doctrine of natural law, were prominent among those who equated morality with facets of the doctrine of human dignity. Some judicial pronouncements (as, for example, in *Shaw v DPP* (1962)) referred to the need to enforce 'the supreme and fundamental purpose of the law ... to conserve the moral welfare of the State'. Here was reference to the purposes of the law as propounded by earlier natural-law jurists.

Intensification of interest in human rights and legal doctrines upon which they were based, followed the formation of the United Nations. Its Charter, published in 1945, spoke of the principle of equal rights of *all* peoples. A Commission on Human

Rights was set up under UN auspices in 1946, followed by a Universal Declaration of Human Rights in 1948. A statute of the Council of Europe required its members to accept the principles of the rule of law and of 'human rights and fundamental freedoms' which applied to all peoples. In 1954 members adopted a Convention on Human Rights. At a later date, European Community law recognised human rights as forming an integral part of the general principles of law (*Nold v EC Commission* (1974)). In the debates which accompanied these events the precepts of natural law, particularly those involving the need for respect to be shown to all people, were referred to and discussed repeatedly, so that the maxims of the classical natural law were re-examined within the context of a changing world.

Outside Europe, a ferment of ideas in relation to rights was widespread. Obvious racial discrimination (as embodied in the laws of South Africa, and the denial of full rights to ethnic minorities in the United States) led to debate on 'self-evident truths and the need for human fulfilment' - major themes within natural law teachings.

Within Britain legislation against some manifestations of racial and sexual discrimination resulted in the Race Relations Acts of 1965 and 1976 and the Sex Discrimination Act 1975. The discussions which preceded this legislation were often predicated on an acknowledgement of 'the fundamental right to equality of treatment', 'the inalienable right to respect and dignity', which had been debated for centuries past in the writings of natural-law jurists. The age-old preoccupation of jurists with the 'right to life and security' found an echo in demands for a Bill of Rights for the UK and a renewed concern with the 'immutable rights of the person', which contributed to the recognition of the offence of torture, under the Criminal Justice Act 1988, s134(1).

Continuing tensions within the Marxist regimes of the USSR and Eastern Europe reflected, in part, disillusion with the claims of legal systems aimed (in theory) at the protection of 'the people's rights'. Revolution does breed reaction, and widespread opposition to the theory and practice of 'relativist' socialist law grew. Denigration by the regimes' jurists of 'bourgeois rights' and the equating of antagonism to the State with criminal liability resulted in hostility to legal doctrine which stressed the relativism of 'right' and mocked the examination of legal universals, such as 'fairness' and 'equitable principles'. The need for 'touchstones' of legal doctrine and administrative action were perceived as essential for the creation of a 'true' legal system. There is now evidence of a revival within Eastern Europe of interest in arguments relating to the impossibility of law without non-relativist principles and to the ideas of 'external touchstones' as advocated by the natural law.

The marked growth of religious practices in many parts of the world, following the Second World War, has created a fertile ground for the proliferation of doctrines based on natural law. Movements within the Roman Catholic Church (which has been associated for many centuries with the promulgation of natural law doctrine) have been of significance. The Second Vatican Council (1962-5) set in motion extensive discussions on the social responsibilities of the Church, which involved an examination of the place of law in modern society. One result, probably not foreseen by the Council and its jurisprudential advisers, was the birth and growth of 'liberation theology' in South America. In some countries, jurists, priests and politicians met to examine ways in which natural law doctrine might be embodied within legal practice so as to secure freedom and dignity under the law. One such conference examined specific ways in which the law might become 'a vehicle for the recognition in practice of the absolute value of the person'. In Europe, attempts - generally unsuccessful - were made to bridge the ideological divide separating Marxist jurists from Catholic advocates of natural law. The French dissident Marxist, Bloch, made a powerful attempt, in his *Natural Law and Human Dignity*, to present Aquinas in a manner which might facilitate a synthesis of 'law and the cause of rights' and 'the agenda of social revolution'. His book was, in its own way, a testimony to the continuing vigour of natural law concepts.

In more general terms, it may be suggested that interest in natural law theories has grown as the dogmas of materialism continue to be questioned during an era of failed values and deepening doubts. A search for values based upon idealistic principles has been renewed. Relativism - in theory and in practice - has been seen as having failed to provide an effective barrier to barbarism, so that a turning towards the 'verities' proclaimed by the natural law as immutable *and rational*, has followed. Restatements by Finnis, for example, who has sought to express natural law in terms which do not avoid consideration of some of its deeper problems (such as the 'ought-from-is' argument) have allowed jurists to respond with increasing interest to the very broad claims of a doctrine which views law as 'rational guidance for all created things'.

Notes

Friedmann considers the revival of natural law theories in ch 14. Lloyd, ch 3, and Harris, ch 2, comment on natural law. Davies and Holdcroft examine the fundamentals of the theory and its modern formulations in ch 6. Stone touches upon the general claims of natural law in his book, *Human Law and Human Justice*.

Question 14

What are the main features of the Neo-Scholastic movement in jurisprudence?

Answer plan

The Neo-Scholastic movement is a twentieth-century development of thought based on the ideology associated primarily with St Thomas Aquinas. The effect of the movement on jurisprudence has been to revive interest in the application of natural law doctrine to contemporary life. An answer to this question should bring out the point that not all the Neo-Scholastics accept the theology of Aquinas. Reference should be made to a representative selection of jurists who represent this school of thought. The following skeleton plan is suggested:

Introduction - essence of Neo-Scholasticism - characteristics of Neo-Scholasticism as viewed by Adler and Cavanaugh - Dabin - Rommen - Le Fur - Renard - Maritain - Adler - Lucey - conclusion, Neo-Scholasticism and man's common good.

Answer

Neo-Scholasticism comprises several philosophies founded upon medieval Scholasticism (an endeavour to discover 'the whole of attainable truth' through Catholic doctrine). Particularly prominent within the Neo-Scholastic school is Neo-Thomism which, in relation to jurisprudence, is concerned with the development and adaptation of the teachings on natural law enunciated by St Thomas Aquinas. He had defined law as 'an ordinance of reason for the common good made by him who has the care of the community, and promulgated'. He considered 'natural law' to be derived from Divine law as revealed in man's reason. The natural law provided limits for the positive law. Noted below are some representatives of the Neo-Scholastic movement in jurisprudence - European jurists such as Dabin, Rommen, Le Fur, Renard and Maritain, and American writers, such as Adler and Lucey.

Adler, whose views are expounded below, sees Neo-Scholasticism as characterised by six widely-held doctrines concerning natural law. First: government-made laws are not the only directions of conduct which apply to persons living within society. Second: there are rules and principles applicable to *all* persons, not merely to one person or even one society of a given time or place. Third: there are vital rules of conduct which are not man-made. Fourth: through the exercise of his reason man may discover these principles. Fifth: these principles are the source of all particular rules of conduct. Finally: these principles provide the standard by which all other rules are to be judged good or bad, right or wrong, just or unjust. Cavanaugh has restated the Thomist doctrine in emphasising that natural law is not an ideal but a reality. 'It is not a product of men's minds, but a product of God's will. It is as real and binding as the statutes in the United States Code'.

Dabin, a Belgian jurist, set out in *The General Theory of Law* (1929) a view of the legal order as the sum total of the rules of conduct laid down by civil society under the sanction of public compulsion so as to realise the general order postulated by the ends of civil society and the maintenance of that society as an instrument devoted to those ends. Natural law should dominate the positive law; indeed, positive law is prohibited *absolutely* from contradicting the natural law. (This is an interesting modern development of the view of Aquinas that a positive law, even though it serves the end of society, may, nevertheless, be of no moral significance.) Dabin stressed his belief that the precepts of natural law must be accepted as possessing a universal and immutable validity, 'suffering neither doubt nor discussion'. They are capable of being deduced from the very nature of man as revealed in the basic inclinations of his nature, 'under the control of reason, independently of any formal intervention by any legislator whatever'.

Dabin's theory of justice owes much to mediaeval thought. Justice takes three forms. 'Legal justice' is a merger of law and morals; it is concerned with 'ordination for the common good', ie, the determination of the duties owed by members of society to the social world - effectively, obedience to laws. It is the virtue most necessary for the public good because its objective *is* the public good. 'Distributive justice' determines the duties of the collectivity towards its members; it provides for the distribution, under the law, of rights and powers. 'Commutative justice' is embodied in the adjustment of private relationships. It is the task of legislators to work for the public good; therefore, anything contrary to 'natural morality', eg, immoral legal rules, must be condemned as contrary to the public good.

Rommen, a German jurist, published in 1947 *The Natural Law* in which he provided a restatement of Catholic doctrine concerning natural law. He wrote with memories of the lawlessness of the Nazi regime, and suggested that the true foundation of the natural law was to be found in the essential, immutable 'dignity of human personality'. Two self-evident propositions could be discerned within the content of natural law: 'What is just is to be done and injustice is to be avoided', and, 'Give to everyone his due'. The natural law will always reflect reason, and man's duty is to act in accordance with reason so as to fulfil 'the order of being'. Immoral laws are devoid of obligation. Ultimately the true and the just are one, and true freedom will be found in being bound by justice. Rommen envisages a variety of different social and political systems in which human dignity might find guarantees; these systems would express the diversity of peoples and changes in socio-political evolution.

Le Fur, a French writer on legal theory, set out in his *Problems of Law* (1947) a statement on rules of law as comprising duties and rights *granted* to members of a community. Problems of law arising within a community could be solved by the imposition of sanctions based on force, by the will of the majority who would act, in the words of Aquinas, with consciousness of 'the ultimate need of preserving the life of the community'. The community's laws must rest on reason, ie, the principles of the natural law. Reason will work best when basic ethical principles, reflecting the harmony of God's creation, are applied to 'social facts' and, in particular, those concerning history and economics. Fundamental principles of natural law involve: the keeping of freely-concluded contracts ('the sanctity of obligations'), respect for properly-constituted authority, and the duty to repair, or compensate for, unlawfully-inflicted damage. Modern legislators should seek to provide for the building of the positive law, with its detailed rules, upon the foundation of these three principles.

Renard, a French professor of law, published *The Theory of the Institution* in 1930. In it he developed a concept of the natural law as finding expression in 'the institution' - the embodiment of that social order which is a part of God's order. The 'institution' was to be viewed as 'the communion of men in an idea'. The most important institutions were the State and the nation. Renard seems to have attempted to develop the mediaeval theory which favoured the concept of a community as based on a 'cooperative union of guilds'. The twentieth century could learn from this type of institution by developing an organic, unified society which would reflect 'self-sufficient constituent groups'. The natural law would be the key to the solution of society's problems. Legislation was to be interpreted as the product of the wills of those who form the legislative organs of the community's institutions. The *enacted laws* are valid only if they do not enunciate ideas contrary to those proclaimed by the institutions. The *judicial acts* of the institutions are valid only if in accordance with the natural law. For Renard, the Neo-Scholastic approach to jurisprudence involves an acceptance of the necessity of subordinating individual purpose to the collective objectives of the institutions. Some loss of freedom might result, but security for the individual would increase.

Maritain, a French philosopher and a convert to Catholicism, published in 1947 his highly-acclaimed *Rights of Man and Natural Law*. His views are rooted in the philosophies of Aristotle and Aquinas, and he affirms natural law as 'an expression of what is natural in the world'. Man's dignity is derived from his having been created in the image of God, and his human rights are also derived from God. The natural law which is rooted in man's nature follows the eternal law which exists in the very nature of God. Man is naturally inclined towards the moral law and, by using his reason, he is able to know and implement that law. The natural law allows us to attune ourselves to the necessary ends of humanity. As our moral conscience has developed so our knowledge of the natural law has increased. Man's very important right to freedom is derived from natural law. When the positive lawmakers decide on matters related to 'promotion of the public interest', they must keep in mind the dictates of the natural law concerning the dignity of man. Above all, says Maritain, jurists must assert with force that an 'unjust law' is not a law.

Adler, former professor of law at Chicago University, epitomises those Neo-Scholastics who do not accept the theology of Aquinas, but who are attracted to the doctrine of natural law. *A Dialectic of Morals* (1941) called for a bulwark against legal positivism and for the mapping of a road which would lead sceptics back to those paths of reason which lead to the truth about man and his nature. Human conduct *can* be based on a knowledge of right and wrong, and moral judgments are *not* merely matters of opinion. When legislators make laws they must keep this in mind. But it must not be forgotten that positive law remains qualitatively distinct from the natural law - they do not share the same essence. Thus, positive law compels obedience by an exercise of external force; natural law does not. Positive law requires promulgation through extrinsic channels; natural law emerges from natural enquiry. The rules of positive law may be evaluated in relation to the constitution of a country; natural law is beyond such relativity.

A restatement of natural law associated with the earlier Scholastic jurists requires, according to Adler, an assertion that without principles of natural justice there can be no meaning attached to the concept of natural rights, and, without a meaningful concept, there can be no settlement of disputes except through power, prejudice and pressure. Natural law is, in itself, inadequate in the face of modern demands for government under the law. A place must be found for positive law within the framework of the natural so that positive law approximates increasingly to 'a perfect embodiment of natural justice'. In this way the virtues of the mediaeval concept of justice as reflecting God's plan may be developed for the contemporary world and its legal institutions.

Lucey, an American jurist and priest, has called for emphasis to be given to man's dignity and to his fundamental duties and rights 'given to him by God, which no man has a right to destroy'. 'Those duties and rights make him *sui juris* as far as others are concerned'. They do not change basically, although their application and exercise will vary according to time and place. Because man is social by nature he is impelled toward civil society and this necessitates a civil law which must be respected. In man is a God-implanted necessity for authority, and respect for it. Within society, government, as well as those who are governed, must be subject to the law. The Neo-Scholastic approach should recognise that although natural law is immutable, the positive law must alter in accordance with perceptions and requirements of 'the common good'.

Essentially, the Neo-Scholastic movement is able to embrace those who see the natural law as embedded within the theology associated with Aquinas, and those for whom that theology is not entirely relevant but who see natural law as emerging from the very attributes of human beings. Natural law is accepted by most adherents to the movement as being immutable; but there is an acceptance of the need for recognition by the positive law of changes in the quality of men's needs, Maritain sums up for many jurists within the Neo-Scholastic movement: 'Natural law is the ensemble of things to do and not to do which follow (for example, that we should do good and avoid evil) in necessary fashion from the simple fact that *man is man*, nothing else being taken into account'.

Notes

Friedmann, ch 19, and Bodenheimer, ch 19, consider the central features of Neo-Scholasticism. Hall criticises Maritain in 'Integrative Jurisprudence', in *Interpretations of Modern Legal Philosophers*. Reuschlin writes on 'The Neo-Scholastics' in *Jurisprudence: Its American Prophets*.

Question 15

MacCormick, commenting on Finnis' *Natural Law and Human Rights*, states that the text necessitates our abandoning 'our caricature version of what a natural law theory is'.

Do you agree?

Finnis has attempted in recent years to restate the natural law in terms acceptable to contemporary society. This has involved him in the enumeration of 'human goods', ie, fundamental values of man's existence that are 'self-evident', the securing of which requires a system of law. The 'human goods' must be discussed in the answer. Consideration should be given to the claim that Finnis has restored 'meaning' to the natural law which has been discredited because of distorted versions of its pretensions. Criticisms of Finnis ought to be mentioned. A skeleton plan is presented as follows:

Introduction -the caricature of natural law - essence of Finnis' restatement of natural law - the seven 'human goods' - law's end as the common good - criticism of Finnis' catalogue - imprecision of his categories - problem of the 'self-evident' nature of the goods - conclusion, misgivings remain.

Answer

'Natural law' is seen here as the system of jurisprudential thought which asserts the existence in nature of a rational order from which we can derive universal and eternal value-statements allowing us to evaluate the legal structure with objectivity. The 'caricature' version which MacCormick has in mind is, presumably, sketched from the claims of those jurists who see natural law as based rigidly upon a unique revelation of truth, as flaunting the principle that 'ought' cannot be derived from 'is', and as proclaiming a set of immutable principles, including the assertion that unjust laws cannot be law. Some of Finnis' attempts to straighten distortions of the image are considered below. It will be suggested that his attempts create their own problems.

Natural Law and Human Rights (1980) is, in essence, a restatement of natural law in novel terms. Finnis' central thesis consists of two major propositions. First: there are certain 'human goods', ie, *basic values of human existence*, that are self-evident, and that can be secured only through the law. Second: these goods may be achieved through 'practical reasonableness', and this, too, necessitates law. The human goods constitute a catalogue of forms of 'human flourishing', exemplifying the conditions required by individuals if they are to attain their full potential (an end which was reiterated in earlier versions of the natural law). 'Practical reasonableness' involves a use of the word 'practical' in an Aristotelian sense, as meaning 'with a view to decision and action'; it is an aspect of 'human flourishing'. Finnis is seeking, in his categorisation of human goods to provide a rational basis for morality and a justification for law.

The forms of human goods that are 'irreducibly basic' are *seven* in number: life, knowledge, play, aesthetic experience, sociability (friendship), practical reasonableness, religion. These constitute 'human well-being', and any real understanding of law or justice must rest on a comprehension of the nature of these 'goods'. Although there may be innumerable forms of human goods, Finnis claims that those outside his list are merely ways, or combinations of ways, of attaining any of the seven enumerated. By 'life' he has in mind the drive for self-preservation. The term signifies every aspect of vitality, including anything done by mankind to further its preservation. 'Knowledge' corresponds to man's basic drive of 'curiosity'. It is knowledge for its own sake, and ranges widely from scientific and philosophical speculation to mundane questions. 'Play' involves engaging in performances which have no point beyond the performances themselves.

'Aesthetic experience', perception and enjoyment of 'dance or song or football', for example, may involve actions of one's own, or mere contemplation. 'Sociability' necessitates being in a relationship of friendship with at least one other person. 'Practical reasonableness' refers to freedom and reason, integrity and authenticity. It relates to bringing one's own intelligence to bear effectively on the problems of choosing one's actions and life-style and shaping one's character. Finnis uses the term 'religion' in an unusual sense as referring to a concern for an order of things 'beyond' each and every individual.

These human goods are, according to Finnis, 'basic' because any other value will be seen as merely subordinate to them, and 'objective', which may be evidenced from a survey of anthropological research which reveals that 'all human societies show a concern for the value of human life'. They are also 'self-evident': thus the 'good' of 'knowledge' is self-evident in that it cannot be demonstrated, but, equally, it needs no demonstration. Finnis insists that all self-evident principles are not validated by individual feelings and that in every field of human enquiry there is, and must be at some point, an end to derivation and inference. At that point we find ourselves 'in face of the self-evident'. The goods are also equally 'fundamental': none can be *shown* to be more fundamental than any of the others and, therefore, there is no objective priority of values among them.

'Practical reasonableness', which is a human good, is also a proposition in Finnis' overall scheme: it comprises *ten* principles allowing the individual to distinguish the social from the unsocial type of thinking, thereby enabling him to distinguish morally right and wrong actions. First, an individual should have a rational plan of life, reflecting a harmonious set of purposes and effective commitments. He should pay equal regard to all the human goods and should not neglect the significance of others' participation in those goods. He should have a certain detachment from the projects he undertakes and should not abandon his commitments lightly. Opportunities ought not to be wasted by using needlessly inefficient methods and there must be respect for the human good in any act performed. One should foster the common good and act according to one's conscience. (In a later work Finnis added a further principle, namely, that one should not choose 'apparent goods', knowing them to be a mere simulation of real goods.)

Finnis views the law as involving rules made by 'a determinate and effective authority' for a 'complete community', strengthened by appropriate sanctions, and directed at the reasonable resolution of the community's problems of co-ordination. Law is a means to an end: its end is the community's good, and its manner and form should be adapted to that good by specificity, minimisation of arbitrariness and 'maintenance of a quality of reciprocity between the subjects of the law' among themselves and in their relations with the authorities.

The maxim *lex injusta non est lex* is viewed by Finnis as pure nonsense. He denies the correctness of its attribution to Aquinas and stresses that in natural law tradition wicked laws may have legal validity where they are enacted constitutionally and where accepted by the courts as guides to judicial decisions. One may, have, according to natural law tradition, a 'collateral obligation' to conform to some iniquitous laws so as to uphold respect for the legal system as a whole.

A perusal of Finnis' theory suggests to many critics a number of unsolved problems. Thus, the list of 'human goods' may be no more than a subjective addition to the long list of similar catalogues, such as the ancient Chinese Six Virtues and Eight Happinesses. Such catalogues tend to reflect personal preferences, class and social mores and religious principles, indicating reactions to compelling, but temporary, crises within society. Finnis, it is argued, may be reflecting little more than attitudes held desirable by a small group. His list of human goods is value-laden and in no sense universal. There is evidence to suggest that some of the goods might be rejected as desirable ends by some sections of the community. What measure of agreement could be hoped for among nihilists, liberals and Marxists on matters of 'play' or 'aesthetic experience'?

Some of Finnis' categories are presented in wide and imprecise terms, making their significance difficult to grasp. 'Knowledge', in his words, embraces a spectrum from 'the intellectual cathedrals of science and philosophy' to 'everyday mundane gossip'. This is a very wide heading for activities of such a disparate nature. Also, it has been pointed out that the pursuit of knowledge 'for its own sake' is forbidden to some sects and religious orders for whom the very questioning of fundamentals may constitute an undesirable practice, if not a heresy. Further, Finnis' category of 'religion' has a meaning which is so wide as to rob it of any significance as a guide to thought and action.

The problem of the 'self-evident nature' of the 'human goods' is an obstacle for those jurists who search for a rationale behind the catalogue. The history of much endeavour in the realm of speculation is a story of a refusal to accept any statement as 'self-evident'. Indeed, according to critics, the term is an abnegation of the individual's duty to seek continuously for verification of theories. The same critics express doubts as to the 'self-evident' nature of, say, 'play' (in Finnis' sense) as a basic 'human good'. Weinreb, in a trenchant criticism of Finnis, notes that the text states or suggests repeatedly that those who are against the 'human goods theses' have not thought out their position carefully, or are 'blinded by bias', whereas, in fact, each of Finnis' conclusions has been contested by many thoughtful, morally committed persons.

Finnis' view of the law in terms of what it achieves, rather than what it is, has been considered less than helpful. It suggests a mere instrumental view of law and fails to examine the question - vital for advocates of the natural law - of the fundamental *nature* of law in our society. His argument concerning *lex injusta* has been criticised as resting on casuistry and as providing no guide for action to individuals within a community in which the law is perceived as oppressive.

There is doubt as to Finnis' general attitude to 'the good' and 'the just'. It has been suggested that his exposition is far too abstract to be of use in the resolution of day-to-day problems relating to disputes and the law. Yet there is a powerful attraction in his restatement of natural law doctrine. It calls for a fundamental examination of the place of the individual within society. In the tradition of the natural law he urges for emphasis to be placed on the human condition and on the ways in which man may fulfil himself. His greatest achievement, in the eyes of some jurists, may be, in Weinreb's words, that 'he has helped us to recognise the level of agreement about human ends and how to achieve them, and he has provided a shelter from the wind of moral relativism' - an accomplishment in itself.

Notes

Extracts from Finnis, and a useful commentary are to be found in Davies and Holdcroft, pp 186-204. Dias, ch 22 and Lloyd, ch 3, comment on the 'human goods' theory. Ridall, ch 11, outlines the essence of the theory. A criticism of Finnis is contained in *Natural Law and Justice* by Weinreb. MacCormick writes on 'Natural Law Reconsidered' in *The Oxford Journal of Legal Studies* (1981).

Utilitarianism

Introduction

This chapter is made up of questions concerning the doctrine associated with Bentham (1748-1832) and J S Mill (1806-73). The principles of utilitarianism which they expounded made a direct impact on jurisprudence, particularly in areas involving the criminal law. Utilitarianism perceived the 'true good' as happiness and argued that each person always pursues what he considers to be his personal happiness. The legislator's task is to effect a balance of public and private interests. Hence the criminal law may be viewed as a mode of producing a coincidence of the interests of the community and of the individual. Bentham was concerned, in particular, with influencing legislation and policy along utilitarian lines. Mill was less dogmatic. His major interest was in the liberty of the individual and the consequent need to set limits to government action. Questions in this area of jurisprudential thought require an understanding of the general principles of utilitarianism and the arguments used by Bentham and Mill in support of the particular policies they put forward concerning reform of the law.

Checklist

Ensure that you are acquainted with the following topics:

- essence of utilitarianism
- felicific calculus
- Bentham's views on punishment
- Mill's fundamentals of liberty
- paternalistic legislation
- legitimate role of government
- utilitarianism and the criminal law

Question 16

How did Bentham apply the general principles of utilitarianism to the specific problem of punishment for criminal offences?

Answer plan

The general principles of utilitarianism should be set out, together
with a brief indication of Bentham's view of the criminal law. It is
in this setting that the question of punishment has to be
considered. The following skeleton plan is suggested:

Introduction -Bentham's general views - essence of
utilitarianism - aim of legislation - essence of the criminal
law - fundamentals of punishment and its rationale -
criticism of Bentham's concepts - conclusion, positive
features of Bentham's approach.

Answer

Philosopher, economist, jurist and legal reformer, Bentham was
able to spin from the thread of the 'principle of utility' a vast
tapestry of ethics and jurisprudential doctrine, known as
'utilitarianism', which sought an answer to the question, 'What
ought an individual to do?' Bentham's answer was that he should
act so as to produce 'the best consequences possible'.
'Consequences' include all that is produced by an act, whether
arising during or after its performance. A summary of the
principles of utilitarianism is given below together with details
concerning Bentham's application of those principles to the
problem of punishment for criminals - a matter with which he
was closely involved in his campaigns for a revision of the
criminal law.

The 'principle of utility' was set out by Bentham in his
Introduction to the Principles of Morals and Legislation (1789). He
defined it as 'that property in any object whereby it tends to
produce pleasure, good or happiness, or to prevent the happening
of mischief, pain or evil and unhappiness to the party whose
interest is considered'. Nature had placed mankind 'under the
governance of two sovereign masters, pain and pleasure'; they
indicate what we *ought* to do and determine what we *shall* do. The
fact that we desire pleasure and wish to avoid pain is utilised by
Bentham so as to make the judgment that we *ought* to pursue
pleasure. The principle of utility cannot be demonstrated because
it is not susceptible to proof; indeed, says Bentham, it is needless
to attempt a demonstration.

Bentham attempted to give the theory some mathematical precision. A thing will promote the interest of an individual when it tends to add to the *sum total* of his pleasure, or to diminish the *sum total* of his pains. It was possible, he argued, to make a *quantitative comparison* of the pleasure and pain likely to result as the consequences of alternative courses of action. A person should sum up the likely pleasures and pains so as to arrive at the 'good' or 'bad' tendency of the act in question - the 'felicific calculus'. An account of the number of persons whose interests appear to be involved should be taken, and the calculus applied to each. The result would be an estimate of the good or evil likely to be produced within the community as a whole.

The aim of the legislator, according to Bentham, should be to produce *the greatest happiness of the greatest number*. 'Community interest' was no more than the sum of the interests of those who compose a society. The art of legislation involves the discovery of the means to realise 'the good'. The legislator must take into account the fact that the acts he desires to prevent are 'evils' and that they are greater evils than the laws (which are infractions of liberty) to be used to prevent them. Legislation ought to aim at four goals: subsistence, abundance, security (the protection of status and property) and the diminution of inequality. The laws which a legislator should seek to promote should be seen in relation to desirable conduct to be expected from persons or classes of persons.

In considering the criminal law, Bentham applied the principle of utility in rigorous fashion. First, the mischief of an act should be measured. 'Mischief' consisted of the pain or evil inflicted by the act. If an act tended to produce evil, it must be discouraged. 'Evil' could be 'primary' or 'secondary'. If X steals from Y, this is 'primary' evil. 'Secondary' evil arises where X's theft weakens respect for property. Bentham stresses that secondary evils may often outweigh primary evils.

Because the legislator is concerned to increase the total happiness of the community, he must discourage acts likely to produce evil consequences. A criminal act is one which is obviously detrimental to the happiness of the community; hence the law should be concerned solely with acts that diminish the pleasure of persons by the infliction of pain. The criminal law is intended to assist in the active promotion of the community's total happiness by punishing those who commit offences characterised as 'evil' according to the principle of utility.

Bentham would not accept a division of offences into *mala in se* (acts wrong in themselves) and *mala prohibita* (acts wrong because the law prohibits them). The principle of utility demands that an act cannot be wrong 'in itself'; whether it is right or wrong depends on consequences. If it is highly probable that an act will produce harm, it should be prohibited; if unlikely to produce harm, its prohibition is unjustified. We prohibit murder and theft and punish those responsible, not because the acts are wrong in themselves but because of the evil consequences for others. For precisely the same reasons we punish also those who commit minor offences.

Punishment, said Bentham, is in itself, an evil: it necessarily inflicts suffering on the offender. But the object of the criminal law is the augmentation of the community's happiness; hence if punishment is to be administered, it must be shown that the pain to be inflicted will prevent or exclude some greater pain. The 'usefulness' of punishment emerges only if it achieves a greater measure of happiness for the community. It has no value if it merely adds more units of pain to the community as a whole. Mere retribution is valueless because it only adds to the quantum of pain caused by the offences.

Bentham insisted on an examination of *why* society ought to punish offenders. There is no value in inflicting punishment where it is 'groundless'; hence an offence which admits of compensation, and which will be followed by such compensation, ought not to be punished. Punishment which is too expensive ought not to be inflicted. The proportion between punishment and the offence must be kept in mind. Punishment should be great enough to outweigh profit derived by the criminal. The greater the offence, the greater should be the punishment.

Punishment ought to be variable and adapted to suit circumstances, but the same punishment should be given for the same type of offence. The quantum of punishment should never exceed the amount required to make it effective, so that extravagant punishment should be rejected as wasteful. The more uncertain it is that a criminal will be caught, the greater should be the punishment when he is apprehended and convicted. Punishment should act as a deterrent, should be reformatory where that is possible and should have wide popular support.

Bentham's utilitarian principles as applied to the criminal law and punishment led him to prepare practical schemes for the 'rational punishment' of offenders. Among a large number of such plans, which were often worked out in considerable detail, was the design of a *Panopticon* - a prison in which the conduct of the inmates was to be controlled by total surveillance throughout the day. Bentham stated that its object was 'to grind rogues honest'. This process was to be achieved by an uninterrupted survey of behaviour, which would result in the remodelling of the offenders' attitudes. Bentham had in mind reform of the prisoners - mere punishment with no objective other than detention seemed to him a wasted opportunity.

Bentham's radical approach to law and punishment was vigorously opposed in his time, although a number of penal reforms may be attributed to him. Controversy surrounds his approach to punishment even today. It is argued that the utilitarians disregarded the claims of justice in determining whether or not a punishment was 'right'. For them the utility of the punishment was the sole consideration, but for many jurists other matters would have to be taken into account before accepting the 'correctness' of a particular type of punishment. Objection is taken, too, to the 'pleasure-pain calculus' which is considered unreal and absurd. Principles of punishment derived from a construct of this nature are considered flawed and, therefore, unreliable.

Opposition to Bentham's views also stems from jurists who cannot accept his reasoning concerning the general happiness of society as constituting the *summum bonum*. It is thought that Bentham's view of mankind was naive in the extreme, People are much more complex than the principle of utility suggests, and the causes of crime may be much more complicated than the utilitarian model indicates. Modern investigations of criminal psychology put forward a picture of anti-social motivation which is at odds with Bentham's views.

Plamenatz, the historian of the utilitarian movement, suggests that although much of Bentham's work was often superficial and

crude, it was far ahead of its time in proposing new methods of
analysing social and legal problems. These methods and the
resulting proposals for reform of the criminal law can be
accepted, Plamenatz argues, on their own terms. It is not
necessary, therefore, to accept Bentham's 'felicific calculus' or his
belief in 'the greatest happiness of the greatest number' in order
to agree with his powerful pleas for a rethinking of the purposes
and modes of punishment. There is much in his analysis which is
ingenious, original and thought-provoking. It remains worthy of
consideration by jurists of all persuasions.

Notes

Bentham's *Introduction to the Principles of Morals and Legislation* is
published in an edition by Burns and Hart. Ogden has edited his
Theory of Legislation. Summaries of Bentham's views are given in
Dias, ch 20, Harris, ch 4, Lloyd, ch 4, Bodenheimer, ch 6. Extracts
from Bentham's work are presented in Davies and Holdcroft, ch
7. Interesting background material is provided by *Utilitarianism:
For and Against*, by Smart and Williams, and *Bentham: An Odyssey
of Ideas*, by Mack. *The English Utilitarians*, by Plamenatz, contains a
history of the movement. For the extraordinary story of the trial
and execution of Bentham's servant, Franks, on a charge of
'burglarously breaking and entering the dwelling house' of his
master, see chapter 10 of *The London Hanged: Crime and Civil
Society in the Eighteenth Century*, by Linebaugh.

Question 17

To what extent might a modern legislator find J S Mill's views on
the limits of toleration and government powers in relation to the
individual to be of relevance to contemporary problems?

Answer plan

Mill's eloquent plea on behalf of freedom of speech, contained in
his essay *On Liberty*, contemplates a society in which interference
with individual rights is kept to a minimum. Freedom will
flourish only where there is respect for citizens and where

conditions prevail allowing for the recognition of points of view, no matter how unpopular they may be. An answer to this question should seek to consider some of the many ways in which Mill's conclusions on matters concerning the freedom of the individual might be relevant to problems of our own day. A skeleton plan along the following lines is suggested:

Introduction - Mill's insistence on a synthesis of justice and utility - liberty as a 'good' and as a means to an end - freedom of expression - 'paternalistic' legislation - duties towards others - principles of government interference - conclusion, relevance of Mill's analysis.

Answer

Mill's views, set out in his essay *On Liberty* (1859), constitute a statement as to the fundamentals of a desirable balance of interests between the State and the individual citizen. His powerful plea for individual liberty emerges from an analysis of relationships of individual and general interests, of 'justice' and 'utility'. The philosophy of utilitarianism suffuses the essay: liberty, for Mill, rests on no 'natural law' or other metaphysical doctrine, but on a synthesis of the essential features of justice and the concept of utility. A modern legislator would be interested in Mill's warning of the dangers of the oppression of minorities by majorities, in his insistence on the need for safeguards against those forces that might deny an individual's free and full self-development, and in the intensity of his concern for the preservation of liberty by imposing limits to government action. The legislator will find no detailed instructions for legal and governmental action, but rather a basic appraisal of principles in the area of State intervention designed 'for the good of the people'.

What better can be said of any condition of human affairs, asked Mill, than that it brings human beings nearer to 'the best thing they can be'? Mill's interest in State, law and society centres on their ability to provide the circumstances in which individuals might flourish. Liberty, which in itself is 'a good', is also a means to an end: the end is man's attaining his optimum development, including his full freedom. Mill is reminding legislators and others that in arranging a social and legal framework, they have to keep in mind the long-term goal of justice and human development. Further, asks Mill, when should society enact legislation which interferes with an individual's liberty of action? Our legislator might understand the import of Mill's question in relation, say, to the Children Act 1989: what *right* (apart from its democratic mandate) has a government to enact legislation of this nature?

Mill's answers to the questions he poses form a key to an understanding of his concept of liberty as essential for the development of society. There is only one purpose, according to Mill, for which a government can rightfully exercise power over a citizen *against his will*, and that is to prevent harm to others. The citizen's own physical or moral good will not constitute a sufficient warrant. Legislators are urged by Mill to consider the thesis that they may not *compel* a citizen against his will 'to do or forbear' because it is better for him to do so or because his happiness will be intensified as a result; they may remonstrate or reason with him, but they may not force him. The exception is where harm may be caused to others. Conduct which is calculated to produce evil to some other person provides a sufficient reason for the exercise of power against the person who intends such a course of action.

Legislators contemplating current problems relating to liberty of thought and expression would find Mill's views to be highly relevant. He is emphatic in his insistence that a society in which this liberty is not respected cannot be free, and that such freedom must be absolute and unqualified. Indeed, if all mankind minus one individual shared one opinion, mankind would be no more justified in silencing that individual than he, if he had the power, would be justified in silencing mankind. To silence the expression of opinion is to rob the human race of the opportunity of exchanging error for truth or of the opportunity of acquiring a clearer perception of truth as produced when it collides with error.

Mill stresses this theme by stating a case for the free expression of opinion. A contemporary legislator, under pressure to support or oppose enactments relating to the suppression of a highly-unpopular type of opinion, might wish to contemplate this case. First, says Mill, if an opinion is silenced, that opinion, for aught we know, may be true; if we deny this we are assuming our infallibility. Secondly, even though the silenced opinion be erroneous, it may contain a portion of truth ('truth often comes on the scene riding on the back of error'); but since current opinion on any matter is rarely the whole truth, it is only through the collision of contrary opinions that the remainder of a truth might emerge. Thirdly, unless received opinion is subjected to vigorous and earnest challenge, it may be held with little comprehension and may take on the character of mere prejudice. Finally, if the opinion is unchallenged and degenerates into dogma, it prevents the growth of any real conviction from reason or personal experience.

The modern legislator will probably respond that this line of reasoning ignores practical necessity. What of the demands of the community for protection against the expression of opinion in circumstances which might inflame sentiment and lead to public disorder? Was it 'wrong' to enact, for example, the Public Order Act 1986, s23 (dealing with possession of racially inflammatory material)? Is freedom of expression to be allowed to overt racism? Mill replies in measured terms.

No one claims, he argues, that men should be free to act upon their opinions; no one claims that actions should be as free as opinions. Quite to the contrary, opinions lose their immunity when the very circumstances of their expression constitute a mischievous act. Mill gives as an example of an intolerable expression of opinion a speech delivered to a mob gathered before a corn dealer's home, in which corn dealers are stated to be starvers of the poor. The liberty of an individual must be limited to the extent that he may not make himself a nuisance to other people. However, if a person merely acts according to his opinion in matters *which concern himself* he should be allowed to carry his opinions into practice at his own cost. In matters which do not primarily concern others, individuality may be permitted to assert itself; but where there is a chance of injury to others, a person may be restrained.

The modern legislator may respond further by questioning the relevance of this type of theory in the face of a growing tendency to 'paternalistic legislation'. Mill's reply would be based on his belief that, in general, it is the privilege of an individual who has arrived 'at the maturity of his faculties' to use and interpret experience in his own way. Mill intends that his principles shall be applicable only to *mature persons* (he excludes, for example, minors). Today's legislators might consider the relevance of Mill's thesis to the contemporary theory of 'the least restrictive alternative', which suggests that if there is an alternative way of accomplishing some desired end without restricting an individual's liberty, then, although it will probably involve considerable inconvenience and expense, it should be adopted.

To an individual, says Mill, should belong that part of his life in which he is largely interested, and to society, the part which largely interests society. A modern legislator may consider this thesis relevant to today's problems only if it casts light on the basic problem - where does society's (ie, government's) authority begin? The problem might be posed thus: what are the 'rightful' limits to an individual's sovereignty over himself?

Mill's answer begins with an assertion that society is not founded on any type of 'contract' and there is no purpose in inventing one so as to deduce social obligations from it. All persons who receive the protection of society owe some return; the fact that one lives in society makes it necessary that each individual should be obliged to observe a specific mode of conduct towards others. That conduct involves not hurting the interests of others (that is, those interests which by express enactment and tacit understanding are classified as 'rights'). Further, each individual must bear a share of the efforts incurred in protecting society from injury. Wherever and whenever a person behaves in a way which affects the interests of others in a prejudicial manner, society, through its legal institutions, must have jurisdiction. But where it is obvious that the interests of no person apart from himself will be affected by an action, that person must have the freedom (legal and social) to perform the action and accept its consequences.

This is not to suggest that members of society, or its government, ought not to be concerned with individuals' conduct of their own lives. There is, Mill claims, need of 'disinterested exertion' intended to promote the good of others. But that benevolence, he insists, can and must find other methods of persuading people to their good rather than 'whips and scourges either of the literal or metaphorical sort'. Nor must it be forgotten that no individual, no group, no government, has a right to say to an individual 'of ripe years' that he shall not do with his life for his own benefit what he chooses to do with it. In the same vein Mill emphasises that whenever there is a definite risk of damage to an individual or to the public, a case must be removed from 'the province of liberty' and must be considered as falling within the area of morality or law.

Given that there is a legitimate role for government to play in the affairs of individuals, Mill advocates three important principles to be kept in mind by legislators. First, government interference which does not involve the infringement of liberty should be considered very carefully when that which has to be done is likely to be better done by individuals than by the government. Mill is suggesting that legislators ought to remember that there are no better persons to determine how or by whom an undertaking should be conducted than those who are personally interested in it. Secondly, although individuals may not perform administrative tasks as competently as government officials, nevertheless they should be allowed, as a mode of furthering their development and social education, to carry them out. Thirdly - and Mill sees this as a most cogent reason for restricting government interference - there is the 'great evil' of a government adding unnecessarily to its powers by creating a bureaucracy. Large-scale ownership by the State would seriously diminish freedom. Not all the freedom of the press and the existence of a popular constitution would make a country dominated by a government bureaucracy, free, otherwise than in name.

A modern legislator may find, indeed, that the problems which Mill posed and attempted to answer are of particular relevance to contemporary legislators and those who administer the law. Today's problems may be outwardly different from those which confronted Mill, but, fundamentally, many of the problems are based on precisely the same tensions which arise in any society committed to individual liberty, social order and cohesion.

Notes

Mill's *On Liberty* appears in a variety of editions. His theories are considered in Riddall, ch 14, Bodenheimer, ch 6, Friedmann, ch 26. Dworkin examines government paternalism in *Morality and the Law*, ed Wasserstrom. Mill's background is analysed in *John Stuart Mill*, by Britton.

Legal Positivism

Introduction

The essence of legal positivism is summed up by Fuller in *The Law in Quest of Itself* (1940): all those associated with the law are called upon to choose between two competing directions of legal thought, namely natural law and legal positivism. *Natural law* denies the possibility of a rigid separation of 'is' and 'ought' and tolerates a confusion of them in legal discussion. *Legal positivism* insists on drawing a sharp distinction between the law 'that is' and the law that 'ought to be'. Questions on legal positivism tend to concentrate on the essence of the doctrine, the criticisms it has attracted, and the work of leading proponents of positivism, such as Austin, Hart and Kelsen. Each of these jurists is represented in the questions forming this chapter.

Checklist

Ensure that you are acquainted with the following topics:

- definitions of legal positivism
- empiricism

- Austin's concept of law

- Austin's doctrine of sovereigny
- Hart's criticism of Austin

- Hart's concept of a legal system
- Hart's primary and secondary rules
- essentials of Kelsen's pure law theory
- norms and Grundnorm
- criticisms of the Grundnorm

Question 18

What do you understand by 'legal positivism'?

Answer plan

The question calls for an outline of the general doctrine associated with legal positivism and provides an opportunity for criticism. The background to the doctrine, associated with the empiricism of Hume and Comte, should be mentioned. Hart's enumeration of the various uses of the term 'positivism' ought to be explained. Account should be taken of the objection to legal positivism stemming from the belief that it downgrades the significance of 'right' and 'justice' in relation to the law. The following skeleton plan is presented:

Introduction - legal positivism as a mode of legal analysis - philosophical and logical positivism - Hume and Comte - Hart's analysis of the use of the term 'positivism' - methodology of the legal positivists - criticisms of the doctrine - conclusion, legal positivism considered as having advanced from its early preoccupations with the 'natural fallacy'.

Answer

The term 'legal positivism' is used here to signify a doctrine which rejects any metaphysical speculation concerning the law and which studies a community's laws precisely as they are, without taking into account matters such as social context, political and psychological background, which are considered extraneous. The basic features of the doctrine, its methodology and claims are noted below, together with some criticisms of positivism and its implications.

It is important, initially, to distinguish the term 'legal positivism' from 'philosophical' and 'logical positivism', although it should be noted that legal positivism has been influenced by the writings of the philosophical and logical positivists. 'Philosophical positivism' (which is mentioned below in comments on Hume and Comte) is a doctrine which holds that our knowledge of matters of fact is derived solely from the data of experience; metaphysical, so-called 'transcendental' knowledge, which is not based on experience, is held to be of no worth. 'Logical positivism', which stems from the writings of Carnap, Wittgenstein, Ayer and others of the 'Vienna Circle', involves a total rejection of statements that are not based on tested and verified experience of the senses; 'meaning' is ultimately to be established solely in terms of experience, so that metaphysical assertions are dismissed as meaningless. This doctrine has influenced the writings of the legal positivist, Hart, who urges the significance of understanding the mode in which statements about the law are couched.

Fundamental to legal positivism is its attitude to the problem of 'is' and 'ought'. Positivists ask us to consider the use of 'ought' in sentences such as: 'If I release the pen I am holding, it *ought* to fall to the ground'; 'You *ought* not to steal'; 'Those who kill *ought* to be punished severely'. The term 'ought' may refer to what is likely to happen as a physical probability, or it may be used as a 'moral ought'. May one, without fallacy, deduce 'ought' from 'is'? May we infer a normative statement from a merely factual statement? The answer of the legal positivists is that if normative rules reflect no more than subjective opinions, they *cannot* be deduced from physical reality. What, then, is the value said to be derived from a search for the 'moral verities' presumed to be at the basis of the law? What is the point in basing legislation on so-called 'immutable principles' which, in themselves, possess no veracity? Analysis, for legal positivists, involves concentrating on a study of the law *as it is*, ie, the law 'posited', that is, laid down, for citizens.

Hume, the eighteenth-century Scottish philosopher, developed the doctrines of empiricism, which called for a detailed observation of phenomena as the basis for scientific investigation. He used this method of enquiry in an examination of 'natural law'. To Hume the natural law was 'real' only in the sense that some persons entertained feelings that it existed; there was no other sense in which its 'truth' might be asserted meaningfully. The 'truths' which some jurists saw in natural law based upon 'reasonable human conduct' could not be demonstrated. So-called 'guides to human action' were mere values inspired directly by human motives; they required no 'eternal framework'. Hume's thoughts were enlarged by Comte in the following century. He taught that *a priori* metaphysical speculation had no validity and that all theories should be subjected to rigorous, empirical investigation. Comte's writings were the first to contain the term 'positivism' used in a philosophical sense.

The teachings of Hume and Comte cleared the way for the application of precise modes of reasoning to problems of jurisprudence. The law, hitherto the object of metaphysical speculation, was subjected to analysis on the basis of experience.

In particular, a growing number of jurists insisted on the separation of 'ought' and 'is'. It was felt that some of the methods of the natural sciences might be considered appropriate to the study of the social sciences, including legal theory.

In Hart's *The Concept of Law* (1961), five uses of the term 'positivism' in relation to Anglo-American jurisprudence, are noted. First, the term is used to describe the concept of law, favoured by Bentham and Austin, in which laws are seen as the commands of human beings. Second, the term is used to describe the view that there is no necessary link between law and morals, as emphasised by Kelsen. Third, the term is employed to name the idea of analysis or study of meanings of legal concepts. Fourth, the term denotes the view that a legal system is a 'closed logical system' in which logical means alone are to be used to deduce correct decisions from pre-determined legal rules. Finally, the term is used to indicate the theory that moral judgments cannot be established, as can statements of fact, by rational argument or evidence or proof. Hart himself uses the term 'legal positivism', in his chapter on 'Natural Law and Legal Positivism', to show that it is *not* a necessary truth that laws reproduce or satisfy certain demands of morality (though they may often have done so). Raz suggests, in the same vein, that a jurisprudential theory is acceptable only if its tests for identifying the content of the law and determining its existence depend totally on those facts of human behaviour capable of description in terms which are *value-neutral*, and which are applied without using moral argument.

Among many legal positivists there is a shared approach to methodology of *investigation* of legal problems. This approach involves an investigation of the structure of laws within a legal system so as to reveal their real foundation. A *classification* of the functions of the legal system is undertaken. Concepts within the legal structure require *identification* and *analysis*. The legal positivist uses these techniques to answer questions such as: What is 'law'? What are 'laws'? What are the essential functions of law?

As noted above, positivists seek to *exclude value judgments and moral considerations* from their examination of the law. In Austin's words: 'The existence of law is one thing, but its merit or demerit is another'. This is not to imply that positivists are not interested in matters of morality in relation to the law, for this is demonstrably not so. Many leading positivists have contributed to debate and social movements associated with problems of social morality. It is in the *examination of legal phenomena* that positivists will set aside moral considerations, as will an epidemiologist investigating the incidence of a disease within the community. The positivist's data are intended to emerge from a study of social reality only. Further, legal positivists seek to confine their investigations to the law which has been enacted and promulgated by the legislative organs of the State, namely, the 'positive law', which is equated, therefore, with the juridical norms laid down by the State.

Criticisms of legal positivism are headed by a general attack on the theoretical foundations of Humean doctrine. The theory, it is said, is flawed and its rejection of metaphysical speculation has resulted in attempts to remove from the attention of jurists large areas of significant, intellectual human activity. The positivists are not convinced that the 'flaws' in Humean analysis have been demonstrated satisfactorily. Hume has, they say, constructed a system of investigation which *can* explain the phenomena of the world, including law and the workings of legal institutions. Further condemnation of legal positivism, stemming from dissatisfaction with its basic position, is centred on its preoccupation with a search for facts without giving any attention to the possibility of an underlying, unifying purpose in the law. The positivist answer declares that the search for facts is a necessary prelude to any search by others for 'purpose'.

The positivists' exclusion from an investigation of legal facts of the entire context of the law is criticised by those who maintain that law exists *only* within a social setting and that it cannot be investigated adequately if that setting is ignored. Fuller reminds positivists that the law is a product of human effort, and that we risk absurdity if we try to describe it in disregard of the aims of those who brought it into being. The positivists' response states that the context of law is a matter for the considered judgment of the historian, the sociologist and the economist; it is not for the jurist.

Two specific criticisms relating to positivism, morality and justice, have been heard increasingly in recent times. First, it is said that it is an error to ignore the 'reality of absolute morality' which often guides communities. Society's belief in *what ought to be* has been a powerful stimulus to change. The positivist answer draws attention to the 'relative nature' of much social morality (as, for example, in the decriminalisation of some deviant sexual behaviour), making objective investigation of this phenomenon very difficult. A second criticism suggests that the positivist approach leads to a downgrading of concepts of 'right' and 'justice'. The positivist retorts that he does not deny the significance of these concepts; he is attempting to investigate their positive manifestations and has no intention of downgrading their importance within a legal system.

Fuller takes issue with the positivists' claim that their intention is, primarily, to promote clearer thinking in the law. Is the end sought in this quest worthwhile? Would clarity in legal discussion really be advanced if positivism could attain its goal of some clear distinction between law and morality? Drawing a distinction of this type cannot be justified as an end in itself. Additionally, says Fuller, positivism exerts a 'serious inhibitive influence' over legal scholarship by fencing in the legal writer with the question: does what you have written state the law or only your idea of what the law ought to be?

These are powerful criticisms but they have not deflected the legal positivists from their course. Early preoccupations with the 'naturalistic fallacy' (ie, the non-separation of 'ought' and 'is') have given way to a more intensive analysis of matters such as the phenomenon of language in the law. Positivist studies continue to analyse the legal order while, at the same time, calling attention to the difficulties of accepting as valid those ideas of law which are based on attempts to transcend the empirical reality of existing legal systems.

Notes

The essential features of *legal positivism* are discussed in Friedmann, ch 21, Bodenheimer, chs 7 and 8, and in Lloyd, ch 6. Shuman's *Legal Positivism*, and Raz' *The Authority of Law* expound the problems associated with positivism. Simmonds comments on the discussion in 'Between Positivism and Idealism' (1991) CLJ 308. Hart's *The Concept of Law* and Fuller's *The Law in Quest of Itself* consider the doctrine of positivism and its implications.

Question 19

'Austin's theory is in the last analysis a psychological one': Jones (*Historical Introduction to the Theory of Law*).

Do you agree?

Answer plan

Austin (1790-1859), a friend of Bentham and J S Mill, was one of the earlier positivists who sought to explain law in terms of commands issued by 'a sovereign'. His best-known work, *The Province of Jurisprudence Determined* (1832), attempts to clarify the distinction between law and morality and to ascertain the limits of jurisprudential investigation. Examination questions concerning Austin tend to concentrate on the detail of his theory and on criticisms of that theory. This question, somewhat unusually, calls for a consideration of Austinian doctrine in relation to psychology. The answer should deal with the main features of the theory and should note those points at which Austin seems to touch upon psychological matters. There should be comment on the problems which must arise in jurisprudence (as elsewhere) when the work of a jurist who lived in a past era is analysed in terms of the science of the twentieth century. The following skeleton plan is suggested:

> Introduction -psychological overtones in Austin's theory - Austin's description of law - commands - sanctions - Austin's analysis of sovereignty - psychological nature of Austin's comments on law - Allen's comments on Manning's views concerning Austin - the psychological school of jurisprudence - conclusion, doubtful classification of Austin as a member of the 'psychological school'.

Answer

'Austin's theory' is taken to mean, within the context of Jones' statement, the concept of law as a species of command, and the analysis of sovereignty. In *The Province of Jurisprudence Determined* (1832), which contains the essence of his theory, Austin attempted to define the precise scope of jurisprudence. This involved drawing a clear line between 'law' and 'morality'. For Austin, jurisprudence was concerned *solely* with positive laws 'as considered without regard to their goodness or badness'. Law was to be viewed as a species of command issued by a person or body of persons to whom habitual obedience is rendered. There are undeniable overtones within Austin's theory of matters which are properly within the province of psychology - command, obedience, habit - and it *can* be argued with force that a theory based on concepts of this nature is to be classified as 'psychological'. It would be wrong, however, to read into Austin's work, produced at a time when the science of psychology was almost unknown in England, suggestions of an attempt by the author to view the essence of jurisprudence in terms of percepts and intellectual constructs which are well beyond his time.

A law, according to Austin, is a description of a rule laid down 'for the guidance of an intelligent being by an intelligent being having power over him'. Within this description are terms rooted in the 'mentalistic' terminology of scientific psychology. 'Intelligent being' refers clearly to sentient persons exercising their mental faculties; the term 'power' may have wider connotations than mere physical might, and can be explained in psychological terms as a perception by one person of another's ability to exercise coercion. Austin's description of law is of orders ('rules') promulgated by one person or body of persons and *perceived* by those individuals to whom they are directed as 'directions concerning conduct'. This view of law is, fundamentally, of a psychological nature in that it rests upon perceptions by 'the governed' within a community.

Laws, says Austin, may be 'improperly so called' and 'properly so called'. The former category is divided into laws 'by analogy', and 'laws by metaphor'. Laws by analogy are rules set out and enforced by mere opinion, such as a communal 'law of honour'. Such laws are aspects of 'positive morality': they are 'positive' in that they are man-made, and they relate to a 'morality' which has to be distinguished from the positive law. Laws by metaphor describe natural law, eg, those describing the determination of movement of inanimate bodies.

The laws 'properly so called' are *general commands*, comprising the laws set by God to his human creatures, and laws set by men to men. The laws of God do not fall within the province of jurisprudence. The laws set by men to men may be categorised according to the nature of the relationship existing among them. If this relationship involves men who have political superiority over others, or who exercise legal rights conferred by their superiors, their 'laws' comprise 'positive law' or 'law' in its strict, simple sense. *The aggregate of such laws is, according to Austin, the essential and appropriate matter of jurisprudence.* By contrast, where laws are set by men who are not political superiors, or who do not exercise legal rights conferred by superiors, these 'laws' are mere examples of 'positive morality', as where rules relating to membership of a private club are published.

The *general commands* given to the community are by their nature 'continuing commands', ie, they determine more than specific acts. Further, they are promulgated to persons 'in a state of subjection' to the author. It is possible to interpret this concept as resting upon psychological data. A 'state of subjection' may arise from political and social status: those who are disenfranchised and who play no part in the enactment of the community's 'rules' will tend to view themselves as 'inferior', and will be aware of a 'state of subjection'. 'Subjection' is a *mental state*, fundamentally.

Austin's analysis of the nature of a 'command' gives support to those who view his theory as 'psychological'. If, says Austin, you express or intimate a wish that I should or should not perform an act, and if I am sure that you will 'visit me with an evil' if I fail to comply with your wish, then the expression or intimation of your wish is *a command*. Further, a command is distinguished from other significations of desire not by the *style* in which the desire is signified, but by the *power and purpose* of the party commanding to inflict an evil or pain in case the desire be disregarded. The psychological basis of Austin's 'command' is clear. The command arises from the expression of a 'wish'; its 'power' depends on 'awareness' by the person to whom the wish is made known that evil will follow upon failure to conform to the wish, and upon his perception of the strength of those undesired consequences likely to emerge as the result of disobedience.

Here is 'command' viewed by Austin in terms of *perception* - the essence of psychological interpretations of the law.

Austin sees 'command' and 'duty' as 'correlative terms', the meaning denoted by each being implied or supposed by the other. Because X is 'liable to evil' from Y if he fails to comply with Y's signified wish, X is 'bound' or 'obliged' by Y's command, ie, he is under a *duty* to obey it. Again, Austin is viewing an essential feature of his theory - the concept of duty - in terms of *personal responses* to the actions of others.

The enforcement of obedience, the 'sanction', is analysed by Austin as 'the evil which will probably be increased in case a command is disobeyed', ie, in the case of a duty being disregarded. Such an evil may be styled 'a punishment'. It is the sanction - the 'fear of evil', of the power of another to inflict punishment in the event of non-compliance with a wish - which transforms the expression of a mere wish into a 'command'. Punitive sanctions are, in Austin's view, essential for valid law. In psychological terms, the motivating force behind conduct which is consciously directed to the carrying out of the wishes embodied in a law is the 'fear' of being visited with 'an evil'.

Austin's analysis of sovereignty is an important part of his teachings. He distinguishes sovereignty from other types of superiority. The essence of sovereignty is to be found in the phenomenon of 'obedience to a perceived superior'. The bulk of members of society are, according to Austin, in the *habit* of obedience or submission to a *determinate and common superior* (a person or body of persons, eg, a monarch or a Parliament); that person or body is not in the habit of obedience to any determinate human superior. Hence, if a determinate human superior, not in the habit of obedience to a like superior receives habitual obedience from the majority of members of a society, *that superior is 'sovereign' in that society* (and the society is 'political and independent'). Essentially, therefore, sovereignty involves the very fact of 'obedience' - a psychological state which reflects subjection, submission, and perceptions of a 'superior-inferior' relationship. 'Habitual' obedience suggests, in psychological terms, attitudes resulting from the force of habit; that habit may have resulted from repeated reactions to the acts of the sovereign power. In modern psychological parlance, it may be the result of deliberate 'conditioning', as where the sovereign so acts as to intend the creation of a set of desired responses to stimuli, eg, obedience induced by exposure to the trappings of majesty and power.

To deny the force of the psychological concepts at the basis of Austin's theory is to reject the essential features of *law within society* as he viewed that phenomenon. It should be remembered that Austin was a utilitarian, closely influenced by his friends, Bentham and J S Mill. For Austin, the proper purpose or end of a sovereign government is 'the greatest possible advancement of human happiness' - an objective which is not easily separated from the states of mind with which psychology is concerned in its investigations. For Austin, law rests on the perception of the nature and consequences of commands. It involves acknowledgement of a person or body as a sovereign to whom habitual obedience must be given. The force of personal attitudes is at the heart of Austin's theory, which, to a considerable extent, may be described in Jones' words, as 'a psychological one'.

It would be unproductive, however, to seek to read into Austin's theory the constructs of twentieth-century psychology. An attempt of this nature was made by Manning in his article on 'Austin Today' (1933). Allen's reply is of particular interest. Manning had suggested that Austin had given merely 'a particular account of the relation between law and communal psychology', and that the Austinian concept of sovereignty was based on the idea of a sovereign as 'a mere abstraction, and his sovereignty just a brace of ideas'. Allen notes that one cannot extract this meaning from anything Austin wrote or meant. Manning is merely transferring ideas and arguments 'from one place to another, both in time and conception' at his will. This is, indeed, the problem raised by attempts to read into Austin's formulations a methodology of which he can have had no possible understanding. The danger is, says Allen, of taking the dogmatic and explicit doctrines of one age and attempting to paraphrase them into 'the terminology and philosophical facts of a later era'.

To employ, for example, Freudian or Jungian theories of human obedience in a modern 'interpretation' of Austin may be valid for us, since our age has at its disposal knowledge of techniques of investigation which were denied to earlier times.

But to use these techniques so as to imply that Austin himself had in mind ideas which were generally beyond his time is invalid. In a very general sense it is true to say that, because jurisprudence concerns human beings, and because all human activities have a psychological dimension, then jurists must recognise that their theories are touched, if only tangentially, by the phenomena which psychology investigates. This observation may be applied with justification to the 'psychological' interpretations of Austinian doctrine.

To say, however, that it is possible to classify that doctrine as belonging to the 'psychological school of jurisprudence' gives rise to difficulty. A full-fledged psychological theory of law is one predicated on the fundamental and decisive significance of mental phenomena in legal events. Thus, Petrazycki, for whom rights and duties are 'phantasmata', existing only in the mind, but creating 'imperative-attributed experiences', may be considered a member of the 'psychological school'. Ehrenzweig, who views the legal order as an enterprise structured in order to moderate conflicting individual views of justice, and who sees those conflicts as explicable in Freudian terms as a product of individual 'early personality development', may be considered as belonging to that school. Jurists who perceive the tensions within a legal system as reflecting Freudian categories, or as mirroring Jung's 'split in the individual between the ego and the shadow', may be classified as members of the 'psychological school'. But Austin, for whom the formal relationships of sovereign and subjects comprise the essence of the socio-legal framework, could be placed within that school only as a result of an unwarranted extension of the aims, framework and methodology attributed to the 'psychological jurisprudence' movement.

Notes

Austin's teachings are considered by Lloyd, ch 4, Dias, ch 16, Harris, ch 3, Friedmann, ch 22, and Riddall, ch 2. There is a full treatment of the Austinian theory, together with extracts from *The Province of Jurisprudence Determined* in Davies and Holdcroft, ch 2. Allen, ch 1, examines the 'psychological interpretation' of Austin's views propounded by Manning in 'Austin Today', which appears in Jennings' edition of *Modern Theories of Law*.

The Thoughts of John Austin, by Rumble, provides useful background information.

Question 20

'Criticisms of Austin's theory of law mounted steadily in the nineteenth century; but it was Hart who delivered the *coup de grâce* a century later'.

Explain.

Answer plan

Austin was criticised in his lifetime for a variety of reasons, but largely because of his uncompromising positivist approach to interpretations of the law. Specifically, it was claimed that he had misunderstood the significance of the social functions of law and that he had failed to separate the concepts of legal authority and political power. Hart later subjected the 'command theory' to intensive scrutiny in *The Concept of Law* (1961). The question calls for an awareness of the criticisms faced by Austin in his lifetime and the general lines of the attack mounted by Hart. The following skeleton plan is suggested:

> Introduction -reminder of Austin's theory - narrowness of his perspective - simplistic view of the law - linguistic looseness - restricted view of sovereignty - Hart's criticisms - conclusion, noting Austin's failure to understand significance of 'rules'.

Answer

The essence of Austin's much-criticised theory is to be found in his basing the very nature of law not on ideas of 'good' or 'bad', 'just' or 'unjust', but on the concept of power exercised by a superior. Positive law, or, as he terms it, 'law properly so called', can be understood only if there is a separation of questions of law and those of morality. The law is characterised by its constituent elements of command, sanction, duty and sovereignty. It may be comprehended in terms of the command of a sovereign backed by sanctions. The theory was published in the first half of the nineteenth century, in a year which witnessed the death of Bentham and the passing of the Reform Act. It bears the marks of the philosophical and jurisprudential thought associated with Austin's friends, Bentham and J S Mill, in particular their positivism and utilitarianism. Early criticisms of Austin turned on his positivism - denounced as 'a sterile verbalism which produced a travesty of reality' - and on an apparent narrowness of perspective. By the time of his death in 1859 the theory had been condemned as a totally inadequate explanation of law based on a misunderstanding of the nature of 'command' and 'obedience'. Hart's detailed examination of Austin's theory in *The Concept of Law* (1961) underlined the essential weaknesses of 'the command theory of law'.

'Narrowness of perspective' was a criticism directed at Austin with particular force by those who saw him as a 'naive empiricist'. It was claimed that he had not understood the implications of the positivism he espoused and that his separation of questions of law from those of morality shut him off from awareness of the real complexities of law within society. This same narrowness of vision was detected by those critics who claimed that Austin's preparatory work for the exposition of his theory had been confined to an enquiry into certain aspects of English law and an investigation of Roman legal theory of the classical era. This appeared to constitute too narrow a base for the construction of a *general* theory of jurisprudence. The result, said the critics, was a doctrine founded upon mere abstractions with few roots in established historical fact.

Further criticism emerged from what was perceived as Austin's 'simplistic view' of law. It was argued that he had confused 'law' with the mere product of legislation. He had failed to understand that 'law' was much more than legislative enactments; it included, for example, customary law and international law, neither of which received adequate treatment in his analysis. Above all, perhaps, the analysis did not extend to an adequate examination of judge-made law. Much law results from the decisions of the courts. It is not easy to see, therefore, in what sense judge-made law may be considered as emanating from 'the commands of a sovereign', unless one accepts the doubtful view of judges as mere delegates of the State.

Critics noted, too, some 'linguistic looseness', or ambiguity, in Austin's exposition of his command theory. The term 'command' has its own singular connotations and overtones. Its general use suggests a person who 'issues orders in a peremptory fashion'. It is difficult to use the word accurately in referring to the content of a large proportion of legislation. The characteristics of a 'command' are often absent from many contemporary statutes.

Austin's concept of 'sovereignty' was attacked by those who considered it to be over-simplified and incapable of application to a wide range of problems arising from the legal structures of democratic societies in particular. Austin's view of the sovereign as possessing unlimited powers seemed to have no validity within a parliamentary constitution. The idea of 'indivisibility' of the sovereign power created difficulties for those who sought to apply it to the analysis of a federal State. Bryce, writing at the turn of the century, suggested that Austin may have blurred the distinctions between the *de facto* sovereign (who receives the 'habitual obedience' of subjects) and the *de jure* sovereign (the law-enacting institution). Thus, our constitutional law makes a clear distinction between Her Majesty the Queen and the Queen in Parliament. Austin, it was claimed, had concentrated too readily on the *form* of the law, on its outward manifestations in relation to the sovereign, and had neglected the *functional aspects* of sovereign power within society.

It was a weakened theory of 'law as command' that Hart set out to demolish. In *The Concept of Law* (1961) he speaks of his aim in the book as having been 'to further the understanding of law, coercion, and morality as different but related social phenomena'. With this in mind he examines, initially, Austin's concept of law as being, basically, 'orders backed by threats'. Superficially, the criminal law may provide many examples of this view. Thus, the Dangerous Dogs Act 1991, s4, states that a person who has custody of a dog in contravention of an order of disqualification is guilty of an offence and liable to a fine on summary conviction. Here is a precise 'order' backed by 'threat of application of sanction'. But there are very many examples of laws in which there is neither 'order' nor 'threat'. Thus, contract law, creating facilities for individuals to realise their wishes by conferring upon them powers to create structures of rights, is an example. Hart points out, too, that many laws of a public nature (constitutional law, for example) exemplify 'power-conferring' *rules*, not 'order plus threat'. Those who argue, however, that the 'nullity' which may be a consequence of a failure to comply with the law (as illustrated by lack of compliance with the provisions of the Wills Act 1837) and which is, therefore, in effect, a 'sanction', must be met with the counter-argument that the effects of failure to comply with the statute may be to the advantage of persons involved, and will not necessarily involve the 'evil' of a sanction.

Hart points out, further, that in Austin's theory the sovereign law-maker is not himself bound by the orders he issues. He stands, to that extent, above and beyond the law. But in practice the legislator is often bound by the orders he makes and promulgates. Thus the House of Lords - an important part of the legislature - is bound by the Parliament Acts 1911 and 1949 which effectively limit its powers. The House of Commons is bound effectively by its 'standing orders relative to public business', as published in 1989. The Austinian view of the legislature as 'subject to no rules' seems inadequate.

The mode of origin of law cannot be understood correctly, according to Hart, by considering it merely as having emerged from 'order plus threat'. Some very important specific rules of our law (now embodied in mercantile law, for example) originated in custom. It is not possible to explain their origin merely in terms of enactments of the legislature. Thus, the customs of merchants in relation to early forms of bills of exchange were recognised as possessing the force of law within groups of financiers long before the Bills of Exchange Act 1882. No 'sovereign' commanded, in the form of an 'order and threat', that the strict codes of practice binding the early 'money scriveners', which originated in the customs of Florentine and Venetian bankers, should have force among the merchants of London. Austin's command theory is of little value in this context.

Hart places particular emphasis on the total inadequacy of the Austinian concept of 'habit of obedience' in relation to sovereignty. Austin, it will be recalled, explained sovereignty in terms of the obedience displayed by subjects towards their sovereign. The authoritarian ruler ensures that his people are conditioned to acceptance of orders and obedience in all circumstances; the citizens of a parliamentary democracy have the *habit* of obeying legislation promulgated on behalf of the Queen in Parliament. But, says Hart, let us suppose that within a State one ruler is followed by another. How may we account for the continuity generally observed? Citizens were 'in the habit' of obeying their first ruler. At what stage is their obedience 'transferred' to his successor? When may it be said that the citizens become 'habituated' to the power enjoyed by the new ruler? Hart's answer involves a perusal of the *rules* which ensure that there shall be an uninterrupted movement of power from one ruler to another. The simplistic notion of mere 'habits of obedience' is an inadequate explanation of the phenomenon of the transitional transfer of legislative powers. Hart argues that the explanation of the seemingly-paradoxical 'movement of obedience' may be discovered in the existence of accepted fundamental *rules* regarding the right to legislate.

Further deficiencies in Austin's analysis of sovereignty are uncovered by Hart. The concept of 'a sovereign with unlimited power' (the 'omnipotent ruler') has no application to our type of parliamentary democracy. Thus, Parliament may not generally extend its life beyond the period of five years, as stated by the Parliament Act 1911. (There was an exception to this rule in the two World Wars.) The voluntary surrender by Parliament of some aspects of its sovereignty (as noted in *Factortame Ltd v Secretary of State for Transport* (No 2) (1991)) in relation to the need to give full effect to European Community law, is of significance. But in spite of limitations upon its 'omnipotence', Parliament's enactments continue to express validly its sovereign status. Nor is the Austinian dilemma in the face of Parliament's practice resolved by reference to the electorate as 'the true sovereign power'. Hart notes that the power of the electorate is undeniably limited. Its delegation of the exercise of its sovereignty to Parliamentary representatives creates in practice a situation in which large sections of the electorate may be subjected to rules and orders of which they may not approve. There is doubt, for example, as to whether Parliament's decision not to restore capital punishment for the offence of murder represents the views of the majority of 'the sovereign electorate'.

Little remains of the Austinian edifice. Hart uncovered and demolished its basic structure. Austin's inability to recognise the significance of 'rules' in a system of law accounts, in Hart's view, for his failure to comprehend the nature of law. Hart points out that the Austinian theory was fashioned from elements such as orders, threats, and obedience; this did not allow for the emergence of the idea of 'a rule', 'without which we cannot hope to elucidate even the most elementary forms of law'. It would be left to Hart himself to construct a concept of law based on the idea of a combination of 'primary and secondary rules', which would provide a credible alternative to the Austinian theory of 'law as command'.

Notes

Austin's theory is outlined in *The Province of Jurisprudence Determined*. Hart's criticisms are contained in *The Concept of Law* (chs 2, 3 and 4 in particular). Appropriate extracts from Austin and his critics appear in Davies and Holdcroft, ch 2. A useful article by Tapper, 'Austin on Sanctions', appears in the Cambridge Law Journal (1965) p 271. Lloyd, ch 4, Harris, ch 3, and Riddall, ch 2, comment on the criticisms of Austinian doctrine.

Question 21

What is Hart's concept of 'a legal system'?

Answer plan

Hart (b 1907) envisages a legal system as derived from 'a union of primary and secondary rules'. His theory is expounded in *The Concept of Law* (1961) (which should be read 'from cover to cover' by all students of jurisprudence). Hart's view is that a legal system can exist *only* when certain conditions are fulfilled: obedience must be given by citizens to certain rules, the validity of which depends on the system's basic 'rules of recognition', and that system's secondary rules must be accepted as common public standards by the community's officials. This question is straightforward and demands an exposition of the fundamentals of Hart's system of primary and secondary rules. The following skeleton plan is suggested:

Introduction -Hart's 'characteristics of the human condition' - social habits and social rules - primary rules - secondary rules - rules of recognition, change and adjudication - essence of a 'legal system' - conclusion, meaning of 'the existence of a legal system'.

Answer

Hart views the concept of a legal system from the perspective of a positivist. Legal institutions and other phenomena related to the law must be studied exactly *as they are*; law is, in general, to be considered apart from morality and is to be subjected to a systematic analysis. Law as a 'social phenomenon', which is how Hart views it, involves, for those who wish to study it, reference to 'the characteristics of the human condition'. In *The Concept of Law* (1961) in which Hart articulates his concept of the essential features of a legal system, he lists those characteristics as: human vulnerability (each one of us can be subjected to undesired physical violence); approximate equality (making necessary mutual forbearance and compromise); limited altruism (tendencies to aggression which require control); limited resources (we need food, shelter, clothing, all of which are in limited supply); and limited understanding and strength of will (our understanding of long-term interests cannot be taken for granted). There arises, therefore, within society, a need for *rules* to protect 'persons, property and promises'. It is the problem of rules - their constituent features and interrelationships - which dominates Hart's interpretation of the essence of a legal system. We note below Hart's system of 'primary and secondary rules' and his view of the circumstances necessary for the existence of what may properly be called 'a legal system'.

Hart's view may be summarised as follows: if a legal system is to obtain within a community, two circumstances must co-exist. First, there must be a variety of 'valid obligation rules' which are generally obeyed by the bulk of members of society. Secondly, the officials within that society must accept, additionally, certain rules of 'change, adjudication and responsibility'. This terminology must now be examined.

The term 'rule' is not to be viewed in Austin's terms, as 'a command'. Within a society there are 'social habits' and 'social rules'. *Social habits* (which are not conterminous with 'rules') may be exemplified by members of a group who visit the theatre every Friday evening. Failure by some members to attend the theatre on Friday evenings will not be perceived as a 'fault' which should attract criticism. *Social rules* are more significant: where they are broken (as in matters pertaining to morality, etc) criticism will result because a 'fault' is thought to have been committed. Existence of a social rule involves its acceptance by social groups as a whole. Awareness of a rule, and support for its significance and acceptance within the group, are termed by Hart 'the internal aspects of that rule'. The 'external aspects of a rule' refer to the fact that an observer outside the group could be aware of its existence. Social habits have an external aspect only; social rules have an external *and* an internal aspect. Hart attaches particular significance to the internal aspect of rules: it involves a 'critical, reflective attitude to certain patters of behaviour and a common standard', and this ought to be displayed in criticism and self-criticism, demands for conformity to standards, and an acknowledgement that such criticism and demands are justified.

Social rules are, under Hart's classification, of two kinds - mere 'social conventions' and 'rules constituting obligations'. The former phrase refers to, eg, rules of correct behaviour in a place of public worship. The latter phrase involves conformity, which is considered essential if society's life - its components and quality - are to be maintained. An example might be the general rules forbidding violence to individuals. The 'rules' relating to obligations impinge on the idea of 'moral duties', and are *what we understand by 'law'*. 'Moral duties' constitute a significant and important portion of a society's moral code; some may have originated in ancient customs. The breach of a moral obligation does not usually result in punishment of the offender, but, nevertheless, there are often intense pressures to carry out those duties.

The rules relating to obligations which we speak of as 'legal rules' are of two types. Hart refers to them as 'primary' and 'secondary' rules. Essentially, the primary rules of obligation may be epitomised by the criminal law and those parts of the law of torts involving obligations. Thus, the Road Traffic Act 1988 imposes duties on those who drive motor vehicles on the roads. The rule in *Rylands v Fletcher* (1865) imposes strict obligations on those who, for their own purposes, bring on their land and collect and keep there anything likely to do damage if it escapes. Primary rules, in Hart's sense, generally concern requirements to do or abstain from certain actions.

Hart argues that a small community, closely knit by common sentiment and belief, and placed in a stable environment, might be able to live with a set of rules approximating to the 'primary rules of obligation' he has described. But this would not be possible in a large community because of the very nature of the primary rules. Thus, doubts might arise as to what the rules are, or as to the basis on which those doubts are to be settled: the problem would be one of *uncertainty*. Further, the *static nature* of the primary rules might create a further problem: deliberate adaptation to new circumstances might be difficult. A third defect would be the *inefficiency* of the diffuse social pressures by which the rules are maintained: there would be no specialised official agency empowered to ascertain whether or not a rule had been broken. Primary rules would not, in themselves, suffice as 'building bricks' for the construction of a legal system; something more would be required.

A supplementary system of 'secondary rules' would be needed, and these rules would be 'parasitic' on the primary rules. They will provide that members of the community may, by performing actions or saying things, introduce new rules of the primary sort, modify old rules, and control the operations of primary rules. The conferring of public or private powers will result from the application of the secondary rules. These rules would create or vary the obligations of members of the community. *The union of the primary and secondary rules constitutes 'the law'*.

The defect of 'uncertainty', ie, the lack of authoritative procedures for settling disputes as to the precise nature of the primary rules, would be remedied by a secondary rule which Hart terms 'the rule of recognition'. This rule will specify certain features, possession of which will affirm conclusively that the rule in question 'is a rule of the group to be supported by the social pressure it exerts'. References to authoritative texts, to legislative enactments, to custom, to general declarations of specific purpose, or to past judicial decisions, will constitute the authoritative criteria for identification of primary rules of obligation. The rule of recognition may be, indeed, the 'ultimate rule' of a legal system since it is itself the test of legal validity within that system. Hart gives the example of the fundamental rule that what is enacted by the Queen in Parliament is law; that rule provides criteria for assessing the validity of other rules within the system, but there is no rule providing criteria by which its own legal validity might be assessed.

The defect of 'static rules' within a system may be remedied by secondary 'rules of change'. Essentially, they empower specified individuals to make changes in 'legal positions'. Thus, the law of contract may be characterised as a group of secondary rules in that they serve to alter existing legal positions: the rules of consensus, of offer and acceptance, create a situation (of legally enforceable agreements) which alters a previous position in which there was no contract between the parties concerned. The Law of Property Act 1925, s 136, allowing the legal assignment of choses in action, makes possible new situations in relation to debts and other 'legal things in action'. The Wills Act 1837 allows a person who makes a will to alter a position in which his property rights might pass under the rules relating to an intestacy.

The defect of 'inefficiency' may be remedied by the provision of secondary rules giving authorised individuals power to determine in authoritative fashion the question as to whether some person has breached a primary rule. This type of secondary rule is known as the 'rule of adjudication'. Procedures relating to the appointment of judges, courts, and declarations in the form of judgments, will be covered by this rule. The Courts and Legal Services Act 1990 is an example of this type of secondary rule.

Primary and secondary rules (of recognition, change and adjudication) constitute the 'law' which is the essence of a legal system. Hart gives a unique answer to the question: What is meant precisely when it is said that 'a legal system exists'? Two basic conditions must be satisfied before it can be said with accuracy that 'a legal system exists'. First, rules, and, in particular, the rule of recognition, must be obeyed. Secondly, the secondary rules must be accepted by the community's officials as 'common public standards'.

The first of these conditions involves general obedience *in practice* by the mass of citizens to the community's rules which have a validity derived from the rule of recognition. The obedience required must be much more than mere 'lip-service'. It must extend in practice to the community's daily life. Rules imposing obligations concerning the necessity to respect the property of others, for example, must be observed strictly if obedience is to be a reality. It is necessary, too, that obedience be given by the bulk of citizens (but not by all, since that is an impossibility). Obedience to the system's rule of recognition is of great importance; in our system, for example, there must be agreement on the necessity to observe as binding the rules made as the result of legislation enacted in Parliament.

Hart's second condition refers to the relationship of the community's officials to the secondary rules. The officials must not only obey those secondary rules, they must collectively 'accept' them. This applies in particular to acceptance of the 'rules of recognition' as providing common standards for the making and enunciation of judicial decisions. Thus, when a judge asserts that no court of justice may enquire into the mode in which Parliament made a law, he is demonstrating acceptance of the rule of recognition as it refers to the power and authority of Parliament.

Hart suggests that to assert that 'a legal system exists' is to make a 'Janus-faced statement' which looks both towards obedience by ordinary citizens (which, of course, will include an element of acceptance of rules) *and* the acceptance by the community's officials of secondary rules as common standards of official behaviour. In accepting these common standards the officials will show a critical and reflective attitude to the appraisal of their own and one another's performance. The 'internal aspects' of the rules they profess to follow acquire unusual significance as partial indicia of the real existence of a legal system.

Notes

Hart's *The Concept of Law* is analysed in Lloyd, ch 6, Dias, ch 16, Harris, ch 9, Riddall, ch 4. A detailed analysis is given in Davies in Holdcroft, ch 3. MacCormick discusses Hart's theory in *Legal Reasoning and Legal Theory*. A valuable exposition of the theory is given by Summers in 'Hart's Concept of Law' (1963) Duke University Law Journal 629.

Question 22

'A system of coercion imposing norms which are laid down by human acts in accordance with a constitution the validity of which is pre-supposed if it is on the whole efficacious'. Outline the theory from which this definition of law emerged.

Answer plan

The initial problem is the identification of the theory from which the definition emerged. It is, clearly, that associated with Kelsen, the so-called 'pure theory of law'. Kelsen (1881-1973), an Austrian-American jurist, argued that an acceptable theory of law must be 'pure', ie, logically self-supporting and not dependent upon extra-legal values. In every system of law can be found some basic assumption accepted as such by a significant proportion of the community. From that fundamental assumption - the 'Grundnorm' - will be derived the norms which constitute 'the law'. An answer to the question will necessitate an explanation of Kelsen's analysis with particular reference to the concept of the norm. The skeleton plan for an answer is as follows:

Introduction -essence of the pure theory - norms - sanctions - the Grundnorm - illustration of norms - effectiveness and validity of norms - norms and the State - conclusion, pure theory as expression of positivism.

Answer

The quotation is, in fact, a definition of law stated in Kelsen's *General Theory of State and Law* (1945). The reasoning from which the definition stems is his celebrated 'pure theory of law', formulated first in 1911 and revised in its final form in 1964. It is, above all, a theory of *positive law*, concerned exclusively with the process of defining its subject matter with as much accuracy as is possible. Kelsen advances it as a general theory and not as an interpretation of specific legal norms, although it is intended to offer a 'theory of interpretation'. It is designed so as to 'know and describe its subject'.

The theory makes possible the discovery of an answer to the basic question: 'What is the law?' It does not seek to answer the question: 'What *ought* the law to be?' Legal science should be fashioned, according to Kelsen, in terms which will reflect the unique nature of the phenomenon of law. This will involve the building of a framework of concepts having reference only to the law; the 'uncritical mixture of methodically-different disciplines which characterises much legal theory' is to be rejected. The appropriate methodology of investigation, which will be value-free, will require the interpretation of experience and 'the reduction of multiplicity to unity'; indeed for Kelsen, *all* knowledge reflected the endeavour to establish unity from chaos. In such an investigation the concept of natural law would have no place. Kelsen viewed the claims of natural law as worthless, based on no more than speculative claims to immutability resting on 'Nature and Reason' - concepts which seemed to him to clothe with an objective character that which is non-existent.

The purification of the science of law and the removal of subjective, evaluative criteria and elements of ideology, involve a process of re-appraising the place of 'justice' in any definition of the law. Kelsen viewed the concept of justice as little more than the expression of an irrational ideal representing the value-preferences of an individual or a group. However indispensable the ideal of justice may be for the volition and activities of men, it is not subject to cognition. It may be considered 'just' for a general rule to be applied in practice in all those cases where circumstances demand that application. In this sense justice may be perceived 'in the maintenance of a positive order by conscientious application of general rules'. Let justice be identified, therefore, with legality. But the question of what constitutes justice cannot be answered with any scientific precision and is not, therefore, a fruitful subject for the investigation which is to characterise a 'pure theory' of law.

Not only should political and ideological value-laden judgments be expelled from an investigation of law, but all non-legal extraneous matters are to be considered as adulterants. Kelsen insisted on the total rejection of those elements of psychology, sociology and ethics which had found their way into jurisprudence. Such 'alien disciplines' had attracted the attention of jurists because they dealt with matters which might be perceived as having a close connection with the law. The connections of this type are to be neither ignored nor denied, but their uncritical use (which Kelsen referred to as 'methodological syncretism') had obscured the true nature of the science of law. If one were to admit into a precise study of positive law material relating, say, to the economic basis of society, the result would be an admixture which would defy attempts to make a fundamental analysis. The pure theory at which Kelsen aimed is, in his words, 'a science of law (jurisprudence), not legal politics'.

The appropriate materials for a study which will lead to a pure science of law are to be found in those 'norms' which have the character of *legal norms*, in that they make certain acts legal or illegal. The term 'norm' is used by Kelsen in a very precise sense so that it connotes a standard to which individuals should conform. Legal norms do not merely prescribe certain types of human behaviour, they attach to the contrary behaviour specific coercive acts as *sanctions*. Kelsen would argue, therefore, that our law does not merely state that dangerous driving is to be avoided; it makes it an offence, under the Road Traffic Acts 1988 and 1991, attracting specified punishments. The element of coercion, which underpins a sanction, is, according to Kelsen, a vital constituent of the law as he envisages it. *Law is 'a coercive order of human behaviour'*. Sanctions are not merely of a psychological nature; when used by the law they are 'outward' in that they involve, *visibly*, a deprivation of the offender's freedom or property.

In Kelsen's terms, law is based on norms which stipulate sanctions; hence law may be perceived as 'norms addressed to officials' (such as judges). These norms are prescriptive of conduct and may be interpreted in the following manner: if A, then B, ie, if the circumstances in question constitute A, then B should happen. Thus, if X is not in possession of an appropriate licence, and he imports controlled drugs, then a judge is required to apply sanctions in accordance with the Misuse of Drugs Act 1971. If Y, the owner of a pit bull terrier, allows the dog to be in a public place unmuzzled, a judge may apply the sanctions set out in the Dangerous Dogs Act 1991.

The *validity* of a given legal norm depends solely, according to Kelsen, on its having been authorised by another legal norm of a higher rank. An administrative order is valid if authorised by statute; the authorising statute is valid if it has been made in accordance with the provisions of a constitution which, in turn, is valid if it has been promulgated by the authority of an earlier constitution. But if, for example, the constitution is question is the first to be promulgated in a new State, then its validity may be considered in terms of what Kelsen describes as a 'basic norm' (Grundnorm). This is a norm *presupposed by legal thinking*. The basic norm - the 'final postulate' - behind which one cannot go, may take a variety of forms; thus, it might be 'coercion of man against man should be exercised in the style and under the conditions determined by the State's first constitution'. A basic norm may be discovered in any legal order; it is viewed by Kelsen as the ultimate source for the validity of all those other norms belonging to the same legal order.

Within a given legal system it should be possible to discern a *hierarchy* composed of different levels of legal norms, at the apex of which is the Grundnorm, valid only because it is presupposed, and providing authority for all other norms within the system. Assume circumstances in which, under appropriate rules emanating from statute, and subsequent to his conviction by a court, X is imprisoned. The act of the prison officer who effects X's actual imprisonment derives its validity from the sentence ordered by the court following X's trial. The validity of the court's action is derived from an appropriate statute which, in turn, owes its authority to promulgation by the Queen in Parliament. Beyond that promulgation is the law and custom pertaining to the authority of Parliament. Beyond that is a *final, basic, norm*, relating to the acceptance by the community of the overriding nature of Parliamentary pronouncements embodied within statute. In applying statute law in X's case, the judges are, in Kelsen's terms, 'concretising' the general norms controlling that case; the decision in X's particular case constitutes an 'individual norm'. Where the administrative organs within a legal system apply general norms to a particular case so that an administrative decree results, the individual norms created constitute 'the law'.

Kelsen distinguishes the 'effectiveness' of a legal norm from its 'validity'. The term 'validity' implies that a legal norm should be *obeyed* and should be *applied* in given circumstances. 'Effectiveness' means that, in practice, the norm is actually obeyed and applied. In his revised version of the pure theory, Kelsen stated that a norm which is not obeyed by anyone anywhere, ie, which is not effective at least to some degree, cannot be regarded as a 'valid' norm. The implication is that although a legal norm requires authorisation by a higher norm, a further condition of its validity is 'a minimum of effectiveness'. Hence, within a community, universal and total obedience to the basic norm is not essential; there must be within the community, however, a *sufficiency of adherence* to that basic norm, allowing it to be effective in practice. The 'principle of legitimacy' is restricted by 'the principle of effectiveness'. 'The efficacy of the total legal order is a necessary condition for the validity of every single norm of the order'.

The pure theory stresses the concept of law as possessing no moral connotation whatsoever; a decisive criterion in law is derived from the 'element of force' underlying sanctions. The apparatus of the law, its courts and other legal institutions, possess the capacity to protect any type of political structure. (Law may be thought of as a highly-specific technique of social organisation.) Further, the law is all-embracing: in effect, there is no human behaviour which, as such, is excluded from being the content of a legal norm. From this, Kelsen suggests the identity of the State and the law. The State is a political organisation expressing a legal order; it is governed by law (a State not governed by law is, says Kelsen, 'unthinkable'). We may consider the State as *a totality of the norms within a hierarchy*; it is nothing other than 'the sum total of norms ordering compulsion' and is, therefore, co-extensive with the law. The State *is* the law, and the traditional dualism of 'law v State' can no longer be maintained.

The pure theory has been described as 'perhaps the most consistent expression of positivism in legal theory'. Its links with classical positivism and its exponents - Hume, Bentham and Austin - are clear. Rejection of natural law, concern for form and structure, a separating out from legal theory of the social and moral content of law, are obvious in Kelsen's analysis. The pure theory represents, according to Friedmann, 'a quest for pure knowledge in its most uncompromising form, for knowledge free from instinct, volition and desire'. Kelsen's task was to discover what he considered as the true essence of the law and, as a consequence, to reject all that which is clearly in flux or merely accidental. The result is a theory which carries the positivist analysis to an advanced stage and which treats the law, in Bodenheimer's phrase, 'as though it were contained in a hermetically-sealed container'. The pure theory attempts to see law as a systematic, unified concept; a legal order is presented in sparse terms as a *system* of normative relations whose unity stems from the *one reason* for the validity of norms - a *fundamental norm*. The contribution of the pure theory to an understanding of law rests in its enunciation of the relation between the fundamental norm and other, lower norms within the society; it does not pronounce on the 'desirability' of the fundamental norm, for that is a task for the political scientist, not for the jurist.

Notes

Kelsen's *The Pure Theory of Law* has been translated and edited by Ebenstein. *The General Theory of Law and State* appears in a translation by Wedberg. Lauterpacht has written on Kelsen's 'Pure Science of Law', which appears in *Modern Theories of Law*, edited by Jennings. There are useful summaries of the pure theory, and extracts, in Harris, ch 6, Lloyd ch 5, Dias, ch 17, Riddell, ch 10, Davies and Holdcroft, ch 5, and Friedmann, ch 24.

Question 23

'An exercise in logic and not in life'.

Does this statement exemplify the criticisms directed against the 'pure theory of law'?

Answer plan

The statement cited in the question was made by Laski, a prolific writer on politics and jurisprudence, in 1925. It typifies, to a considerable extent, the kind of criticism commonly levelled against Kelsen's 'pure theory'. The search for an 'unadulterated' version of law produced, it is alleged, a theory which is arid, unreal and, therefore, far-removed from the rich complexities of the law in practice. Other types of criticism should also be mentioned in the answer, eg, Kelsen's attitude to an examination of the place of justice in the law, his alleged confusion of duties and sanctions based on coercion, his analysis of international law in the light of the 'pure theory'. A skeleton plan could take the following form:

> Introduction - the essence of criticisms of Kelsen - results of his failure to examine law in its social setting - his attitude to a study of justice and rights - criticisms of the theory in relation to sanctions and obligations - problems of the Grundnorm - investigating law in terms of the pure theory - international law - Allen's criticism - conclusion, unacceptable narrowness of the theory's base.

Answer

The quotation comes from Laski's *Grammar of Politics* (1925), in which he suggests that, given its postulates, Kelsen's 'pure theory' of law is unanswerable, but that its substance is an exercise in logic, not in life. Many of the criticisms directed against the 'pure theory' do rest, indeed, on what is perceived as its aridity and separation from the realities of legal activity within the community. But there are other important criticisms, some of which are mentioned below, based on the implications of Kelsen's methodology of enquiry. The target of these criticisms is a theory which emerges from an attempt to view law *purely in terms of reason* and in a manner which excludes all ethical and political value-judgments. Law is seen as a coercive order, based on a system of norms, the validity of which is derived from a basic norm.

A major criticism, encapsulated in Laski's comment, is that the theory chooses to disregard the *totality* of a society in which law plays a relatively restricted, albeit important, role. To abstract from a consideration of the law its surrounding social and political factors is, it is argued, virtually impossible, even if it were desirable. Law does not exist as an isolate: it is affected in considerable measure by the dynamic nature of the community of which it is a part. A perusal of any aspect of our common law and current legislation indicates the difficulties inherent in any attempt at investigating the law as a phenomenon 'in itself'. Thus, the law relating to theft may have little 'meaning' save as an expression of communal ethical attitudes to the ownership and possession of property. The European Communities Act 1972 expressed political and economic ideologies. The Children Act 1989 articulates deep and complex concepts of the community's social responsibilities. Remove discussion of the inner significance of legislation of this nature, and one is left merely with 'form' as an object of study - it has been given unwarranted primacy over 'meaning'.

An allied criticism is based on Kelsen's decision to ignore the concept of 'justice' and on his apparent lack of concern for the nature and significance of human rights. Kelsen seems to view 'justice' as a mere expression of an irrational idea. Because it is not subject to scientific cognition or investigation, it is not to be considered as having any role in the foundations of law. For Kelsen it involves little more than 'the conscientious application of appropriate general rules'. Justice as a measure of the validity of laws is rejected. Hence a concept which, for many communities and jurists, is seen as expressing the *end* of law, is dismissed by Kelsen because it appears to be beyond the pale of cognition. But because legal life as we know and experience it is *consciously* based upon a desire to act in accordance with the tenets of justice, and because unjust behaviour is generally unacceptable, Kelsen's doctrine gives the impression of ignoring the complex and deeply-held feelings which characterise much legal activity. It is worth noting, too, that the history of this century gives little reason to view with equanimity the promulgation of a systematic interpretation of law from which the concept of justice has been banished.

The exclusion of 'justice' from the 'pure theory' has led some critics to question not only the resulting sterility of its findings, but the claim advanced by Kelsen to have 'explained' the *reality* of the law. It is suggested that, in dogmatic fashion, he has limited the data he wishes to explore to some positive legal matters while ignoring substantive, conceptual legal realities. The result is no more than a highly-selective and incomplete investigation. The 'reality' of the theory is flawed by a misconceived approach to so-called 'objective phenomena'.

The place of force ('coercion') in the 'pure theory' has evoked adverse comment. There is no explicit assertion in the theory that law is *only* force, but there is an inference that the effectiveness of law seems to be based solely on force or sanction. All law must possess 'an apparatus of compulsion', Kelsen argues, and the essence of law is in duty, not in right. One's legal duty is as the law commands, with coercion available for the enforcement of norms. But critics have suggested that this is a confusion of 'coercion' and 'obligation'. It is *because* a rule is considered by the community as obligatory that it is possible to attach to it some measure of coercion; the rule is not obligatory merely because there is coercion. The rules relating to individual physical inviolability are considered by most communities to be of an obligatory nature, and, therefore, penalties are attached to their breach; the rules embodied in the Offences against the Person Act 1861, are not considered as obligatory merely because of the sanctions contained therein. Further, Kelsen is said to have ignored the discussions on communal attitudes to obligation, punishments, etc, which form the content of important work in the social sciences. Kelsen's norms seem to be little more than formal, authoritarian commands enforced by those who happen to have a monopoly of force within the community. This has been criticised as a caricature of real life: laws are not obeyed merely because of threatened sanctions; some statutes impose duties without the threat of any sanction. Duties and sanctions require separate definitions because, in reality, they are not conterminous.

The concept of the Grundnorm (the 'basic norm'), which is central to the 'pure theory', is not without its critics. The basic norm ('presupposed in juristic thinking') is that which is said to give a unity to the legal system in that it tops the pyramid of norms and gives those norms their validity. This has been condemned as mere fiction, or as being little more than Austin's 'sovereign' in disguise, or as a mythical 'first cause' beyond which one ought not to venture in any investigation of law. A statement such as 'the first constitution must be obeyed' is criticised as self-contradictory. The reasons why the law *is* obeyed, argue the critics, are to be found in more than one so-called 'fundamental reason', and certainly not in any fictitious basic norm, the very existence of which rarely figures in the conscious responses of citizens to their legal obligations. Further, if one considers the activities of the community's judges, the Grundnorm will not explain the many 'non-rule standards' which jurists such as Dworkin perceive as entering into decisions of the courts. Judges probably take into account, during the process of adjudication, much more than formal rules: they keep in mind wide principles and communal policies - the very matters which Kelsen seeks to exclude from a formulation of the essence of law.

The very search for a Grundnorm within a legal system will be affected by the personal value-judgments of the investigator - so runs a common criticism of the methodology of Kelsen's supporters. Further, it is very difficult to investigate the validity of Kelsen's test of 'a minimum of support' for a basic norm without enquiring into surrounding political and social facts - an unacceptable state of affairs for advocates of the 'pure theory'. If, for example, it is assumed by these advocates that the basic norm of a community is 'belief in the divinity of the law-giver', or in his charismatic law-making, it would be almost impossible to discover the level of support for that belief without enquiring into ways in which the law-maker's subjects are affected in practice, and that would necessitate investigation of a variety of social matters of a 'non-legal' nature.

The problems raised by the existence of international law have been viewed by critics as constituting a basic objection to the 'pure theory'. In Kelsen's view, international law can be interpreted correctly as a 'juridical order' which may be understood within the boundaries of a 'normative science of law'. But it appears that international law lacks a number of characteristics of a 'legal order' in Kelsen's sense. It has no developed apparatus of compulsion and, apparently no Grundnorm. Kelsen's reply to this objection suggests an acceptance of war and reprisals as constituting the 'international sanction'. This, for many jurists, involves a negation of the spirit and essential purpose of the doctrine of international law. Further, it may be that a multiplicity of basic norms is required for the interpretation of the complex structure of the law of nations, but this would certainly offend the austere sense of parsimony which is characteristic of the 'pure theory'.

There are, then, many points in Kelsen's theory at which evidence emerges suggesting a lack of correspondence of its express and implied doctrines and legal life as we know it to be. The theory, it has been said, has no application to the everyday problems of the law; it solves none of the recurring difficulties which face legislators and judges. If the 'proper business' of a positivist jurist be with the actual operations of the law, then Kelsen might be considered as having contributed little to an understanding of those operations. Allen suggests that, in Kelsen's anxiety to keep perception of the law 'pure', he has raised it to such an inaccessible altitude that 'it has difficulty in drawing the breath of life'. Gény, writing before Kelsen, had warned against the 'palpable illusion' of attempting to erect a pure judicial science on the postulates of 'an inevitable and imperious logic', with the result that what is created is barren and without value. It is, perhaps, this criticism which Laski had in mind in his comment on Kelsen.

It is paradoxical that Kelsen, criticised for remoteness and a predilection for authoritarian jurisprudence, both of which are said to be evident in the 'pure theory', should have been, in fact, a jurist who was intensely concerned with the practicalities of the law. He had rejected authoritarianism by choosing exile from his native Austria which was under totalitarian rule, and he made a fundamental contribution to the legal foundations of the United Nations in his commentaries on the basis of UN proposals for international security. His concern was to give to legal science a methodology which would enable the law - no matter what its form or origins might be - to be understood. The resulting edifice seems to have been constructed, however, from postulates and perceptions which ignored the peculiar richness and complexities of developed legal systems; its basis is now seen by some jurists as being unacceptably narrow. It may be that any attempt to create a rarified 'pure theory' which involves separating law from custom, tradition, communal conceptions of justice and morality, will succeed only in erecting a system of jurisprudential thought which, no matter how logical its methodology may be, is, in the event, at variance with the life of the law.

Notes

Criticisms of Kelsen's doctrines appear in Dias, ch 17, Lloyd, ch 5, Allen, ch 1, and Davies and Holdcroft, ch 5. Snyder's article, 'Hans Kelsen's Pure Theory of Law' (1966) 12 Harvard LJ, is useful. Stone's 'Mystery and Mystique of the Basic Norm' (1963) 26 MLR 34 analyses the theory of the Grundnorm. Moore, *Legal Norms and Legal Science*, provides a detailed examination of Kelsen's doctrine.

Historical Jurisprudence

Introduction

In this chapter reference is made to the 'historical movement' in jurisprudence. The movement centres on the thesis that the study of existing structures of legal thought requires an understanding of its historical roots and its pattern of evolution. Current legal systems and jurisprudential concepts have developed over long periods of time; the common law jurisdictions, in particular, give evidence of a continuous process of evolution. It is in the records of the past that the keys to a comprehension of the present may be discovered. The questions in this chapter refer to Savigny (1799-1861) and Maine (1822-88). Savigny, a Prussian statesman and historian, sought for an understanding of law through an investigation of the ancient and enduring *Volksgeist* - the 'spirit of the people'. Maine, founder of the English school of historical jurisprudence, made an intensive study of ancient law which revealed to him the existence of evolutionary patterns of development. Both Savigny and Maine used the lessons of history to assist in the analysis of jurisprudential problems of their own times.

Checklist

Ensure that you are acquainted with the following topics:

- *Volksgeist*
- codification of law
- Maine's 'static and progressive' societies
- status-to-contract theory
- customary law
- legal fictions

Question 24

'A cry against the rationalistic and cosmopolitan principles of the French Revolution, and a reactionary call for the recognition of law as the product of "internal, silently-operating forces".'

Do you agree with this comment on the work of Savigny in his role as founder of the German 'historical school' of jurisprudence?

Answer plan

Savigny shared with many of his country's thinkers opposition to the French Revolution and its philosophical foundations. His reaction was to stress the significance of authority, tradition and the 'creative force' of a people's 'common consciousness'. Law emerged, he claimed, from a people's 'special genius'. An answer to the question should note the essence of Savigny's teaching on the theme of the *Volksgeist* and should seek to show the background of his thesis within the setting of anti-revolutionary doctrine. The following skeleton plan is suggested:

Introduction -context of French Revolution - Savigny's attitude to codification of law - law as product of the spirit of the people - significance of Roman legal doctrine - criticism of the *Volksgeist* theory - legislation according to Savigny - selectivity of his arguments - Savigny's hostility to revolutionary doctrine - his opposition to rationalism - conclusion, Allen's criticism in the light of the perversion of Savigny's theories.

Answer

An appraisal of the comment on Savigny requires the posing and answering of two questions. First, how deeply was Savigny influenced by his perceptions of the significance of the French Revolution? Second, in what sense may one characterise as 'reactionary' (ie, backward-looking and retrogressive) his belief that the essence of a system of law is a reflection of the *Volksgeist*, ie, the unsophisticated 'national spirit' of the group who evolved it?

Savigny, a Prussian statesman, jurist and authority on the history of Roman law, lived in an era dominated by the effects of the French Revolution which destroyed the French feudal order. The revolutionaries believed that society's 'general will' would be guided by reason, its 'legislative will' would be guided by the *Code Civil*. Savigny shared with many other European jurists deep hostility to revolutionary philosophy; liberty, equality, 'Supreme Reason', became anathema to him. Within Germany a deep reaction set in: tradition, authority and the 'creativity' of a people's folklore and customs were stressed. 'Kindred consciousness of inward necessity' was invoked as the source of strength of a nation's legal system. Cosmopolitanism was rejected in favour of 'creative national character'. There is little doubt as to the basic anti-revolutionary character of Savigny's deliberate espousal of the 'virtues of the past' and his vision of ancient custom as a condition precedent of acceptable legislation.

Savigny opposed codification of the law for Germany. The time was not ripe, Germany had 'no calling' for the construction of a code, and, in any event, a code would merely fetter the development of the law and 'do violence to tradition'. His opposition to codification at that time became generalised in the theory he evolved, which would explain national law as flowing from, and reflecting, the age-old 'spirit of the people' - *the Volksgeist*.

The origin of the law was to be found, according to Savigny, in a study of certain principles. First, all law is formed originally by custom and popular feeling, ie, by 'silently operating forces'. A people's common consciousness is 'externalised' in its customs. Law grows in organic, unconscious fashion. A people's laws embody 'popular genius'. Law resembles language; both evolve gradually from a people's characteristics; both flourish when a people flourishes, and both perish when a people loses its individuality. Laws have neither universal validity nor application: they apply only to a specific people. Law is not static; it develops according to the life of the people. Law emanates from no single law-giver, but from a people's instinctive awareness of right and wrong; legislation, therefore, lacks the vitality of custom as a source of law.

Savigny turned to the ancient Roman law to provide material for a study of the needs of the German people in relation to law. Critics see an inconsistency here: the *Volksgeist* theory should have concerned itself with ancient *Germanic* law, rather than Roman law. The same critics suggest that Savigny's insistence on the utilisation of Roman legal principles reflects a desire to embrace a far-off authoritarian code which was seen as possessing eternal validity.

Savigny did not describe his concept of *Volk* (ie, 'a people') but said that it resembled a 'spiritual communion' of people living together, using a common language and creating a communal conscience and common traditions. This has been condemned as a loose description, incapable of proof and of little use in jurisprudential analysis. His concept of 'communal conscience' is difficult to comprehend. Where is 'communal conscience' when a nation is divided on some legal questions? How does one apply a people's 'feeling for right and wrong' to, say, a multicultural community? What of the important areas of law which have evolved from inter-communal political and legal conflict?

For some critics, the *Volksgeist* is mere fiction or 'reification' of questionable abstractions. It is impossible to prove the axioms Savigny formulated concerning a people's 'folk soul' and its alleged creativeness. Savigny, it is suggested, may not have wished to create a reactionary legal ideology, but, in the event, he did create a framework of concepts which was utilised to support in a later era those who actively desired authoritarian regimes based on mystical ideologies involving 'the people's will'.

Savigny's view of legislation as being of subsidiary importance to custom is of significance. For him, the 'living law' does not result from a sovereign's command; rather does it develop organically from the 'people's spirit'. Hence legislation will be effective only when it is attuned to the voice and aspirations of the people and when it reflects national needs. Doubts within a community could be resolved by declaratory enactments. This view has been criticised. Vinogradoff shows that most customs arise from *local usage* and are rarely of national significance in their early stages. Legal history reveals, too, that formal legislation has often become necessary when custom has failed to respond to novel conditions.

Other critics of Savigny pay attention to the highly-selective historical data on which he draws. It seems that the conditions of his own era coloured his view of the past. In particular, his attitudes towards liberty and egalitarianism, conditioned by his reactions as a Prussian aristocrat to the events of the French Revolution, may have prevented the adoption of the disinterested attitude which should characterise a scholar's work. The fact that he turned to the ancient Roman law for guidance, rather than to the well-researched Roman jurisprudence of the Middle Ages, has been attributed to his personal predilection for the severe authoritarianism which seemed to him to typify Roman legal doctrine. The possibility that the *Corpus Juris* was no more than a reflection of the considered reactions of Roman lawyers and statesmen to everyday economic and social problems seems not to have entered into his commentaries on the 'eternal significance' of Roman legal doctrine.

Further evidence of undue selectivity emerges from Savigny's writings which suggest that the law grows *uniquely* 'within the *Volk*'. There was available to Savigny considerable historical research indicating that law does not always emerge from 'popular conscience, awareness of nationhood and common culture'. The ancient world, and Savigny's own times, had witnessed the transplanting of laws from one country to another. In his role of historian, Savigny should have been aware of the important part played in the development of a nation's law by the imposition of the will of alien conquerors. Consider, for example, the Norman conquest of England in 1066. Here the successful invaders were able to effect a transformation of the prevailing English legal order. A few centuries later, important developments of the land law were effected, but it cannot be said with accuracy that they emanated from 'the spirit of the English people'. The great statute, *Quia Emptores* 1290, which assisted in fixing the theory of estates, was in no sense a reflection of 'unconscious forces' moulding the shape of the legal order. *De Donis Conditionalibus* 1285, which had created the entailed estate, cannot be said to have emerged from the popular 'communal conscience'; rather was it a pragmatic reaction to problems arising from the descent of land. Savigny's *Volksgeist* is not to be discerned here.

Savigny seems to pay little attention to the law-making of judges. Those who, under the guise of unfolding and revealing the law effectively modify and extend it, are participating in the process of law-making as if they were legislators. 'Awareness of nationhood' is not easy to discern in activities of this nature. The *Volksgeist* is, clearly, not the unique source of law Savigny would have us believe.

We turn to the statement embodied in the question and to the two problems which require consideration. First, to what extent was Savigny influenced in his jurisprudential thought by the phenomenon of the French Revolution? There can be little doubt as to the answer. Few jurists are willing to stand aside from consideration of the march of events. We have seen this in our own times, as evidenced in the writings of Radbruch, Friedmann, Hart and others. Savigny seems to have provided no exception to this generalisation. For him, the French Revolution was a cataclysm, threatening the very existence of the political, social and legal fabric of Europe. Revolution does breed reaction, and in Savigny's case the reaction took the form of a total rejection of the philosophical and political concepts associated with the revolutionary scholars of France. The result was, for Savigny, a flight to the perceived 'comfortable certainties' of the ancient Roman law. The bastions of a remote system of legal thought would stand secure against the impact of revolutionary dogma. Out of the rock of the *Corpus Juris* would be fashioned a fortress within which German philosophical and legal doctrine would hold out against the alien principles of radical rationalism.

The second question, concerning the 'reactionary nature' of Savigny's thought is more complex. The anti-rational nature of *Volksgeist* theory is obvious: it elevates the role of the unconscious and the instinctive and seems to play down the role of reason in the growth and development of the law. Critics have suggested that Savigny generated a 'juristic pessimism' and effectively denigrated the efforts of mankind devoted to conquering its surroundings. The perception of ancient Roman law as a repository of the panaceas which would cure the ills of the nineteenth century engenders an exaggerated reverence for a fictitious 'golden era' in the past and, in reactionary fashion, diverts attention from the necessary analysis of events. There is indeed evidence of the reactionary nature of much of Savigny's juristic thought: it looks backwards, it invokes principles which are rarely amenable to rational interpretation, and it seeks solace in a fabricated mystique.

It would be wrong, however, to follow those critics who condemn Savigny as an unwholesome reactionary, addicted to the type of legal practices which have flourished in the totalitarian regimes of our century. Allen's suggestion that Savigny and his associates were 'National Socialists before the National Socialists', is, surely, unwarranted hyperbole. The fact that later generations of German politicians and jurists drew on Savigny's theories, and distorted them in order to provide justification for a racist tyranny, and that, in Friedmann's words, the sharp edge of State power was turned brutally against those who were perceived as aliens, polluting the party of the *Volk*, does not, in itself, justify total condemnation of Savigny as one who would have supported totalitarian excesses. It is highly probable that Savigny would have recognised the perversion of his doctrines under the Nazi regime. It is almost certain that he could not have foreseen, and would not have approved, the uses to which the theory of the *Volksgeist* was put during the era of dictatorships.

Notes

Extracts from Savigny's *System of Modern Roman Law*, translated by Holloway, are given in Lloyd, ch 10. Friedmann, ch 18, Vinogradoff, ch 6, Bodenheimer, ch 5, and Allen, chs 1 and 2, provide criticisms of the *Volksgeist* theory. 'Sovereignty and the Historical School of Law' by Kantorowicz [1937] 53 LQR 334, is a useful survey of Savigny's contribution to jurisprudence.

Question 25

What do you consider to be Maine's singular contributions to jurisprudence?

Answer plan

Maine brought to the task of interpreting the history of law a very wide knowledge of early societies, from which he constructed a theory of legal development which reflected the vision of inevitable progress prevalent in his day. The history of law is seen as portraying an upward movement made up from consecutive stages of development. Maine's contribution to jurisprudence rests, according to jurists such as Pospisil, in his systematic method of investigation. Others stress the acuity of his insight into ancient societies and their law. Two aspects of Maine's work are selected for discussion below: first, his view of legal ideas and institutions as possessing their own course of development, and, second, the concept of individual progress as resting on a move from fixed relationships based on individual status to relationships reflecting the free agreement of individuals. The following skeleton plan has been used:

Introduction -Maine's significant contributions to jurisprudence - the three epochs constituting legal development - the importance of fictions, equity and legislation - from status to contract - criticisms of Maine - conclusion, the overall importance of Maine's work.

Answer

Jurist, historian and pioneer in the study of anthropology as applied to the evolution of legal ideas and institutions, Maine made a considerable contribution to the study of jurisprudence in the second half of the nineteenth century. Writing with unusual knowledge of the classical Roman tradition, primitive law, Biblical and Indian legal ideas, he was able to produce a systematic account of the evolution of law. His principal work was *Ancient Law: Its Connection with the Earlier History of Society and Its Relation to Modern Ideas* (1861), in which he ranged widely over early law and embryonic legal systems. For Maine, history was no record of humanity's 'essential reasonableness'; rather did it reveal the pervasive influence of emotions, deep instinctive reactions and habits. We select from his work two unique concepts: first, the view that legal history may be read as revealing an *evolutionary pattern* which affects in different measure 'static' and 'progressive' societies, and, second, the idea that within progressive societies can be traced a movement in individual relationships marked by a change *'from status to contract'*.

The development of law involves three stages. The first stage emerges solely from the personal commands and judgments of *patriarchal rulers* - kings, for example - who propagate the notion that they are divinely inspired. Judgments precede rules; the judge exists before the law-maker. Maine uses the Homeric term *Themistes* to describe the kings' judgments which are, essentially, separate, and are not connected by principles.

The epoch of kingly rule ends when royal power decays as a result of a weakening of belief in royal charisma and sacredness. Royal authority vanishes to a shadow and the *era of oligarchies* emerges. Elites of a political, military and religious nature appear, claiming a monopoly of control over the law and its institutions. The law in this era is based generally on customs upheld by judgments. In this second development period, which Maine refers to as 'the epoch of customary law', the ruling oligarchies claim to enjoy exclusive possession of the principles used in the settling of disputes. At this stage law is largely unwritten; the interpreters of the law enjoy, therefore, monopolistic powers of explanation. This epoch does not endure; in particular, the spread of writing prepares the ground for a transition to a third era.

The third, sharply-defined, epoch is dominated by *Codes*: this is, indeed, the 'era of the Codes' which, according to Maine, all arose at similar points in the progress of Greece, Rome and parts of Western Asia. The Codes, such as the Roman Twelve Tables, promulgated in the fifth century BC, and Solon's Attic Code, which remained the basis of Athenian law until the end of that century, were, in some cases a mere statement of existing customs and, in other cases, sets of rules which declared the law as it ought to be. Maine saw the principal advantage of codes in the protection they claimed to offer against the results of debasement of national institutions. But the codes marked an end to spontaneity in legal development; henceforth the law would be characterised by *purpose*. Changes in the law would be effected deliberately, often out of a conscious desire for improvements.

Having constructed a framework for systematising the interpretation of legal development, Maine introduced a remarkable concept of further progress being conditional on the very *nature* of a given society. He drew a distinction between 'stationary' and 'progressive' societies. The stationary societies (which were the rule) did not progress beyond the concept of law based on, and dominated by, a code. The progressive societies (which were the exception, and included most societies in Western Europe) tended to expand and refine the law and legal institutions. Maine believed that the stationary nature of most societies reflected a lack of desire on the part of their members to improve their legal institutions beyond the stage at which the law had been embodied in the permanence of a code. The result was an inflexible law which acted as a brake on legal development. By contrast, the progressive societies exhibited a dynamism which allowed them to engage in modification of the law, so that the gap between formal legal doctrines and the pressing needs of a developing society was narrowed.

The dynamic stage of legal development, confined to progressive societies, was characterised by the use of three agencies, *legal fictions, equity and legislation* (in that historical order). The term 'legal fiction' is used to refer to suppositions or assumptions of law that something which is, or may be, false is true, or that some fact exists when, in reality, it does not. Fictions are designed to assist in overcoming the rigidities of the law and to advance the ends of justice. Their use affects to conceal the fact that a legal rule has been altered or its operation modified, although the letter of the law remains unchanged. Maine gives as an example the Roman fiction of adoption which allowed vital family ties to be created in an artificial manner.

The second mode of adapting the law to the requirements of a progressive society is the development of equity - a corpus of rules co-existing with the original law, founded on distinct principles and claiming an inherent 'sanctity' allowing it to supersede the original law. Equity involves open interference with original law, which separates it from legal fictions. It differs from legislation in that its principles are often expressed in terms of a 'higher authoritativeness'. Equity assists in the advance of society in that it softens the rigours of the law and is concerned with the spirit of the law rather than its letter. It suggests, too, according to Maine, a more advanced state of thought than that which created the legal fiction.

Legislation is the final 'ameliorating instrumentality' of the progressive societies in their process of legal development. It involves the enactments of a legislature (a parliamentary assembly, for example) which is, according to Maine, 'the assumed organ of the entire society'. It is important to note that, for Maine, civilisation presupposed legislation carried out by *formal bodies*; he was not favourably disposed towards 'judicial legislation' and thought that judge-made law had serious weaknesses. Here, then, is the ultimate stage in legal development within the progressive societies. The order of stages in legal development is not invariable, according to Maine, but he stressed that legislation, in its final and highest form of 'codification', marked a pinnacle of achievement.

Ancient Law includes a chapter entitled 'Law in Primitive Society', in which Maine produces a 'formula', which is considered here as the second of his singular contributions to jurisprudence. 'The movement of progressive societies', he declares, 'has hitherto been a movement from status to contract.' Maine used the term 'status' to signify those personal conditions of an individual which are not the immediate or remote result of agreement. It is in this sense that Maine speaks of 'the status of a slave', or 'the status of the Roman female under tutelage'. He sees, in the history of some ancient societies, status as the fixed result of dominant family relationships. The Roman *pater familias* exercising *patria potestas*, wife, sons and daughters in a subordinate status, slaves serving the family but enjoying the lowest type of status - here are examples of 'family-determined status'. In time, the dynamism of the progressive society loosened the chains of familial status; Roman women were emancipated from tutelage, the *filius familias* was freed from his father's power, and even the slave might change his status through the process of manumission. Relationships began to emerge from the free agreement of individuals. Slavery eventually disappears, serfdom is abolished, the free links, based on agreement between master and servant, burgeon into the employer-employee contract. In sum, one of the hallmarks of a progressive society is, according to Maine, an inexorable move by its people from legal relationships determined by a seemingly-fixed status to the creation of conditions through free negotiations.

Maine's jurisprudential concepts have attracted criticism. It is suggested that he may have oversimplified the early stages of society's development. The move from 'charismatic judgment' through 'autocratic interpretation' to 'code' is doubted by a number of anthropologists. Childe, for example, suggests that divisions based on the relative importance of hunting, agriculture and pastoralism may provide an important key to the understanding of legal development. Childe doubts the basis of Maine's interpretation, which he finds 'simplistic'. Further, recent investigation suggests that not all primitive peoples pass through the stages suggested by Maine: some may 'jump' a stage. It may be that there is no *universal* pattern of legal development as he pictured in *Ancient Law* and that the evolutionary movement described in its pages may be true for Europe and some parts of India, but not for *all* societies. Additionally, Maine appears to imply a rigidity of thought among primitive peoples which has been challenged by some contemporary anthropologists who note the adaptive skills of the early societies.

Further criticism has centred on Maine's methodology of enquiry, dismissed by some jurists as totally inadequate for the tasks he set for himself. He is held to have extrapolated beyond his data, ie, to have assumed for societies in general the existence of patterns which characterised *unique groups* at specific stages in their development. The evidence for some of his generalisations has been held to be inadequate; it is noted, for example, that some of his illustrations derive from the evidence of epic poetry only. Allen suggests that the broad principle formulated by Maine 'needs larger corroboration than this'.

The 'status-to-contract- theory' has also attracted critical comment. Friedmann observes that the development of feudalism seems to indicate a move from contract to status. He notes, too, that there are modern tendencies to replace individual bargaining by collective group agreements, and he points out the significance of the appearance of standardised contracts which result in the imposition of status-like conditions in the case of mortgages, lessor-lessee agreements and some insurance contracts. It has to be observed, however, that Maine spoke of the movement of progressive societies 'hitherto'.

Criticism of Maine should not be allowed to dim the overall significance of his work. He was writing in the era of pre-scientific anthropology - at a time when, for example, the very existence of the Palaeolithic Age was unknown. Frazer and Malinowski, who changed the direction of anthropological studies, were yet to come. It is, however, the *general pattern* of Maine's studies which constitutes his legacy for jurisprudence: his long-range vision of the law as resulting from a continuous process of development, his view of law as an important aspect of general social evolution, his stress on the significance of the written word in the history of legal change, continue to play a role in the work of jurists who emphasise that the law does possess *a history of its own*.

Notes

Ancient Law, by Maine, appears in a number of editions. Comments on Maine's doctrines appear in Lloyd, ch 10, Dias, ch 18, and Friedmann, ch 18. Maine is criticised by Diamond in *Primitive Law*. There are interesting biographical details of Maine in *From Status to Contract: a Biography of Sir Henry Maine*, by Feaver, and *Sir Henry Maine: A Study in Victorian Jurisprudence*, by Cocks.

The Anthropological and Sociological Movements in Jurisprudence

Introduction

Anthropology may be described in general terms as 'the study of mankind'; more specifically it is concerned with the behaviour, beliefs, culture, customs and other diversities of humanity. *Sociology* studies the causes and effects of the participation of individuals in groups and structured organisations. Both disciplines have attracted the attention of jurists who see law as a reflection of human beliefs and behaviour and as a product of certain types of social organisation. Hence there has grown a body of jurists who have turned increasingly to a study of the data produced by anthropologists and sociologists. In this chapter the single question on anthropology is intended to elicit an answer concerning its general significance for jurisprudence. Five prominent sociologists and jurists are singled out for attention: Jhering (1818-92), Ehrlich (1862-1922), Weber (1864-1920), Durkheim (1858-1917) and Pound (1870-1964). The outlines of their contribution to the sociological movement in jurisprudence should be known.

Checklist

Ensure that you are acquainted with the following topics:

- functional school of anthropology
- law as purpose
- norms for decision and conduct
- traditional and charismatic authority
- legal-rational authority
- mechanical solidarity
- organic solidarity
- the theory of interests
- jural postulates
- law as social engineering

Question 26

Has anthropology any significant contribution to make to jurisprudence?

Answer plan

The anthropological movement in jurisprudence sees law as an important aspect of a society's integrated characteristics. Basic beliefs, patterns of culture, traditions concerning the place of the individual in relation to his fellows and superiors, and rules concerning obligations are among the data collected and studied by modern anthropologists. Much of this material has been used to clarify some problems in jurisprudence concerned with the *origins of law*. Attention should be drawn to the work of Hoebel (b 1906) and Malinowski (1884-1942), who produced studies of direct relevance to the interpretation of law in terms of 'institutionalised relationships'. The following skeleton plan is suggested:

Introduction -essence of anthropology - problems of methodology - functional anthropology - Malinowski's work - significance of some recent studies - Hoebel's work - value of anthropology for jurisprudence - conclusion, anthropology has corrected a number of misconceptions prevalent in jurisprudence.

Answer

It would be surprising if an area of studies described in literal terms as 'the study of man' were unable to offer anything of significance to jurisprudence, which is concerned essentially with man and his laws. The anthropologist who seeks to understand man by studying, for example, social attitudes to human behaviour, to the establishing of norms of conduct, and to those who ignore those norms, will, of necessity, follow paths of investigation which ought to lead to the discovery of data which will throw light on the development of legal ideas and structures. Thus, when Hoebel, in a study of primitive culture, is led to an analysis of what is understood by 'a legal norm', it becomes difficult to argue that the work of the anthropologist can be of *no* relevance to jurisprudence. It can be argued that a study of those areas of anthropology concerned with a society's 'integrated total behaviour characteristics' (ie, its culture) can probably enrich jurisprudence by broadening its perspective.

Cultural anthropology is based today on field work, in contrast to the studies associated with, say, Maine and Durkheim.

The work is carried out, where possible, among existing so-called 'primitive societies', largely characterised by their non-industrialised basis and their lack of written communication. An objective of this type of study, which is of much interest to jurists, is the discovery and analysis of the patterns of 'institutionalised relationships', ie, the regulatory mechanisms by which a group seeks to formalise and control attitudes and activities among individuals. Two important problems, not unknown to the historical movement in jurisprudence, have arisen in recent anthropological studies of this nature. The first concerns the difficulty, if not impossibility, of translating the terms used by a primitive people into the investigator's language, so that he may be wrong in translating as 'unlawful homicide' the description of the activities of one who kills a member of his tribe in apparent defiance of a tribal rule. A second problem emerges from an attitude labelled by the anthropologist, 'ethnocentricity' - the inclination to interpret and evaluate other cultures by reference to one's own, resulting in absurdities such as attempting to interpret a primitive culture by considering the presence or absence of features of the common law in its methods of punishing wrongdoers. Errors of this nature are not unknown in some contemporary evaluations of legal systems by comparative jurists and others

The principles of study utilised by the 'functional school' of anthropology may be considered as of direct relevance to jurists who are concerned with what the law does *in practice*. One of the founders of this school, Malinowski, in his study of crime and custom in an undeveloped Melanesian society, suggested that if one wished to explain the actions of the Melanesians in dealing with unacceptable deviations from norms, one had to *define* those actions *at the time they were carried out*. A culture and its legal components make up a unique reality, so that comparisons often make little sense. Malinowski's celebrated dictum, 'There are no survivals', suggests that everything that is current has *some sort of function* - custom, as such, is of little significance. The relevance of this type of study for comparative law and historical jurisprudence will be obvious. The techniques of macrocomparison and microcomparison, which are utilised by jurists attempting to discern similarities within legal systems, owe much to the weighting of data suggested by Malinowski.

The significance for jurisprudence of recent anthropological discoveries will emerge from even a cursory glance at some relatively recent field work. Moore, for example, has studied developments in 'legal structures' affecting the life of the Chagga tribe of Mount Kilimanjaro. The effect on their activities of governmental abolition of private freehold ownership has been analysed. Changes effected by legislation in 'lineage-neighbourhood complexes' have been investigated. The spontaneity of everyday rules employed by the Chagga has been contrasted with the formalism of court-made regulations. In similar fashion, Fortes has analysed the concept of debt among the Tallensi of Ghana. The significance of 'group raiding' as an aspect of self-help against debtors and of 'counter-borrowing' has been explored so as to provide material for a general consideration of some complex legal relationships. There is, in studies of this type, much data of importance for the jurist who wishes to analyse the very basis of early concepts of debt.

In a remarkable study of the Lozi, who live in Zambia, Gluckman has analysed the functions of their legal processes, revealing the existence of 'hierarchies of principles'. High in that hierarchy are very wide, general rules; lower come specific, precise rules. The hierarchy of rules allows for the working of the legal process in a large variety of circumstances. Gluckman suggests that the Lozi appear to have their own concept of 'the upright man', whose behaviour is used as a norm by which the behaviour of parties to a dispute might be assessed. Bohannan studied the Tiv people in Nigeria and concluded that they had 'laws', but no 'law'. He made the important point that an analysis of the legal system of a primitive group might involve a study, not only of practices and institutions, but also of indigenous terminology. Findings of this nature are certainly of relevance to jurists who are interested in early forms of law from which *our* present practices have grown.

One of the most important of recent anthropological studies of the law of primitive man has been made by Hoebel, in conjunction with the American jurist, Llewellyn. Law among the Cheyenne tribe (a North American Plains Indian people) was studied by questioning elderly Cheyenne persons who were able to recall ways in which violators of tribal rules were treated.

Hoebel believed that the place of law within a total social structure can be analysed correctly only by an investigation of society at large. All tribal groups, he suggested, possess some kind of legal system: the concept of 'lawless tribal society' was pure myth. Law seemed to Hoebel, as the result of his investigations, to possess three essential elements: *regularity* (relating to continuously-applied standards of behaviour); *official authority* (involving an enforceable imperative relating to behaviour); and *sanction* (involving general social acceptance of its legitimacy of application). Hoebel saw no 'straight-line development' of the law; it seemed no more than a mere part of a much larger system of social control, and its inevitable changes mirror society's varying attitudes towards *problems of control*. A shift of the right to impose measures of control from wronged individuals to officials representing the wide social group, is a sign of increasing maturity of society. There is much to be learned from the primitive group, argued Hoebel, if we wish to study the fundamentals of our own attitudes to wrongs and penal sanctions.

Hoebel generalises from his anthropological studies the existence of four functions of law within society's cultural pattern. First, laws are concerned with the determination and promulgation of rules of acceptable relationships among members of a defined group; this involves general acceptance by the group of the necessity to prohibit certain types of misbehaviour. Secondly, laws are related to the process of allocating authority in relation to activities necessitated by the ignoring of norms and the punishment of those who choose to defy those norms. Thirdly, laws are needed for the resolution of disputes in order that social cohesion might be maintained. Fourthly, the law must reflect and adapt to change; the continuous examination of social problems and social relationships is essential if laws are to be appropriate and relevant. From Hoebel's field studies and his analysis of collected data has emerged a perspective of law which is of immediate relevance for jurisprudence.

The overall value of anthropology for jurisprudential studies has, however, been doubted. It is suggested that the anthropologist seeks for universalities where none can exist, that he presupposes basic cultural traits in spite of evidence suggesting their non-existence, and that he employs a methodology of enquiry which is suspect. Some interpretations of law within primitive society have been criticised as resting on a misunderstanding of the *totality* of those societies and a failure to note the very restricted role played by the so-called 'legal institutions'. Further, the immediate relevance to an understanding of the developed world's legal systems of data derived from a study of primitive social groups is not always clear - another criticism of those jurists who have used the findings of anthropology in indiscriminate fashion. Law, it is suggested, requires for its understanding, in a basic sense, data of a very different nature to those produced by the anthropologists.

The case for the significance and relevance of anthropology in the study of jurisprudence rests, it has been said, on its inherent capacity for a broadening of perspectives. Anthropology has added, it is argued, a new dimension to the study of law. The anthropologists have shown that a study of the basis of law ought not to be confined to a mere survey and interpretation of existing legal forms and institutions. Society is a vast system, *with a number of sub-systems* including that constituted by legal institutions. Those institutions and the underlying patterns of thought do not exist in isolation from other sub-systems. Anthropology has taught some jurists the significance of viewing legal phenomena as part of a systematic whole.

Modern anthropology has drawn attention to the importance of the historical development of law. At any given time the law can be considered, in large part, as the product of historical forces and it requires interpretation as an embodiment of changing patterns of thought. By drawing attention to primitive societies which mirror, even in a distorted fashion, changing cultural patterns, the anthropologist is able to ensure that the significance of a culture in flux is not overlooked. Thus, anthropologists have corrected a number of myths concerning societies in the process of change. Some of Maine's assertions concerning the movement of society, as evidenced by his interpretation of the transition 'from king to code', have been disproved by anthropological research. The 'primitive communist societies', which appear in various Marxist interpretations of legal history, have been exposed as myth.

In attempting to analyse society in terms of its socio-cultural phenomena, anthropologists have succeeded in drawing the attention of jurists to the interrelationships of various elements - legal, ethical, political - within a culture. However separable in practice these elements may be, the anthropologist insists that they be considered as constituent elements of an effectively-functioning whole. Law, they maintain, cannot be studied merely 'in itself'; it has to be analysed as part of a wider system. This, claim the anthropologists, is as true of a study of the rules of the Chagga people as it is for an investigation of the workings of the Queen's Bench Division or the International Court of Justice.

Notes

Lloyd, ch 10, contains a variety of extracts from the writings of jurists associated with the 'anthropological school'. Studies of law, based on anthropological data, include Malinowski's *Crime and Custom in Savage and Society*, Moore's *Law as Process*, Pospisil's *Anthropology of Law*, Bohannan's *Justice and Judgment among the Tiv*, Gluckman's *Judicial Process among the Barotse* and Fortes' *The Web of Kinship among the Tallensi*. *The Cheyenne Way* by Hoebel and Llewellyn is of unusual interest for those who wish to study the significance of field work in anthropological jurisprudence.

Question 27

'Law is the sum of the conditions of social life, in the widest sense of that term, as secured by the power of the State through the means of external compulsion.'

Show how Jhering's jurisprudential thought led him to this definition.

Answer plan

The nineteenth-century German jurist, Jhering, viewed the essence of law in the relationship of man to the society in which he lived. Neither man nor his law could be understood save within the context of society. There was a profound purpose to society - the enabling of man to add to the very quality of his existence. This study of society - sociology - would throw light on the central problem of jurisprudence: 'What is the law?' An answer to the question involves an account of Jhering's views on 'purpose' and law in relation to 'social reality'. The following skeleton plan is suggested:

Introduction -Jhering's views on law and the balancing of interests - law and purpose - individual and common interests - the levers of social motion - law and change - the State and coercion - conclusion, Jhering's definition of law considered.

Answer

Jhering achieved his reputation largely on the basis of his research into Roman law which culminated in the publication of *The Spirit of Roman Law* (1852). His later influential treatise, *Law as a Means to an End* (1877), was described by Friedmann as one of the most important events in the history of legal thought. In it, Jhering develops his theme of law as expressing 'purpose', and analyses the role of law in the protection and balancing of individual and social interests. It is from these concepts that Jhering derives the definition of law which is cited in the quotation above.

Jhering's early work in Roman law moved him towards an interpretation of law in terms of *purpose*. He analysed the Roman concept of 'possession' in very great detail and was able to construct a theory which explained the praetorian interdicts related to possession. Jhering emphasised the form of the interdicts in relation to their *purpose*. The praetors had in mind the *need* to protect those in control of property; hence interdicted possession could be described as a 'reflection of purpose'. His studies of Roman law led him into total opposition to what he described as 'the jurisprudence of concepts'. The true significance of Roman law resided not in its logical refinement of concepts, but rather in its capacity (as illustrated by the case of interdicted possession) to provide a *basis* on which concepts might be moulded *so as to serve practical purposes*. Life, he said, did not exist for the sake of concepts; to sacrifice the true interest of life to dialectic, and to turn jurisprudence into a sort of 'legal mathematics', was to act on mere illusion. The 'jurisprudence of concepts' was basically a misdirection of logical principle; it resulted in plausible abstractions which, in terms of the reality of life, were irrelevant.

Purpose, social reality and a jurisprudence which would reflect those principles emerged as the foundations of Jhering's approach to the law. *Purpose was all-important.* In his preface to *Law as a Means to an End* he states that the fundamental idea of the text is to demonstrate that 'purpose is the creator of the entire law'. There is no legal rule which does not have its origin in some practical purpose, that is, in some practical motive. This he had demonstrated in his study of Roman law-making. The creating of legal rules resulted from an exercise of human will, and such an exercise was to be understood only in terms of a purpose. Human activity is undertaken in order that objectives might be attained. *Volition involves and reflects purpose.*

Enunciation of the principle of 'purpose' in relation to the law marked, for Jhering, a turning away from the doctrines of the German 'historical jurisprudence' movement to which he had been attached. Law could not be understood in terms of the product of 'silently-operating forces of the people's spirit'; it did not well up from the springs of the nation's 'unconscious folk-soul'. On the contrary, it was to be interpreted as a *direct social response to perceived purpose.* Law emerged in order that problems might be solved and social needs met. It was purposive and existed for ends determined by society. *Outside society's problems and needs, law had no meaning, no rationale.*

Jhering asked what dictated the very purposes to be effected by law. His answer was: *interests dictate purpose.* A person's individual interests should be linked to the interests of others so that a social purpose might be enunciated and achieved. The linking of interests, the fusing of many sets of individual interests into a unity which reflected common, social purpose ('to effectuate every force in the service of humanity'), is one of the most important functions of the law. The demands of the individual are to be viewed within the context of society *as a whole,* and the social framework, in which law plays a prominent role, exists so as to ease the pursuit and attainment of social purpose.

For Jhering, the common interest of all was more important than particular individual interests. *'Every person exists for the world, and the world exists for everybody.'* Jhering refers to this aphorism as embodying the essence of culture and morality. It is the disproportion between man's needs and his purposes which necessitates his associating with others, so as to attain all those purposes to which he is, on his own, unequal. Nature 'refers' man to the outside world, to his fellows, from whom he may derive the assistance he requires. Common interest, which will emerge only from the very nature of social life, will require protection and it is the prime purpose of 'the protection of society' which must dominate the law, its ideology and institutions. Purpose, not abstract 'concepts', characterises the law within society.

Because of the superiority of the common interest, it is necessary that the conditions in which it will thrive shall be developed. The active encouragement of all those aspects of life which will intensify social cohesion is of great importance. This necessitates, on the part of the State, a recognition of the need to minimise the conflicts which may arise from the opposition of some individual and social interests. The reconciliation of those interests, in which the law will play a significant part, requires the utilisation of what Jhering refers to as 'the levers of social motion'. Those 'levers' are of two types: 'egoistic' and 'altruistic'. The 'egoistic levers' are reward and coercion. Reward is seen in terms of private gain. The threat of coercion is a vital element in law; Jhering sees the effectiveness of legal rules within society as depending on compulsion and force. Without this element, rules of law will be 'like a fire which does not burn'. The 'altruistic levers', eg, feelings of duty, are of particular significance in the creation of social interest. Jhering suggests that the levers be utilised in a combination which will create and intensify the significance of 'social ends'. *The object of society - the very purpose for which it is brought into existence - is the securing of the satisfaction of the totality of human wants.* In that process, which involves coercion and the reconciliation of apparently-contradictory interests, the law will be of much importance.

Jhering categorises society's wants (the satisfaction of which is the purpose of the social structure) in an unusual fashion. These wants are termed 'extra-legal', 'mixed-legal', and 'purely legal'.

The category of 'extra-legal wants' involves nature as the sole supplier. Food is an example: it is a basic requirement offered to man, but with the requirement of an effort from him. The 'mixed-legal' category refers to the conditions of social life, preservation of life, labour, trade, which are peculiar to humanity and which are generally independent of legal coercion. The third category, 'purely legal', refers to conditions *depending in their entirety upon legal commands*, eg, orders of the legal authorities requiring the payment of taxes and the settling of debts. Rewards, coercion, duty (the 'levers'), have to be used by the State in providing the setting within which human wants may be satisfied. The satisfying of these wants necessitates a system determined by 'social purpose'. In brief, Jhering is viewing the law, with its appropriate apparatus of coercion, as assisting in the attainment of those ends which characterise social activity and purpose.

The 'balancing' of individual and social interests so as to realise an appropriate equilibrium, which Jhering refers to as 'a realised partnership of the individual and society', is a necessary objective for society. It is the function of the law to act as a *mediator* in disputes which will stem from the opposition of interests. The mediating function of the law - its contribution to the creation of social harmony - has to be exercised, however, within the context of *changing social purposes and standards*. Hence, argues Jhering, the 'natural law', with its immutable, eternal standards, is of no use in this task. A law based on permanent and 'universally-valid' principle and content is, he says, no better than medical treatment which is administered in the same way for all patients. *Purpose is all*, and purpose is relative; the law must have the capacity to adapt to changing circumstances and to varying levels of individual and social needs.

Jhering's definition of law, to which we now turn, requires consideration in the light of his view of man, society and the law. Bodenheimer suggests that the definition comprises '*a substantive and a formal element*'. The essential features of the *substantive element* may be recapitulated. Law is to be perceived solely in terms of aims and purpose; to view it in the context of mere 'concepts' is to deny its true basis. The substantive aim of the law is 'social' and related entirely to the securing of the conditions of the life of society. Jhering interprets the phrase 'conditions of the life of society' as embracing much more than mere physical existence and self-preservation of its members; it includes all the goods and pleasures which give life its true value. Among these goods and pleasures are to be found honour, art and science, which give a savour to the individual's life. When Jhering speaks of the conditions of life 'in the widest sense of that term', he has in mind the quality of a society and the character of its individual members.

The values which underpin the social conditions of existence must be assured by the State's coercive powers - the 'means of external compulsion' mentioned in Jhering's definition. The means utilised by the State to achieve its purposes will vary according to social needs of a given period and according to the level of civilisation reached by the society in question. These means cannot be established by reference to so-called 'immutable principles'. Hence, says Bodenheimer, the *formal element* of Jhering's definition involves the principle of 'power of constraint', ie, the coercion which will be applied by the State when it perceives social cohesion and standards to be in peril. Coercion, constraint will be employed to attain the State's overriding purposes. The law is to be comprehended only within an appreciation of this context.

In the final analysis, Jhering views law as a *social, purposive phenomenon enabling man to add to the quality of his being*. Individually, his powers of achievement are severely limited by his restricted capacities. In collaboration with his fellows he becomes a member of society - a unit possessing powers allowing him to achieve more for himself and enabling him to contribute to the welfare of the community in general. The law's purpose is to provide assistance in the creation and maintenance of the circumstances in which he adds to his capacities for self-realisation. A study of law within society is a study of rules and their purposes. The 'jurisprudence of concepts' is rejected in favour of legal study based upon an awareness of the *social nature* of law and its institutions.

Notes

Jhering's *Law as a Means to an End* appears in a translation by Hussik. Summaries of his theory are contained in Lloyd, ch 7, Bodenheimer, ch 6, Dias, ch 20, and Friedmann, ch 26 (which includes a criticism of Jhering's view of law as 'the protection of interests').

Question 28

'At the present as well as at any other time, the centre of gravity of legal development lies not in legislation, nor in juristic science, nor in judicial decision, but in society itself': Ehrlich. How did Ehrlich view law in the light of this thesis?

Answer plan

Ehrlich, an Austrian legal scholar, produced a sociology of law which suggested the existence of two complementary sources of law within society, the formal law and the 'living law', as evidenced by current social custom. If jurists wished to understand the real basis of the law they would have to investigate the many activities of society. Studies of fact, enquiries into social structures and conditions, would be found to be of as much significance as analytical jurisprudence in discovering the foundations of the law. An outline of Ehrlich's view of law requires a discussion of 'norms of conduct' and 'norms for decision' and an examination of the differences between the formal law and the so-called 'living law'. The following skeleton plan is suggested:

> Introduction -law as a function of society - norms for decision and norms for conduct - the law in its formal sense - the 'living law' - examples of the 'living law' - discovering the 'living law' - significance of extra-legal data in investigations of the foundations of law - Allen's criticism of 'megalomaniac jurisprudence' - conclusion, Ehrlich's 'centre of gravity' and the need for studying social conditions.

Answer

Ehrlich's area of interest was in the impact of law on society as a whole, and the interaction of social and legal institutions. In his *Fundamental Principles of the Sociology of Law* (1912) he emphasised the importance of the 'living law' which dominates life itself even though it has not been transferred in its entirety to the propositions of the formally-promulgated law. To study the real nature of law is to recognise and analyse those *unformulated rules of conduct* accepted within a society; these 'vital rules' are often of greater significance than the 'lifeless provisions of codes'. Law can be comprehended only as a function of society. Within a society are two complementary sources of law: *first*, legal history, jurisprudence (ie, useful precedents and written commentaries) and formal rules; *secondly*, the 'living law', derived from current customs within society and, in particular, from the 'norm-creating activities' of the many groupings of members of that society.

Two types of norm emerge from Ehrlich's view of the functions of law within a society. 'Norms for decision' are the legal norms enunciated in statutes, codes or common law doctrines. They are intended primarily for the adjudication of disputes and they act also as 'rules of conduct' for those whose professional activities involve the settling of legal disputes. Thus, the Sale of Goods Act 1979, Part III, provides 'rules' enabling the courts to arrive at decisions relating to the transfer of property as between buyer and seller. The Children Act 1989, Part IX, sets out precise rules relating to arrangements for the private fostering of children. 'Norms for decision' are, in fact, equivalent to what are generally known as 'laws'.

'Norms of conduct' are the innumerable, self-generating rules to be found within society. They are generally efficacious, although not dependent upon any superior sanctioning or sovereign authority. These 'fact-norms' affect groups and relationships within those groups. The State may act so that 'norms for decision' confirm fact-norms, giving them new, potent authority. The Bills of Exchange Act 1882 is an example. It codified a number of enactments based on the recognition of certain types of practice among merchants. 'Norms of conduct' form what Ehrlich describes as 'an inner order of associations', reflecting social practices, often in contrast to the law enacted by the State.

Ehrlich draws further distinctions between the two types of norm by advancing a conceptual analysis of 'the facts of law'. Underlying the formal, enacted law may be found, he suggests, certain 'vital facts' which jurists must uncover and study. These facts are based on the phenomena of 'usage, possession, domination and declaration of the individual will'. The State should be aware of these 'facts' and should recognise their social significance by acting upon the relationships to which they give rise, ie, by seeking to encourage, regularise, or prohibit them.

It is, however, the 'living law' which is the centre of Ehrlich's thesis. 'Living law' grows within society and may dominate its life, even though it lacks a cloak of legal formality. Because it reflects the changing values of society, the 'living law' can never remain static. As social values change, so society's culture patterns will be transformed, and the 'living law' which reflects those patterns will be altered. In our own times, the community's attitudes to persons who are unfit to plead at criminal trials have changed and the State's recognition of these altered perceptions has culminated in the enactment of the Criminal Procedure (Insanity and Unfitness to Plead) Act 1991.

There is, said Ehrlich, a gap between the 'living law' and the formal law. The dynamism of the former ensures that it is in continuous evolution, often 'outpacing the rigid and immobile State law'. Indeed, one of the important tasks for jurisprudence, he said, is to solve this 'eternal tension'. Ehrlich saw in the commercial world of his day considerable differences between the actual day-to-day procedures of the business community and formal commercial law. Evidence from our own times might support this observation. The Consumer Credit Act 1974, for example, was interpreted by some jurists as a belated recognition of established practices within the area of credit provision and the supply of goods on hire. Recent case law concerning 'letters of comfort' issued by commercial organisations (see, eg, *Benson Ltd v Malaysia Mining Corporation* (1989)) suggests a wide gap between existing commercial practice and judicial opinion concerning this area of activity.

Where legislators insist on the recognition of formal law only, then, Ehrlich notes, they are ignoring the practices of a 'living law' based on wide popular acceptance of standards and modes of conduct created by groups within society. (Ehrlich's definition of society is of relevance: 'the sum total of the human associations that have mutual relations with one another'.) The legislator, assisted by the jurist, should attempt to integrate the 'living law' and the State's formal rules. In that way formal expression might be given to 'the innermost feelings of society'. The Financial Services Act 1986 may be viewed as an example of the State working with, and through, 'recognised self-regulating organisations' (as defined in s 8). The Act refers to 'the practices of clearing houses', and 'recognised bodies' and 'designated agencies' feature in its provisions in ways which suggest that legislators have taken into account the actual practices of the financial community. Legislation can effect a coalescence of 'living law' and formally-enacted rules.

Ehrlich insists that legislators shall recognise the fact that members of society perform many duties without any threat of legal compulsion. He considers the existence of a 'psychological rule' allowing norms to function through suggestion. Individual, unconscious obedience to 'the call of duty', as reflected in social obligations, might be an aspect of the 'living law'. There are cases in which citizens respond intuitively to the need to carry out duties. Commands and prohibitions involving legal duties may be, according to Ehrlich, less a matter of consciously thought-out responses than of an unconscious habituation to the demands of the social environment.

The discovery of the 'living law' is a task for legislators, judges and jurists. The uncovering of its nature will emerge from a deep examination of judicial decisions, an intensive analysis of documents related to social activity, and, above all, from observation of people engaged in their daily activities. A careful study of documents such as mortgages, leases and assignments will provide insight into social principles concerning the holding and disposition of one's property. Business documents reveal much more than the operation of rules; according to Ehrlich they reflect deeply-held attitudes towards relationships within society.

The deep examination of judicial decisions, which Ehrlich recommends as an important aid to an understanding of the 'living law', can reveal the significance of the judge as an individual whose actions are coloured by social rules of conduct. Ehrlich believes that 'juristic logic' often obscures the part played by the 'personality' of the judge. Judicial citation of authority, for example, may rationalise a decision reached by a judge who is, intuitively, weighing competing social and individual interests.

'Logical and legalistic concepts' must not blind us to the 'pull' exerted by the 'living law' on members of society.

Because the facts of the 'living law' are the facts of social life itself, it is necessary to study the large variety of organised social activities if one is to understand the law. To analyse the 'living law' as it relates to business necessitates a study of the production-distribution-exchange process in its entirety. The many intricate paths leading through the maze of commercial transactions must be charted if a full picture of the practices, procedures, codes of conduct and relationships constituting the 'living law' is to be obtained.

Ehrlich disapproves of investigation based on casual observation only. In a celebrated 'seminar of living law' held at Czernowitz (now in the Ukraine), he organised groups of students who investigated the attitudes and practices of neighbouring communities. Data collected were considered alongside private documents and showed the existence of a wide gulf between the customs and practices of diverse ethnic groups and the so-called 'sovereign code' under which they lived. The gathering of extra-legal data as part of the investigation of a problem in law was emphasised by Ehrlich in all his work.

Links between jurisprudence and the social sciences were valued by Ehrlich. The jurist can and must learn from the economist and the social scientist. All knowledge must be taken as the province of jurisprudence because the 'vital facts of the living law' are the facts of social life in its entirety. *There ought, therefore, to be no bounds to jurisprudence.*

Allen criticises Ehrlich on this point. Ehrlich's refusal to recognise any boundaries to jurisprudence leads to a concept of the subject as 'a compendium of all the social sciences'. Allen notes that a knowledge of everything usually ends 'in wisdom in nothing'. Ehrlich's 'Czernowitz-style' method of enquiry suggests to Allen a 'megalomaniac jurisprudence', utterly inappropriate for the investigation of legal phenomena. Other critics point out that the gap perceived by Ehrlich between the 'living law' and State enactments is not always as wide as he suggests. Contemporary society often involves the State playing an important part in the regulation of life on the basis of changing perceptions by the community of the quality of life. The Environmental Protection

Act 1990 may typify this. Further, there are occasions when the
State may have to move *ahead* of prevalent social attitudes: thus,
the abolition of capital punishment in Britain, almost certainly
against the wishes of the majority of the population, is cited as an
example of the formal law being 'in advance' (according to some
jurists) of the 'living law'.

Ehrlich's comment on 'the centre of gravity of legal
development' - society itself - reminds us that the enactment and
administration of the formal law require an understanding of
social requirements and a study of the precise conditions within
which the law is intended to operate. This may involve an
extension of the range of enquiry usually associated with the
positive law. As law-makers recognise in increasing measure the
significance of the relationship of promulgated law to the needs
and aspirations of society, so the formal law and the 'living law'
draw closer together.

Notes

Lloyd, ch 7, Dias, ch 21, and Allen, ch 1 provide concise accounts
of the idea of the 'living law'. Friedmann, ch 20, comments on
Ehrlich as one of the founders of modern sociological theories of
the law. Gurvitch's *Sociology of the Law* outlines the background
and methodology associated with Ehrlich.

Question 29

'Starting from an analysis of the mundane economic phenomenon
of division of labour, Durkheim was able to fashion a compelling
theory of law.'

Explain this statement.

Answer plan

Durkheim, founder of the French school of sociology, was
interested in the distinctions between individual and collective
consciousness as they affected social needs and actions. He
propounded a theory of 'social solidarity', a concept which

allowed him to examine the law as an 'index' to solidarity and cohesion within society. His view of society, of 'solidarity' and of the significance of law ought to figure in the answer. Some of the criticisms of Durkheim ought to be mentioned. A skeleton plan on the following lines is suggested:

Introduction -Durkheim's perception of law - division of labour and types of social solidarity - law as an index - law and social morality - Durkheim's view of criminal conduct - criticisms of Durkheim's mode of investigation - conclusion, force of criticisms of Durkheim's theory.

Answer

Durkheim was a social scientist, concerned essentially with a study of social forces and institutions; he was neither a jurist nor a teacher of law. His interest in the place of law within society emerged from an investigation of the factors underlying 'social cohesion' - a phenomenon which he referred to as 'organic solidarity'. Law might be perceived as an 'index' to the level of development within a given society, and, hence, its study could provide valuable data for social scientists. Durkheim's methodology of investigation involved an examination of what he termed 'the inner nature' of society, from which a knowledge of its 'real' basis could be deduced.

It was in an examination of the division of labour that Durkheim found a vital clue concerning social development and the structure of law within society. The term 'division of labour' refers to the specialisation of labour-power among individuals and groups. The process is characterised by individuals or groups concentrating on particular aspects of a productive process rather than on the whole product. The father of classical economics, Adam Smith, had subjected the process to a methodical investigation and had concluded, in 1776, that it was the most important cause of improvement in the productive powers of labour. Durkheim saw it in very different terms: it was, for him, a key to an understanding of the very development of society.

There were, according to Durkheim's analysis, two kinds of needs and aptitudes of men living within society. First, there are common needs; these can be satisfied by men giving one another mutual assistance and combining their similar aptitudes. This produces 'solidarity by similitude' or 'mechanical solidarity'. But men have also diverse needs and different aptitudes, and these needs may be satisfied by their exchanging the services they are able to offer, with each individual using his specific aptitudes to satisfy the needs of other persons. This produces 'solidarity by division of labour' or 'organic solidarity'. Division of labour and social cohesion tend to co-exist and, argues Durkheim, the greater the development of free, individual activities, the more intense will be social solidarity.

Durkheim differentiates the situations within early homogeneous societies and later complex societies. Early societies were, he claims, simple, their values uniform, and production was carried out *collectively*, in the absence of division of labour. Individualism was at a low level. More advanced societies required that their members should be interdependent; their work was differentiated by function, ie, division of labour was widespread, with persons experiencing different life styles. *Collectivism was replaced by individualism*. The two types of society produced different types of social solidarity. The 'mechanical solidarity' which characterised the undeveloped society involved a strong 'collective conscience' which reflected shared life styles and experiences. The 'organic solidarity' of the more developed society reflected the varied individual life styles of its members and arose from the functional interdependence of producers. Each type of society produced its own attitudes and type of law.

Law was perceived by Durkheim as *an external index to the level of social solidarity within a society*. Indeed, if it is possible to understand the type of law which obtains within a given community it should be possible to deduce from that the accompanying type of social organisation. Law reproduces in its styles and functions the principal forms of social cohesion. In the societies characterised by 'mechanical solidarity' the law will tend to be strict and repressive. Deviations from the norm will be interpreted as meriting severe, condign punishment. Durkheim refers, in this context to the 'passionate reaction' of a community to activities which, at this level, offend the collective conscience of society. In more highly-developed societies in which 'organic solidarity' is prevalent, law has moved away from the use of those penal sanctions which reflect a desire for vengeance, towards restitutive sanctions. The State, through its legal institutions, will be concerned, where there is 'organic solidarity', with the *legislation of norms*. Punishment may tend to take the form of deprivation of liberty rather than the forms associated with mere revenge.

Law will assist in the spread of cohesion within the community. It will,in the developed societies, strengthen contractual relationships. It will emphasise, through its sanctions, common reactions to threats. It will introduce into the legal process a pattern of uniformity which will *intensify* the level of cohesion and solidarity.

Durkheim views law and morality as being very closely-related phenomena. Because law is derived from the morality of society it tends to express it. *Law may be said to symbolise morality*. Together, law and morality constitute a 'totality of ties', binding every individual to society and assisting in the transformation of a mass of individuals into a unified, coherent aggregate. Anything which is a source of social solidarity is 'moral', anything which forces one individual to take account of others is 'moral', and the morality of a society is as strong as the 'totality of ties'. No metaphysical premises underpin this concept of morality which emerges from the mere fact of the existence of individuals *within a society*. Law allows an individual to adjust himself and his moral concepts to those of society. In that way he is given 'moral guidance' by the law and is able to free himself from the effects of *'anomie'* - a term used by Durkheim to describe a mental state in which an individual feels that he lacks an identity because his life lacks meaning.

Durkheim applied his theory to an understanding of crime. He considered an act to be 'criminal' when it offended strong and defined states of the collective conscience, which he viewed as 'a totality of beliefs and sentiments common to average citizens of the same society'. Crime has, as one of its effects, the bringing together of 'society's upright consciences, and concentrating them'. Hence, the criminalisation of certain types of disapproved modes of conduct arises from an exercise by the community of its collective conscience. An action does not shock society because it is criminal; rather it is criminal because it shocks the common conscience. Durkheim notes that certain types of criminal offence are abhorred by most societies. Thus, every society has a respect for life, 'the intensity of which is determined by and commensurate with, the relative weight of the penalties attached to homicide'. The nature of the law in relation to penalties for criminal conduct is, for Durkheim, an index of the general level of social development and cohesion.

In his comments on contracts, Durkheim stresses the importance of 'social influence' in a paradoxical aphorism: 'Not everything in the contract is contractual'. The law of contract is not to be considered solely in terms of individuals reaching an agreement. Social norms, derived from social attitudes and *practices* in relation to agreements, such as the significance of a promise (which will reflect the prevailing level of social cohesion), regulate contractual behaviour, making some actions acceptable in relation to agreements, while others are proscribed.

'Law as an index' is, without doubt, a 'compelling theory', which calls for legal institutions to be considered in terms of society, its development, its economic background *and* the level of social cohesion it indicates. There are criticisms of the theory which should be noted. It is suggested that Durkheim has adopted a 'consensus' model of society which seems to underestimate the phenomenon of social conflict. There is little evidence that Durkheim gave sufficient weight to the significance of moral conflicts among members of a community or that he accepted the importance of the phenomenon of 'law *v* morality' disputes. There is criticism, too, of Durkheim's view of societies held together by 'mechanical solidarity'. Recent investigations by some anthropologists and sociologists suggest that there are many examples of the division of labour within primitive societies, and the existence of non-repressive forms of regulation within undeveloped communities. The 'mechanical solidarity' which Durkheim postulated as characterising undeveloped societies is not always evident. Conclusive evidence as to the correlation between levels of social development, economic specialisation, repressive attitudes towards unacceptable behaviour, is not easy to find.

It is suggested that Durkheim's views concerning the transition from 'mechanical' to 'organic solidarity' fail to consider the importance of the *intermediate stages* of that transition. Durkheim appears to imply a sharply-defined transition from one society to another, whereas modern research points to social transitions marked by gradual evolution. Nor does research support the thesis which suggests that, whereas repressive law characterised the early stages of a society, modern, highly-developed societies view law in terms of restitution where that is practicable. A survey of contemporary law might be interpreted as suggesting that, in many societies, retribution is often an aspect of guidelines in sentencing policy, for example. A further criticism of Durkheim, arising from his attitude to the significance of 'penalties' in the legal order, points to his lack of understanding of the legal *process*. His investigations were confined to legal *rules* within society; he said little concerning the structure, purposes and functions of the *institutions of the law*, such as the courts and the legal profession. In practice, legal institutions occupy an important place in developed societies; their operations have an effect upon 'social cohesion' which ought not to be ignored.

None of these criticisms weakens the 'compelling nature' of Durkheim's theory. They serve, however, to remind those who adhere to the general tenets of the sociological school of jurisprudence of the importance of testing speculation against fact, of carrying out extensive field work (which Durkheim neglected) and of utilising such work and its results in a continuing examination of theories of law based largely on investigations of so-called 'primitive societies'.

Notes

Durkheim's *The Division of Labour in Society* has been translated by Simpson. Summaries of the principal points in Durkheim's theory appear in Lloyd, ch 7, and Friedmann, ch 19. *Durkheim and the Law* by Lukes and Scull is a contemporary interpretation of the 'social solidarity' theory. Hunt's *The Sociological Movement in Law* considers the implications of Durkheim's interpretation of law. *The Power to Punish*, edited by Garland and Young, includes a critique of Durkheim's attitude to law and punishment of offenders.

Question 30

What are the principal theoretical conclusions concerning the nature of law which Weber derived from his sociological investigations?

Answer plan

It has been said that few scholars have had as powerful an influence on this century's social sciences as Weber. A polymath who had mastered the disciplines of sociology, history, economics and jurisprudence, he stressed the need for objectivity in *all* areas of research and emphasised the importance of studying human actions in terms of the actors' motives. His studies in sociology and history, carried out in Germany, produced a theory of law in which typology (a study and interpretation of 'types') predominated. The types of law which form the basis of his classification should be outlined in the answer, and attention should be given to his general attitude to the *development* of the law. The following skeleton plan is used:

Introduction -Weber and the methodology of *'Verstehen'* - order and authority - types of legitimate authority - criticism of Weber's typology - rational and irrational systems - Weber's views on English law - conclusion, law and reciprocal relationships.

Answer

A theme which runs through Weber's work is the necessity for recognition of the human individual as the basic unit of any social enquiry. The motives of individuals who find themselves in situations such as legal disputes must be understood. Weber utilised a methodology of enquiry known as *Verstehen* ('to understand'), which concentrates on comprehending the *states of mind* of persons involved in events, and on the construction of *'ideal types'*, ie, generalised models of situations which could be applied to analogous cases. *Why* persons obeyed the law, *why* power was respected, *why* authority was accepted as legitimate, were of great interest to Weber.

Specifically, Weber was concerned with 'answering Marx', with refuting the doctrinaire finalities which had become associated with historical materialism. The Marxist search for a single, primal cause of social change was, in Weber's view, futile - there was much more to society than the relationships arising from the ownership of the means of production. Further, capitalism was not to be viewed, in Marxist terms, as a mere 'passing phase' in social development. The problems of law in relation to society in general, and capitalism in particular, could not be reduced to questions of class domination. A review of the history of law, and its recasting in terms of a typology, would, according to Weber, underline the deficiencies of Marx's interpretation of law in society.

Society and its law could be comprehended clearly if the significance of 'order' were investigated. Order requires norms and the power to enforce those norms. Weber perceived the phenomenon of power as the probability that a person within a social relationship will be able to carry out his will in spite of possible resistance, and regardless of the basis upon which the probability rests. (One is reminded of Bertrand Russell's statement that power is 'the production of intended effects'.) Power is needed if law is to be effective, but unrestricted power is the antithesis of law. It is 'legitimate authority' which must be accepted as underlying the exercise of power. A relationship of legitimate authority exists only where the ruled accept the ruler as embodying the concept of 'power through authority'. Weber discerned three types of legitimate authority in his investigation of the history of societies: the 'traditional', the 'charismatic', and the 'legal rational'. Each had its own appropriate type of law.

'Traditional authority' was determined by ingrained habituation: legitimacy arose from the sanctity of age-old rules and powers. The ruled owed obedience, not to enacted rules, but rather to persons who occupied position of authority by tradition, or who had been chosen by traditional rules. The law in societies characterised by this type of authority was not created openly; often, new rules were legitimised by their presentation as reaffirmations of ancient rules. Rule by elders, powerful patriarchies, seems to typify authority of this nature.

'Charismatic authority' ('*charisma*' means 'the gift of grace') involves devotion to a perceived sanctity or heroism of an extraordinary person, and to the norms revealed or ordained by him. Heroes, prophets endowed with superhuman powers and qualities are examples. Authority of this nature often arises in revolutionary situations in which there is a sharp repudiation of the past. In such circumstances a 'charismatic type' of law is enforced, but becomes difficult to maintain at a later stage when it comes into conflict with the demands of everyday routine structures.

The 'legal rational authority' requires from ruler and ruled a belief in the legality of enacted rules and in the right of those who enjoy authority under these rules to issue commands. Authority in this context is justified by the obvious 'rationality' of the rules promulgated. It is this type of authority and its appropriate pattern of law, which, according to Weber, may be seen as characteristic of capitalism. Thus, the general law within a capitalist society provides an ambience of certainty and predictability within which a law of contract, essential for this type of society, might grow and flourish. The law of Western societies is characterised, according to Weber, by strictly formal rules and procedures which command respect and obedience, not necessarily because of their content, but because they are *perceived* as fundamentally rational. They have been created and enforced by the State in conditions which are accepted by society as reflecting appropriate norms. The authority of the capitalist State rests fundamentally on the acceptance by society of the rules related to the exercise of power and the promulgation of 'rational' laws.

Weber stressed the significance within the 'legal rational order' of acceptance by society of the principle that authority attaches 'to the office rather than to the person'. The authority of a particular prime minister, for example, derives from the office he holds, and obedience to him stems from attitudes to that office. The authoritative nature of decisions of the House of Lords stems from its place in the hierarchy of the courts rather than the personal reputation of the Lords of Appeal in Ordinary.

The 'legal rational order' provides a basis for Weber's definition of law. We may refer to a rule as 'law' if it is promulgated and is externally guaranteed by the probability that physical or psychological coercion to produce conformity or 'to avenge violation' will be applied by a group of persons holding themselves in readiness for that purpose. The law is viewed here in terms of expectations and probabilities acceptable to the individuals who make up society. Weber's attachment to the significance of *Verstehen*, of understanding the states of mind of members of society in relation to events in which they participate, is obvious here.

Weber's classification of law into three 'types' has been criticised by jurists such as Berman, who points out that no explanation is given of the similarities and differences among various historical legal orders. Weber provides no answer to the question of why charismatic law becomes 'routinised' in one society, but not in another. Nor does he explain the fact that the legal tradition in the West seems to be a combination of aspects of *all* three 'types' of law. Thus, within our own legal tradition, the position of the Monarchy, the conventions and prerogatives of Parliament, the phenomenon of Equity, may be viewed as containing principles derived from each of the three types of law.

Weber uses another typology to underline the importance of procedures within legal systems. He suggests a division of systems based on 'rationality' and 'irrationality' and a sub-division reflecting the 'substantive' or 'formal' nature of procedures, and produces four categories: 'substantively irrational', 'formally irrational', 'substantively rational' and 'formally rational'.

The essence of the 'substantively irrational' system is that cases are decided entirely on their own merits. There is no reference to general principles (which are rarely acknowledged). Those who dispense this form of justice make ad hoc decisions, taking into account ethical and political considerations. Intuition often controls decision. In the 'formally irrational' system, decisions tend to be made on the basis of 'tests' beyond the control of the human mind. Intuitive pronouncement is replaced by reliance on some ordeal or oracle, from which an indication of guilt or innocence will emerge. The establishing of guilt will require more than a pronouncement by an individual invested with authority. There is an appeal to *judicium Dei* (the judgment of God). Ordeal by fire or water is interpreted as showing guilt or innocence established by outside intervention. The fundamental irrationality of the system is clothed in formality.

The 'substantively rational' system supposes no separation of law from morality. Theocratic systems provide an example - the Divine Word *is* the law. Rules and principles may be constructed and codified, but justice may be administered in the name of the Divinity; its sanctions may derive from an interpretation of the Revealed Word. Its procedures may be heavily dependent on traditional concepts of what should be done so as to restore a social balance which might have been broken, or so as to repair a breach in the ordained relationship between God and man.

The 'formally rational' system, exemplified in part by the codes of civil law based upon the classical Roman law, is characterised by an apparently 'seamless web' of principles, rules and procedures which are intended to provide answers to all types of legal problem. The norms underlying such a system are perceived as rational and impersonal; the rules are formulated and applied by processes requiring logical generalisation. Rules are collected and often codified so that they appear as components of an internally-consistent system. The prime place occupied in the 'substantively rational' system by ethical considerations disappears when the principle of *logical consistency* achieves prominence.

Weber was particularly interested in the application of his typology to the characteristics of law in England, the first developed capitalist society. He suggests that, because of the importance of its political history in the formation of the legal system, England was, perhaps, an exception to the generalisation he had formulated. Capitalism had grown in England *before* full legal rationality had been established there. The common law was a mixture of substantive rationality (as evidenced, for example, by its concern for extra-legal matters such as 'the public good') and formal irrationality (such as the oaths taken by parties to a judicial hearing). He also perceived in English law some important characteristics of the 'charismatic epoch' of law-making, noting, for example, Blackstone's description of the judge as a sort of 'living oracle'. His general conclusion was that the capitalistic supremacy achieved by England over other nations arose in spite of its judicial system.

Weber's perspective of law is on a grand scale. Emanating from his concern with the individual participating in social processes and creating relationships, he interprets the evolution of the law in terms of those relationships within a system based on the legitimisation of authority. It is in the rationality of the law that its ultimate power may be perceived. Weber's answer to Marx is clear: a theory which seeks to explain law solely in terms of relationships founded upon the ownership of the means of production misses many features of law and society and must, therefore, be inadequate.

Notes

Weber on Law in Economy and Society is published in an edition by Rheinstein. Lloyd, ch 7, Harris, ch 19, and Friedmann, ch 19, expound Weber's theory of law. Berman offers a criticism of the theory in *Law and Revolution: The Foundation of the Western Legal Tradition*, in a chapter entitled 'Beyond Marx, Beyond Weber'.

Question 31

'Little remains of Pound's theory of interests save an empty taxonomic shell; the critics have demolished everything else.' Do you agree?

Answer plan

Pound, an American jurist, former Dean of the Harvard Law School, and a leading figure in the American 'sociological jurisprudence movement' considered law as a social institution designed to satisfy society's wants. The 'theory of interests' involved a classification of 'demands, desires and expectations' which the law ought to recognise and secure. Intense criticism of the theory has resulted in a decline in its significance. The answer should include a general exposition of the theory and an outline of the more important criticisms, particularly those centring on the inadequacy of Pound's 'jural postulates'. The following skeleton plan is suggested:

> Introduction -essence of the theory of interests - the balancing of individual and social interests - jural postulates - criticisms of the theory - conclusion, the shell of the theory acts as a reminder of the concept of law as a means to an end.

Answer

Pound was concerned with the working of the law rather than its abstract content, with its social purposes and institutions within the context of social progress. His attitude was essentially 'functional': 'law', as distinct from 'laws', was a system which provided the foundation for judicial and administrative action within an organised society. The theory of interests, the outlines of which are set out below, is based on a belief in the necessity of legal order which demands a classification, securing and protection, of a variety of *interests*. Pound's taxonomy of interests is his specific contribution to the objective of analysing social purposes. The criticism directed against the theory is noted below, together with the suggestion that most of the theory may be considered as effectively demolished.

One of the aims of Pound's jurisprudence is an understanding of the mechanisms appropriate to achieving a *balance* of the security of society and of each individual's life. The law must attempt to satisfy, reconcile and harmonise conflicting claims and demands so that the interests that weigh most in society are given an appropriate prominence. To this end a process of 'balancing' is needed; it will involve reference to *rules* (precepts of a detailed nature), *principles* (starting points for legal reasoning), *conceptions* (the categorisation of causes and situations) and *standards* (markers of the limits of permissible conduct). The appropriate balancing process will reflect the aim of law, which Pound spoke of as 'social engineering', concerned with the ordering of human relations 'with a minimum of waste and friction'.

To secure for society 'the greatest number of interests with the least possible sacrifice of other interests' is a primary function of the law, according to Pound. He defines an interest as a demand or desire which human beings, individually or in groups, seek to satisfy and which must be taken into account in the ordering of social relations. The theory of interests recognises the existence of individual, social and public interests, defines the limits within which they should be recognised and given effect by the law, and emphasises the need to secure them. From an inventory and classification of interests, decisions on their recognition and modes of ensuring their security, will emerge the key task for jurists and legislators - the *balancing* of those interests.

Pound's taxonomy is complex and is based on a division of interests into three basic categories: *individual, social and public.* *Individual interests* are interests of personality or interests in domestic relations or interests of substance. They involve claims and demands related to an individual's life, eg, personality (physical security, freedom of belief, etc), domestic relations (interests of parents, children, protection of marriage, etc), substance (property, freedom of contract). *Social interests* are claims or desires of the group which constitutes the community. These include general security, security of social institutions, general moral standards, conservation of social resources, general progress and individual life (the very important claim of a person to live a full human life according to society's standards). *Public interests* relate to claims viewed from the standpoint of a politically-organised society. They include interests of the State considered as a 'juristic person' (its integrity and security), interests of the State in its role of guardian of social interests.

These interests must be balanced fairly and this can be achieved only by examining a conflict on the appropriate plane or level. One ought not, for example, to weigh an individual interest against a public interest. Further, the satisfaction of as many interests as possible might involve the testing of a claim to a 'new interest'. Pound's solution to the problem of recognising whether or not a claimed 'new interest' shall qualify for recognition is to consider that interest by reference to the *jural postulates* of a civilised society. The postulates encapsulate the underlying *values* of a society. Given these postulates, legislators may modify rules and make new ones so as to conform with general values.

Pound's 'jural postulates' may be stated in the form of assumptions. Men within a civilised society are entitled to assume: that others will commit no intentional aggression upon them; that they may control for beneficial purposes what they have discovered, created and acquired; that others will act in good faith and carry out promises; that others will act reasonably and prudently and will not impose, by want of care, unreasonable risk of injury; that others will restrain or keep within proper bounds, things harmful in their normal action outside the sphere of their use. Pound later added the following postulates: that men should be entitled to assume that the burdens incident to social life shall be borne by society; and that at least a standard human life shall be assured to every individual by way of immediate material satisfaction.

We may summarise the theory as follows: Pound views law functionally, as a necessary social institution created to assist in the satisfaction of human wants. The satisfaction of wants necessitates an analysis of interests so that they may be systematised and secured by society's legal institutions. Conflicts of interests will demand a process of balancing one against another on the same plane. Where conflict follows on a request to recognise a new interest, reference is to be made to the jural postulates which reflect society's (and the law's) values. These postulates are not immutable and will require revision from time to time.

Criticism of Pound's theory has been intense. It is claimed, in general terms, that his theory is not an integrated whole because he failed to synthesise his thought. It is not always possible to see the links between the instrumentalist outlook which dominates his view of law, and his insistence on the significance of values as the basis of the jural postulates. Critics suggest that Pound may have derived his 'purposes' of society from principles which are couched in a form of words making factual proof impossible, and that he made no actual advance in our understanding of the law. He has done no more than 'rationalise the actual'. His views are said to reflect the thinking peculiar to American society of his day and may be difficult to translate to another epoch. The theory has been said to be based too closely on 'making things work better' and to provide little more than a minimalist picture of social needs which is not entirely relevant to our day. His methodology, involving a taxonomy of interests, has been criticised as suffering from the 'reification' inherent in any attempt to classify in systematic form phenomena outside the range of the natural sciences, with the result that personal attitudes and perspectives emerge as aspects of objective reality. These criticisms have certainly undermined the credibility of the theory of interests.

Specific criticism has been directed against the 'consensus model' of law adopted by Pound. This is condemned as founded on a view of society functioning through shared values and ideas, a view which, critics suggested, is distorted. Pound, say the critics, has failed to take into account the deep conflict of values within our society and he has ignored the struggles for the dominance of interests which have characterised much of our history. A theory predicated on a model of a society which does not exist is rejected as unreal.

Attention has been drawn, too, to the so-called 'inadequacies of analogy' as reflected in Pound's description of law, within the terms of the theory of interests, as 'social engineering'. Engineering involves building according to a detailed plan on 'solid ground'. But the essence of law in our society is that it is, in general, unplanned; it involves ad hoc attempts to deal with situations which are often unforeseen, and there may be little 'solid ground' in a rapidly-evolving community. Further, say the critics, 'engineering' involves the creation of 'agreed structures' according to agreed plans; this analogy is of no relevance to a consideration of law within a non-static society in which there is often dissent concerning legal ends and means.

The methodology employed by Pound in the theory of interests is said to be inadequate, giving a spurious air of objectivity to essentially vague ideas, and often based on no more than his reactions to events. The 'interests' are nebulous and it is not easy to see the distinction drawn between 'public' and 'social' interests. Nor is it possible to discern the precise system of classification used in the theory. The result is, say the critics, a classification based on no obvious set of principles, so that what has emerged from Pound's analysis reads like 'a political tract issued by a liberal grouping'. The critics note that whether, for example, an interest is classified as 'individual' or 'social' must be a reflection of changing, relative, political concepts, and little more. Pound's commentary on the classification seems not to acknowledge limitations of this nature.

No real standards are provided, according to critics, for evaluating or weighing interests. In the event, 'weight' is likely to depend upon highly-subjective criteria. 'Balancing' - a concept which Pound favours - implies some objective 'measuring rod', but the word is used in a misleading sense since it suggests a lack of subjective ideals and sentiments which, in reality, will, almost certainly, affect the evaluation upon which the 'balancing' depends. Further, recognition of a 'new interest' cannot be divorced from aspects of social policy - itself a subjective matter. Thus, current controversies on the recognition of a 'right to privacy', or the 'right to a home', will reflect individualist political views.

Finally, the critics have launched a sustained assault on Pound's concept of the 'jural postulates'. Seen by some as derived from 'a cramped and myopic view', by others as an attempt to smuggle in by the back door the 'unchangeable verities' of the natural law, the postulates have been rejected as a mere reflection of the social mores of American society of the 1920s. Pound, it is said, has failed to perceive the relative nature of his postulates. His call for their continued revision does not face up to the problem inherent in their enunciation as the legal values of a 'civilised society' - itself a concept based on personal evaluation. Indeed, Stone has suggested that the postulates require 'a basic reworking' so that they may reflect social changes that have come about since the time of their initial formulation. One wonders whether Pound would have accepted some recent legislative changes within the United States as being consistent with the values of the 'civilised society' he proclaimed.

The criticisms levelled at the theory of interests have removed it from the mainstream of modern jurisprudential thought. The very concept of a taxonomy of interests ('overticketed, overdocketed') is considered as flawed. Little is left of the theory. But the general outlines of Pound's theory do serve as a reminder of the approach to law as a 'means to an end' and as an enunciation of the 'reconciling task' of law. In Friedmann's words, the theory does make inarticulate premises articulate, and serves to remind legislators and jurists of the need to consider the interests of the community when addressing matters relating to the purpose of the law within society.

Notes

The principles of Pound's theory of interests are discussed in Lloyd, ch 20, Friedmann, ch 25, and Dias, ch 20. 'Pound's Theory of Social Interests', by Patterson, appears in *Interpretations of Modern Legal Philosophies*, edited by Sayre. Pound writes on 'A Survey of Social Interests' in 57 Harvard LR 1 (1943) and on 'The Scope and Purpose of Sociological Jurisprudence' in 25 Harvard LR 489 (1921).

Marxist Jurisprudence

Introduction

Marxist jurisprudence stems primarily from the writings of Marx (1818-83), Engels (1820-95) and Lenin (1870-1924), and involves the application of the philosophy of dialectical materialism to a consideration of the nature of society, State and law. The motivating force in history is seen as the class struggle, from which the law and jurisprudence do not stand aside. The questions in this chapter concern Marx's analysis of law in the context of capitalist society, and the contribution of Pashukanis (1891-1937), one of the few Soviet jurists who challenged some of the orthodoxies in Marxist jurisprudence.

Checklist

Ensure that you are acquainted with the following topics:

- dialectical materialism
- historical materialism
- base and superstructure
  - commodity-exchange theory
- class instrumentalism
- State and law
- withering away of the State

Question 32

Addressing the bourgeoisie in his *Communist Manifesto* (1848), Marx stated: 'Your jurisprudence is but the will of your class made into a law for all, a will whose essential character and direction are determined by the economic conditions of existence of your class'. Outline the theory behind Marx's statement and comment on its jurisprudential implications.

Answer plan

The *Communist Manifesto* was an analysis of the history of society in terms of the class struggle, and a 'call to arms'. Marx was concerned to show how law was an ideological weapon of the ruling class (the bourgeoisie) which was deployed by the State through the legal system so as to maintain class rule and oppress the working class. The question demands an explanation of the basis of Marx's theory of law which, in turn, involves a consideration of the 'base and superstructure' explanation of the State. The following skeleton plan is used:

Introduction -Marx's world-outlook - materialist conception of history - laws of economic development - history as class struggle - base and superstructure - law and class instrumentalism - State and law - law in a classless society - conclusion, current rejection of Marx's jurisprudence.

Answer

The *Communist Manifesto* was an outline of principles and a call to action, a combination of the 'theory and practice of revolution' which Marx considered essential if society was to be transformed. 'Up till now', he had declared, 'philosophers have interpreted the world; the point, however, is to change it.' Marx had studied jurisprudence, philosophy and history at the universities of Bonn and Berlin and had been influenced profoundly by the teachings of Hegel which he adapted and transformed in the creation of his own world-outlook. Embedded in that outlook was a unique interpretation of law as reflecting economic relationships within society. The corpus of Marxist jurisprudence grew out of his general philosophy, and some of its essence is contained within the quotation from the *Manifesto*, addressed to the ruling class - the bourgeoisie - whose overthrow was, in Marx's view , necessary, inevitable and imminent.

Marx's jurisprudential thought was based on the doctrines which comprised his philosophical outlook: dialectical materialism, the laws of economic development and the materialist conception of history. Dialectical materialism is Marx's version of the basis of the 'laws of change'; it combines a materialist philosophy and the method of interpretation known as 'dialectics', which is a highly-systematised mode of reasoning involving the examination and resolution of contradictions within phenomena. Marx's materialism embraced *all* phenomena, natural and social. Natural phenomena constitute a unity: everything is in motion and nothing exists (or can be understood) as an isolate. The bases of a system of law, its purposes and manifestations, have to be comprehended in terms of their relationships and changing nature. The Marxist jurist rejects 'idealistic jurisprudence': ideas can have no meaning or significance outside a materialistic framework of analysis. Legal thought has to be interpreted in relation to the social fabric within which it was conceived and nurtured.

The laws of economic development reflect fundamental antagonisms ('contradictions') between those who own the instruments of production (the bourgeoisie) and those who own nothing save their labour power (the proletariat). The latter are exploited by the former; the mode of exploitation characterises the laws of economic development. Methodical exploitation sets in motion a struggle which can be resolved only by the expropriation of the bourgeoisie, together with the abolition of the legal system which has assisted in securing bourgeois class rule.

The materialist conception of history rejects the view of historical development as 'man's movement towards his spiritual destiny' or 'a struggle towards perfect freedom'. For Marx, history is a bleak record of the conflict of class against class, with the law 'taking sides'. The laws of historical development are inexorable in their operation. Society began with conditions in which a legal system was unnecessary because there was common ownership of property. Slave-owning society followed, with laws recognising and protecting the ownership of slaves. Medieval feudalism followed and, in turn, produced capitalism, with a developed legal system. Revolutionary activity will, according to Marx, produce from capitalist society the socialist, classless order in which a legal system will no longer be needed because, with the removal of economic contradictions, crime and other anti-social activities will disappear. Marx's fulminations against the bourgeoisie, recorded in the *Manifesto*, are intended to remind them of the transitory nature of their society and its legal system.

It is from the Marxist thesis of 'base and superstructure' that the significance of law emerges. The basis of a given social order is its economic foundation, which is characterised by relations of production. The relations are determined by the mode in which the factors of production (land, labour and capital) are organised and exploited by those who own the instruments of production (factories, mines, etc). On this foundation society erects a 'superstructure', which includes ideas, ideologies, theories, philosophies relating to religion, ethics, art, etc. Society requires, and, therefore, creates as part of the superstructure, legal rules and institutions, referred to, collectively, as 'the law'.

Legal ideology, according to Marx, owes little to so-called 'eternal categories', 'innate ideas of justice' or 'immutable concepts of right'. It is an identifiable part of the social superstructure, built on the foundation of a certain type of economic production and mirroring the antagonisms of a society characterised by class domination and suppression. The emergence and growth of the common law, rooted in the mores of an exploitative agricultural society, the growth of theories of natural law, are to be understood solely by reference to the framework of economic relationships in which they took root and flourished. It is the relationships engendered by society's economy which determine the nature of legal ideology.

The doctrine of 'class instrumentalism', which exercised a significant influence on many European jurists of the mid-twentieth century, arises from investigation of the nature of superstructure and the concept of struggle. Ideas relating to the law - its content, theoretical basis, principles of legal institutions - must be viewed as aspects of the class interests jurists serve, consciously or unconsciously. Law, according to Marx, is an instrument of class domination, enabling the ruling class to control and suppress those groups which challenge its power. Behind the apparent scholarly and 'disinterested' jurisprudence which advocates 'human rights' or 'reason' or 'natural justice', is the veiled purpose of the *protection and preservation of class interests*. Jurisprudential ideas may be interpreted, therefore, not as 'phenomena in themselves', but as a rationale for the forging of 'ideological weapons' safeguarding those who hold power. It is this facet of law to which Marx is referring in the extract from the *Manifesto*. 'Behind your jurisprudence is your concern for the maintenance of your economic superiority. Your law is a mere expression, a rationalisation, of that concept.'

Also dependent on the theory of 'base and superstructure' is the Marxist concept of State and law, which is implicit in the extract from the *Manifesto*. The State, its apparatus and ideology, may be perceived as a part of the general superstructure of society and resting, therefore, on society's economic base. The State did not exist prior to the emergence of classes; its functions appear and are intensified as class divisions grow. In the era of bourgeois domination, to which Marx is referring in the passage cited in the question, the State is merely the 'executive committee' of the bourgeoisie, providing coercive power in a continuing class conflict of which it is aware. The structural form of the State reflects the prevalent mode of production. The feudal State, according to Marx, with its hierarchy of allegiances, mirrored aspects of the ownership of land. The modern State, with its emphasis on administration, is said to reflect large-scale production systems. Today's State is interpreted by Marxist jurists as an organisation concerned primarily with the task of protecting a ruling class. The law provides assistance in manning the organisations of the State concerned with the protection and reinforcement of class rights, and jurisprudence performs its role of justifying the legal basis of the *status quo*.

Implicit in Marx's criticism of bourgeois law is his notion of 'change'. He gives no exemption to law, class or State from the workings of historical development. Following on the inevitable defeat of the bourgeoisie will come a radical transformation in the role of State and law. The new, victorious, socialist society will see a replacement of 'the government of persons' by 'the administration of things'. Mankind, in the new classless society will have no need of a State apparatus; there will be no classes and, therefore, no tasks for State organs of repression. Exploitation and poverty, the root causes of crime, will vanish, as will the jurisprudential ideology which sought to explain these phenomena as permanent. In effect, the State will not be abolished, but will merely 'wither away'.

There is, therefore, the certainty that law will disappear from the classless society after a 'transitional period'. During that period, when society is shedding its old habits, new, temporary forms of law, designed to strengthen the powers of the new dominant class will be needed. Eventually the law will disappear and man will develop into a 'group creature' who no longer has a need for rules, codes and institutions of law.

Marxist jurisprudence now has few attractions for jurists. Its basic theses appear over-simplified, and its philosophy seems untenable in the face of actual historical development in our times. Marxist legal thought is seen to have been used to underpin authoritarian regimes in which justice and liberty were non-existent. Vestiges of the system of thought originated by Marx may continue to be considered in discussions of the nature of the State and law, but it is unlikely that the school of Marxist legal ideology will long survive the disappearance of the States in which it was encouraged and in which it flourished as official dogma. Theories which proclaimed the withering away of the State under socialism, which foresaw the disappearance of crime and a replacement of the administration of people by the administration of things, now appear to have little credibility in the context of the harsh realities of State power which characterised the Marxist regimes and which were supported by the writings of almost all Marxist jurists.

Notes

The principal works of Marx, including the *Communist Manifesto*, appear in a variety of editions, some annotated by contemporary scholars. Lloyd, ch 11, and Friedmann, ch 29, provide useful commentaries on Marxist jurisprudential thought. Collins' *Marxism and Law* gives a unified, comprehensive account of the Marxist theory of law. Chapter 23 of *An Introduction to Comparative Law* (vol 1) by Zweiger and Kotz, entitled 'The Marxist-Leninist View of Law', is particularly useful. Plamenatz, in *Marx's Philosophy of Man*, outlines aspects of Marxist jurisprudence. A contemporary Marxist analysis of law is given in *Images of Law*, by Bankowski and Maugham.

Question 33

Outline and evaluate the contribution of Pashukanis to jurisprudence.

Answer plan

Pashukanis, a Soviet jurist, professor of law and a Vice-Minister for Justice in the early days of the regime, produced an interpretation of law which was, in some respects, at variance with official, orthodox jurisprudence. In the light of his theory he resisted the call for the creation of a 'proletarian law'. He disappeared in the purges of the 1930s, having been denounced as a 'wrecker'. The question demands an explanation of the 'commodity-exchange' theory from which Pashukanis derived his view of law. An estimate of his significance today is required; this should take into account the apparent excesses of the legal system he helped to create. The following skeleton plan is suggested.

Introduction -Pashukanis' questioning of orthodox Marxist views of law - the political context of his writing - significance of the commodity-exchange theory - Pashukanis as a 'wrecker' - criticisms of the basis of his legal thought - conclusion, Pashukanis' contribution to jurisprudence now seen as interesting but slight.

Answer

It is paradoxical that Pashukanis, generally considered as one of the few outstanding contributors to Marxist jurisprudence in this century, should now be known only for his deviation from orthodox Marxism as applied to law. His *Law and Marxism - a General Theory* (1924), was intended as a first draft of a Marxist critique of fundamental juridical concepts; in Marxist terminology it was envisaged as 'an attempt to approximate the legal form to the commodity form'. Pashukanis proposed a re-thinking of the doctrine of law associated with earlier Marxists and a re-casting of some fundamental concepts of jurisprudence, particularly in relation to 'the withering away of the State'. The result was that he moved outside the mainstream of Marxist thought as interpreted by the official Soviet jurisprudential school, with predictable results.

The significance of political events during which Pashukanis prepared and published his theory should not be forgotten. The Russian Revolution was less than five years old, lawlessness was rife and the draconian legal system which was to characterise the Soviet State was already in embryonic form. By 1930 it had become obvious that world revolution - a basic dogma of Marxist official thought - was not imminent, and in 1936 a new constitution, which recognised the importance of obedience to the law of the State, was introduced. Pashukanis' work did not escape the attention of the Communist Party's vigilant theoreticians. They viewed it - correctly - as a deviation from orthodoxy and as an implied criticism of the role of law in the State. Pashukanis was denounced in the official press in 1937 and, later that year, was arrested as 'an enemy of the people'. He disappeared in a widespread purge of 'unreliable elements'.

Pashukanis writes as a convinced Marxist who accepts the basic thinking of Marx and Lenin in relation to law. He accepts the doctrine of the class struggle, of class instrumentalism and of the role of law within society. He cites with approval Marx's aphorism: 'It is not consciousness that determines life, but life that determines consciousness'. The relations of production determine society's superstructure, including legal thought, and 'right can never be higher than the economic structure of society'. But he gives a twist to these doctrines in *Law and Marxism* in an unusual emphasis on exchange, rather than production, within society. Further, he calls for the rejection of a growing, popular call for a 'proletarian law' and stresses the significance of the doctrine of the withering away of the State - this at a time when the dominance of law and State was being deliberately intensified.

The commodity-exchange theory is at the basis of Pashukanis' thoughts on jurisprudence. Any theorising in law, he insists, demands deep historical enquiry. This will reveal that the real basis of all law is *the contractual relationship*. Fundamental to capitalism is exchange; goods produced are 'commodities' and are destined largely for exchange on the market. Law emerges when there is a perceived necessity to ensure the smooth running of systems based on trade and barter. The importance of contract grows and a legal structure emerges so as to resolve disputes and conflicts of interest.

Further, says Pashukanis, an analysis of law in the era of commodity exchange epitomised by capitalism reveals that 'the only law is bourgeois law'. The full logic of the very concepts of law and legal system can be asserted, therefore, only under capitalism. The ideal of law comes to fruition at the same time as the ideal of the market, and this is no historical accident. Bourgeois economic doctrine and law are dominated by the concept of commodity-exchange. This had to be accepted by Marxists if they were to understand the historical nature of capitalism.

Calls for the establishment of a 'proletarian law' were rejected by Pashukanis as backward-looking. He argues that the formal patterns of bourgeois commodity-exchange law continue during the transitional period leading to socialism, even though capitalist exploitation has ceased. Law will die out together with the State, and the withering away of categories of bourgeois law will involve the withering away of law *in its entirety*. The juridical factor will disappear from social relations. Lenin's view that there will remain for a time after the revolution not only vestiges of bourgeois law, but that the bourgeois State itself will continue - without the bourgeoisie - had to be remembered. The demand for a 'proletarian law' would delay the transition to socialism and was incorrect in the circumstances. The desirable objective was the withering away of the *entire legal form* as such.

The State will wither away, said Pashukanis, when commodity-exchange in *all* its forms has disappeared. State superstructure, including the law and morality associated with commodity-exchange, will *precede* the dissolution of the State. Law has attained its developmental peak under capitalism; its decline and disappearance will herald the end of the State.

The political implications of Pashukanis' thought were construed as 'objectively anti-Soviet'. His subsequent denunciation as a 'wrecker' was based on an interpretation of his doctrine as a mask for the activities of the State's enemies. At a time when the proletarian nature of the State was receiving official recognition in the constitution, he had chosen to deny the necessity for proletarian law; at the very moment when discipline and obedience to the law were stressed as every citizen's duty, he was emphasising the temporary nature of the law; during a period of the strengthening of State power, he had decided to stress the withering away of the State. Law, which was being proclaimed as an instrument in the maintenance of 'revolutionary vigilance' was being explained by him in terms of commodity-exchange. Here, indeed, was the archetype of the 'intellectual wrecker of Soviet society'.

An evaluation of Pashukanis involves an examination of the doctrinal basis of his thought and his methodology. To a very large extent his work stands or falls according to one's reactions to Marxist jurisprudence as an expression of revolutionary doctrine. There is considerable doubt today as to the logic and veracity of the reasoning behind the economic interpretation of history upon which Pashukanis relies. The doctrines of the withering away of the State and 'base and superstructure' command little intellectual support and there seems to be a minimum of agreement on the worth of the 'laws of development of history' which Pashukanis uses to illustrate his theories.

Pashukanis' work has been dismissed as exemplifying the inadequacies of Marxist jurisprudence in general. Thus, the picture of societies dominated by legal structures based on the ideologies emanating from commodity-exchange is difficult to recognise in the records of economic and legal development. Commodity-exchange is merely one facet of the system of capitalism, and Pashukanis seems not to have noted the relationships arising from the *productive basis* of that system. It is not easy to see why a complex relationship involving producers and the market is to be analysed solely in terms of the final stages of commodity production and exchange. Pashukanis has been extraordinarily selective in his examination of the capitalist processes of production and exchange. The resultant legal theory is, of necessity, unbalanced.

Additionally, there appears to be a lack of empirical evidence to support the view of Pashukanis as to societies entirely dominated, in their economic and social development, by concepts of contract which embody ideas of commodity-exchange, and its significance. It is doubtful whether all primitive societies, with embryonic legal systems, utilised commodity-exchange transactions. It is suggested that Pashukanis was generalising from some few, highly-specific views concerning early development within some parts of Europe. An overall, universal theory has been erected on a narrow, insubstantial foundation.

Claims that Pashukanis made a distinctive contribution to historical jurisprudence by his insistence on the recognition of pre-commodity-exchange societies as lacking legal structures are difficult to substantiate. There are many instances of the existence of complex legal structures within pre-capitalist society. Law *did* pre-date capitalist society in England, for example. Indeed, the very vocabulary of our contemporary land law remains marked indelibly with its feudal origins. The systems of tenure and estates, complex and far-reaching in their effect during the era of feudalism, testify to the existence of legal concepts and appropriate structures. *De Donis Conditionalibus* 1285, estates in fee tail, knight service, indicate a wide and growing network of relationships based on a law existing long before the industrial revolution and the emergence of capitalist society in England.

There is doubt, too, as to the truth of Pashukanis' assertion that communal morality is but a reflection of the commodity-exchange basis of society. There are strong arguments suggesting that morality exists and develops outside the framework of economic relationships. Thus, attitudes in Western society to those acts 'whose harm is plain, grave and universally unwelcome' have not undergone changes which coincide with new eras of economic development. Murder, theft, assault, have been condemned through the ages; the refinement in attitudes towards these offences does not suggest fundamental changes in moral perceptions determined by commodity-exchange relationships.

Pashukanis' forecasts of legal events on the basis of his theoretical analysis of capitalism and socialism have, in the event, been rendered false. No new morality emerged in the Marxist-controlled States; in none of those regimes was there ever any evidence of the withering away of the State; in no Marxist regime was there every any inclination towards the replacement of the administration of persons by the administration of things. Judged by Lenin's own litmus test - 'the veracity of a theory can be tested only by action' - the lasting contribution of Pashukanis to jurisprudence is likely to be slight, save perhaps as a potent reminder of a system of legal thought placed at the service of a regime which could not tolerate any significant deviation from its proclaimed tenets of orthodoxy.

Notes

Pashukanis' *Law and Marxism - a General Theory* has appeared recently in a new translation by Einhorn, edited by Arthur; the volume contains an interesting biography and a critical assessment by the German jurist, Korsch. Lloyd, ch 11, and

Dias, ch 19, discuss Pashukanis' contribution to jurisprudence. Schlesinger's *Soviet Legal Theory* includes material on the commodity-exchange thesis. Articles on Pashukanis' legal thought include 'Pashukanis and Vyshinsky: a Study in the Development of Marxian Legal Theory' by Fuller ([1949] 47 Mich LR 1159), 'Pashukanis and the Commodity Form Theory' by Swann in the International Journal of Sociology of Law (1981)(9), and 'Pashukanis and Liberal Jurisprudence' by Simonds, [1985] 12 Journal of Law and Society 135.

Scandinavian Realism

Introduction

The school of Scandinavian realist jurisprudence is best known through the writings of its founder, Hägerström (1868-1939), Lundstedt (1882-1955), Olivecrona (b 1897) and Ross (b 1899). They were opposed to metaphysical speculation and were concerned with the general investigation of the 'fundamental facts' of legal systems. The nature of rights and duties was of particular interest to them. The questions in this chapter call for a knowledge of the general principles of the Scandinavian school, and of the jurisprudential thought associated with Olivecrona in particular.

Checklist

Ensure that you are acquainted with the following topics:

- mental constructs
- perception of rights and duties
- independent imperatives
- law as creating morality
- word-magic

Question 34

'It is not always easy to perceive the "realist" element in Scandinavian Legal Realism'.

Comment.

Answer plan

The essence of Scandinavian Realism is a reaction against 'pseudo-concepts' which are merely 'shams'. The reality may be discovered by an analysis of the facts. Assertions which cannot be proved, so-called 'inherent qualities' of legal concepts, are worthless. Law creates our morality, not vice-versa. The general principles of the Scandinavian approach require elucidation in the answer, together with a consideration of the criticism that, paradoxically, the Scandinavians have substituted their own 'non-realist' theory in place of the metaphysical speculation they attack. The following skeleton plan is suggested:

Introduction - the Scandinavian reaction against metaphysics - Hägerström's views and criticism of his teaching - Olivecrona's views and criticism of them - teachings of Lundstedt and reactions to them - views of Ross and views of the critics - conclusion, problems of the Scandinavian approach.

Answer

The Scandinavian Legal Realist movement involved, essentially, a reaction against the 'chimera of metaphysics', its inadequacies and distortions, and a concentration on the 'facts' of legal life. It shared few features of the approach of the American Realist movement. The Scandinavians are less concerned than the Americans with the behavioural aspects of adjudication, preferring to raise questions concerning the nature of rights and duties. The 'realism' of the Scandinavians rests in a critique of metaphysics, whereas the American realists are concerned with a pragmatic approach to legal institutions. The Scandinavian realists, Hägerström, Lundstedt, Olivecrona and Ross, were trained philosophers; the American realists were, in general, jurists, judges and teachers of law. Outlines of the views of the leading members of the Scandinavian school are given below, together with criticisms of their basic approach to the law. Whether their jurisprudential thought may be correctly classified as 'realist' will be suggested as open to doubt.

Initially, it is necessary to state the principal features of Scandinavian realism. First, metaphysics is rejected totally; it is interpreted as nothing more than a survival of mysticism, and a meaningless study, because its assertions and conclusions cannot be proved. 'What cannot be verified does not objectively exist.' Hence, objective values were non-existent; 'goodness', for example, is viewed as a mere emotional reaction of approval to certain types of stimulus. Its 'objectivity and absoluteness' are illusion. 'Natural law' jurisprudence is unacceptable - it can be made to support almost any facet of legal theory. In Ross' words:

'natural law is like a harlot - at the disposal of everyone'. A scientific probe of the basis of legal concepts such as 'rights' and 'duties' generally reveals mere conceptualisations which possess no real meaning because they have no counterpart in the physical world. 'Justice' is but feeling engendered by habit and a prevalent ideology which suggests that the legal order is adequate. If, say the Scandinavians, jurisprudence is to aspire to the status of a natural science, rooted in empiricism, it must act on the assumption that there is no cognition other than empirical.

Hägerström, founder of the Scandinavian school believed that metaphysical speculation distorts the 'true basis' of any appreciation of law. We tend to obey the law because of our psychological conditioning, not because of the law's 'inherent qualities'. 'Right' is a concept meaningless in itself: the 'right of ownership', he stated, has no empirical significance unless and until it is infringed and has become the subject matter of litigation. One cannot speak, therefore, of 'rights' in a context separated from remedies and enforcement procedures. Similarly, the concept of 'justice' (associated with rights) is, in itself, meaningless; it represents, says Hägerström, no more than a highly-subjective evaluation which cannot be examined scientifically. The origins of terms such as 'right', 'justice', can be traced to the use of 'word-magic' in ancient, arcane ceremonies. The use of ritual is, according to the Scandinavians, fundamental to the early days of the law, and words spoken in the form of incantation (as, for example, in the Roman ceremony of adoption) tend to give individuals feelings of *power*; hence their significance in law.

It is difficult to observe the 'realism' with which Hägerström claims to have replaced metaphysical interpretations of the law. The rejection of universal standards ('goodness', for example) stems from the questionable dogmas of logical positivism and its insistence on the 'verification' of all statements. (Logical positivism is itself a theory which has not been proved beyond doubt. Is it *ipso facto* an 'illusion'?) The view of 'justice' as meaningless seems somewhat exaggerated: its constituent features have been analysed repeatedly and there is broad general agreement on the desirability of many of them. The concept of word-magic is not always easy to support today. Thus, the words, 'I now pronounce you man and wife', which conclude the authorised marriage ceremony, are perceived correctly as indicating a change in status and a modification of rights and duties, and are acted on accordingly. Far from possessing a connotation of 'magic', they are understood as a precise indicator of the existence of a new relationship. There would seem to be little 'realism' in Hägerström's analysis; it is a highly-speculative interpretation of some aspects of the real world which does not, as a result, become more 'understandable'. The uncertainties of metaphysics have been exchanged for the abstraction of a so-called 'realist investigation'.

Olivecrona pursued the same line of enquiry using the same methodology. Rights, he insisted, are subjective ideas existing only within the mind; there can be no objective 'right' or 'duty'. Psychology will explain the growth, power and persistence of concepts of this nature. The connection between moral standards and the law is of much interest to Olivecrona. He suggests that the promulgation of legal rules and the threat of sanctions are 'internalised' in the form of 'imperative symbols' ('Thou shalt ...'), and when prohibited activities spring to the mind, they are imprinted with the symbols of communal disapproval. After the legal rules become dominant in an individual's psychology, their hold is increased by sanctions. It is the law, therefore, which creates our 'morality'.

Olivecrona produces no empirical evidence in support of his 'realist' theses; his generalisations concerning rights are based on little more than speculation. The suggestion that rights and duties are subjective phenomena, with no existence in the empirical world, would seem to be contradicted by the events which follow on the promulgation of rights. A right is more than a psychological 'feeling of power': it is a phenomenon, the existence of which may be inferred from the events which surround its creation, its enforcement and its infringement. Thus, the mortgagor's 'right' to require the mortgagee to transfer the mortgage to a third party (under the Law of Property Act 1925, s 95) is much more than a mere 'subjective feeling of power' enjoyed by the mortgagor. Further, Olivecrona's 'realism' applied to the question of law and morality produces its own problems. Is it possible to explain adequately in terms of 'law creating morality', the widespread abhorrence of murder, or the feelings against racism which preceded the Race Relations Act 1976? Olivecrona appears to be flying in the face of reality.

Lundstedt argues that feelings of justice do not direct the law; on the contrary, they are directed by the law. Law expresses social and economic interests - all else is illusion. Concepts such as 'guilt' operate only in the individual conscience and have no objective meaning. If we say that D, the defendant, 'acted wrongfully', this is a mere circumlocution for the precise fact that he was adjudged to pay damages. To talk of D's 'violating his duties' is to make a mere value judgment. Law is the result of social pressures reflecting 'inescapable societal needs', that is, 'social interests'.

Here, again, is one set of allegedly-inadequate abstractions exchanged for another set of abstractions. Lundstedt's view of justice has been criticised as a travesty of what has been understood and accepted very widely. 'Violation of duties' is, arguably, a reference to a proven phenomenon, and much more than a 'value judgment'. 'Social interests', which Lundstedt perceives as the basis of law, is itself an abstract concept which involves the very value judgments against which he inveighs.

Ross, too, stresses 'justice' as an expression of emotional feelings. Indeed, to invoke 'justice' is, he says, the same as 'banging on the table'; it is an emotional expression, transforming one's demands into an absolute postulate. Further, he says, to know the legal rules which govern the functioning of legal institutions is to know everything about the existence and extent of the law. Primary rules, which may exist only in the minds of citizens, inform them of how they are obliged to behave; they are followed with regularity, and psychological pressures ensure that they are 'binding'. Secondary rules ('directives') specify sanctions and the conditions under which they will operate. Confidence in, acquiescence towards, and obedience to, the rules is also underlined by their 'predictability'.

Ross' assumptions and interpretations lack supporting evidence. The hypothetical 'pressures' which are said to ensure the binding force of legal rules are conjecture and have not been investigated with the rigour generally used by psychologists in the investigation of theories of this nature. An absence of 'realist' methodology in Ross' work has been commented on by several critics.

The positive features of the Scandinavians' teachings ought not to be forgotten. The specialised vocabulary of the legal process ought not to be sacrosanct: words *can* obfuscate reality, verbal ambiguity may conceal contradiction, abstruseness may disguise error. Nor should any mystique attach to the functions of the law, as the Scandinavians point out. Yet it is difficult to ignore the unrealistic and sterile nature of much of their work. It has produced no useful answers to practical problems posed by jurists and lawyers and it has engendered no valuable discussion on the everyday activities of legal institutions. Its excessive concentration on semantic problems has not resulted in a 'realistic' approach to the law. The forceful rejection of terms such as 'right', 'duty' and 'justice', and their dismissal as mere subjective feelings, have little relevance for those for whom the protection and security offered by the law reside in acknowledgement of the 'reality' of these concepts.

The dismissal of concepts of 'duty', etc, as incapable of factual verification, as 'nonsense' (itself a quasi-metaphysical term), may derive from the fallacy of considering words *solely* as parts of empiric, factual statements, whereas they can be used legitimately in a *normative context*. Further, the suggestion that law creates our moral standards involves an unwarranted rejection of the significance of the community's sensibilities which, in practice, may provide the driving force behind the making and modification of the law. On a number of counts, therefore, doubt may be expressed as to the Scandinavians having produced a body of jurisprudential thought which can be characterised as 'realist' in the sense in which that term is generally understood by jurists.

Notes

The principal works of the Scandinavian Realists are: *Inquiries into the Nature of Law and Morals*, by Hägerström, translated by Broad, *Legal Thinking Revised*, by Lundstedt, *Law as Fact*, by Olivecrona, and *On Law and Justice* by Ross. Summaries of the general approach of the Scandinavians appear in Harris, ch 8, Friedmann, ch 25, Dias, ch 21. Extracts from the principal works mentioned above appear in Lloyd, ch 8, and Davies and Holdcroft, ch 14. Hart's review of 'Scandinavian Legal Realism' (1959) Cambridge LJ 233, is of particular interest.

Question 35

Outline Olivecrona's interpretation of the meaning of 'rights', and rules of law as 'commands'.

Answer plan

Olivecrona follows the general pattern of legal enquiry characteristic of the school of Scandinavian Realism. Law emerges from normative rules based on social facts; it exists through the individual imagination and is concerned with rules which contain patterns of conduct for the exercise of force. The term 'right' as generally used in jurisprudence 'lacks semantic reference', but the subjective idea of 'rights' is a *fact* which must be recognised. The concept of 'command' in relation to law has, he argues, confused the task of understanding legal activities. He presents an analysis of rules in terms of 'independent imperatives'. The following skeleton plan is used:

Introduction -Olivecrona's basic outlook - essence of rights - perception of rights and duties - directive and informative functions of rights - problems of the term 'command' - independent imperatives - conclusion, rights with a factual context.

Answer

Olivecrona sets out his views on 'rights' and the meaning of 'rules of law' in *Law as Fact*, which was published in 1939, and revised in 1971. His general aim was to fit the complex phenomena covered by the word 'law' into 'the spatio-temporal world'. This involves a discussion of mental concepts of 'rights' and an application of the principles of realism to a study of the rules inherent in enacted law. Fundamental to his investigation and analysis is the philosophical outlook of the Scandinavian school of jurisprudence, which demands a rejection of metaphysical speculation and a concentration on the 'real, objective facts' of legal life.

Hägerström, Olivecrona's mentor, had suggested that the reasons for the recognition of abstract conceptions of rights might be traced to historical and psychological sources; the former were to be found in ancient, arcane rituals, the latter were exemplified by the emotional 'power' experienced by an individual who believes that he has 'a just claim'. Olivecrona explored the psychological sources of 'rights', viewing the concept as a 'non-verifiable idea' which, however, could be explained in terms of the *fact* of those psychological feelings which move individuals to action. He considers the commonplace, paradoxical fact that individuals speak of 'rights' as though they exist, but rights cannot be shown to have 'existence'. The citizen is convinced that he possesses a variety of rights and duties - the right to vote and to receive his pension, the duty to repay loans and to refrain from stealing. He is *aware* that institutions exist for the purpose of adjudicating on disputes arising from an invasion of one's rights. Yet, Olivecrona asks, where *are* the empirical realities of 'rights' and 'duties'?

Olivecrona examines and rejects the Benthamist relationship of 'rights' and 'duties'. Bentham had said that it is by creating duties, and by nothing else, that the law creates rights. When the law gives *you* a right it makes *me* liable to punishment if *I* do something which disturbs *you* in the exercise of that right. This, says Olivecrona, is based on a circular definition - the law creates rights by creating duties, but the duties are merely obligations to refrain from disturbing rights. The concept of 'right' has been presupposed in the concept of 'duty'.

Fundamental legal concepts, such as 'rights' and 'duties' belong, says Olivecrona, to the common hoard of concepts needed by people in their everyday contacts and transactions. When we buy, sell, hire, borrow, we require a conceptual understanding (no matter how vague) of what we are *doing*. We *expect* to receive what we have paid for, we are *aware* of the consequences of leaving a debt unpaid, we act on the basis of *expectations* and *awareness*. The mental constructs of 'right' and 'duty' are, in Olivecrona's view, 'vehicles for attaining practical ends', and they enable us to receive and convey information about events in which we are involved. We make personal interpretations of the changes effected in our position within society as the result of our obeying or disobeying rules. It is our *feelings* concerning what we may or may not do which constitute the basis of our perceived 'rights' and 'duties'.

A 'right' may be viewed in terms of 'feelings' and 'sensations of power'. The existence of, say, a document of title to property creates mental constructs ('feelings') or sensations of compulsion or restraint. A 'right' has been perceived. The presence of these feelings may be explained as impressions passed, visually or auditively, to the mind and creating the illusion that we have power over some object. Illusion stems from emotional background. Under certain conditions, particularly in situations of conflict, the idea of possessing a right produces a feeling of strength. The subjective ideas of right cannot be excised from a consideration of 'law as fact'. Their existence is a fact of psychological interpretation - but no more.

'Rights' as mental constructs may have, according to Olivecrona, two functions, directive and informative. The 'directive function' of a 'right' results from the part it plays in, say, commercial transactions when it directs human behaviour. It erects signposts needed to guide conduct. Responses to perceived 'rights' ('You have a right to this property and, therefore, I must react in a certain way') become part of general practice. Eventually these practices may be backed by the power of the State. The 'informative function' of 'rights' is evident where, for example, a person is told that, 'This house belongs to X'. It is not possible, argues Olivecrona, to explain *precisely* what this statement means without referring to the 'rights' of property. The use of the concept 'right' is needed to provide information as to the *nature* of X's title.

'Right' is, therefore, in Olivecrona's reasoning, little more than a useful mental construct. It exists as a 'fact' solely in terms of the 'feelings' its use engenders.

Olivecrona applies his non-metaphysical style of investigation to a study of the rules of law, which he perceives as essentially mental constructs. In general, he declares, it is possible to consider rules of law as 'ideas of imaginary actions'. To apply the rules of law involves using these imaginary actions as *mental models* for actual conduct when corresponding situations are seen to occur in real life.

Is a rule of law a 'command', in the accepted sense of that term? May we correctly interpret, say, the Criminal Justice Act 1991, s 78(1) ('Any person who assaults a court security officer acting in the execution of his duty shall be liable to ... a fine ... or imprisonment ... or to both') as a 'command' not to perform a specified act? Olivecrona is doubtful. A 'command', he claims, presupposes one *person* who commands, and another to whom the command is addressed. But the enormous quantity of rules in the law of a modern State cannot be said to represent the commands of any one human being; this is why such commands are ascribed to the State. Yet the State cannot be said to 'command'. The expression is a loose statement indicating, in reality, that the commands are given by persons 'active in the organisations' of the State. The command relating to assaulting a court security official emanates from the State, from Parliament, and not from any single individual. 'Command' cannot be used here, says Olivecrona, in its 'proper sense'.

It is possible to regard the rules of law as 'independent imperatives'. Although Olivecrona believes that the rules are not real 'commands', they are given in the imperative form ('Any person ... shall be liable ...'). It *shall* be an offence for a person to perform a proscribed act. But because a 'command' in the 'proper sense', according to Olivecrona, implies a *personal relationship*, we are not dealing with a 'true' command. A true command is given by X to Y in words or gestures intended to influence Y's will and his subsequent actions. The words, 'You will perform this action', or a gesture implying 'You will not continue the activity upon which you are now engaged', constitute a command which is personal to X and Y. Nevertheless, the same type of words may be used to the same effect where there are no personal relations whatsoever between the individual who issues rules and those who receive and act upon them. Clearly, the Criminal Justice Act 1991 is not issued by any one person and is certainly not directed to any one individual. It is a generalised statement which functions independently of the context of 'personal command'. It functions as an 'independent imperative'.

It is not possible, argues Olivecrona, to make a *clear* distinction between a command and an independent imperative. He suggests that as the distance between the persons involved grows, so the command assumes the nature of an independent imperative. There is, for example, a difference in immediate perceptions of the 'personal relationship' existing between the motorist commanded in personal terms by a police officer to produce his driving licence, and the 'independent imperative' of the statute sanctioning the conduct of the police officer. It is our general habits of language which allow us to think in *identical terms* of *commands* and *imperatives*. The sight of a padlocked door (interpreted as 'Keep out'), of traffic lights (interpreted as 'Stop' and 'Go'), a perusal of an Act of Parliament, are transformed into the essential features of a command or an imperative.

Olivecrona gives an example of 'independent imperatives' by referring to the Ten Commandments, divinely revealed to Moses on Mount Sinai. The words of the Commandments are said to be the very commands of God, and have been accepted as such. But in reality, Olivecrona argues, they are a 'bundle of imperatives' carried down the centuries by oral tradition and in writing. They have the form of language characteristic of a command ('Thou shalt ...'); but they are 'nobody's words'. The rules of law, Olivecrona maintains, are of a similar character. Thus, in our day, the rules of law are generally independent imperatives that have passed through a series of formal procedures, eg, in Parliament, and have been promulgated. People 'feel' that they are bound by such rules. Olivecrona would insist that they have been 'conditioned' to think about the rules in a manner which *urges* them to comply with orders of a particular type and couched in a certain format. The power of the issuing authority is perceived at all levels of social existence: ceremonies, traditional reverence, interact so as to produce upon citizens the 'mental context' within which imperatives are accepted as 'objectively binding'.

The binding force of the 'independent imperatives' which constitute the law is, therefore, a reality. But in the external world, says Olivecrona, nothing can be found which corresponds to the idea of that binding force, of those imperatives. It must, nevertheless, be taken into account in an investigation of what makes the law. Olivecrona's conclusions are a direct consequence of the rejection of metaphysics; the features of the law are discernible, but only in 'factual circumstances'. Rights, rules of law, may be interpreted as concepts within a context of facts. Divorced from this context, they are without meaning and, therefore, without significance, in an investigation of the nature of law.

Notes

Lloyd, ch 9, and Davies and Holdcroft, ch 14, include extracts from Olivecrona's writings. Harris, ch 8, and Bodenheimer, ch 9, give the essential outlines of Olivecrona's thought. Articles by Olivecrona include 'Legal Language and Reality', in *Essays in honour of Pound*, edited by Newman, and 'The Imperative Element in Law' [1964] 18 Rutgers LR 774.

American Realism

Introduction

The American Realist movement grew during the 1930s from the philosophical views associated with James and Dewey. Both rejected 'closed systems, pretended absolutes and origins' and turned towards 'facts, action and powers'. James insisted upon the study of 'factual reality'; Dewey called for an investigation of probabilities in law and reminded jurists that 'knowledge is successful practice'. The realists studied law on the basis of a rejection of 'myths and preconceived notions' and on the acceptance of recording accurately things as they are, as contrasted with things as they ought to be. A true science of law demands a study of law in action. 'Law is as law does'. The four jurists noted in this chapter are Frank (1889-1957), Llewellyn (1893-1962), Holmes (1841-1985) and Loevinger (b 1913).

Checklist

Ensure that you are acquainted with the following topics:

- legal certainty
- judicial hunches
- law jobs and job clusters
- grand and formal style in judicial reasoning
- law as what the courts do
- jurimetrics
- behavioural research

Question 36

What part was played in Frank's analysis of law by his perception of 'legal uncertainty'?

Answer plan

Frank was motivated in his writings by a strong desire to reform the law in the interests of justice. The law could not be separated from the decisions of the courts. It was necessary, therefore, to understand the real bases of judicial decisions; they were to be found in a variety of factors, some often irrational. A knowledge of legal rules was not in itself adequate for the successful prediction of the courts' decisions. Legal uncertainty, which reflected the wider natural phenomenon of the impossibility of 'complete definiteness', was of fundamental significance in an understanding of the law. The following skeleton answer is suggested:

> Introduction -Frank as fact-sceptic - why we search for certainty - difficulties of prediction in face of judges' and juries' preconceptions - significance of judicial discretion - the judicial 'hunch' - criticism of Frank's 'cult of the single decision' - Frank's propositions concerning legal uncertainty - conclusion, need to qualify some of Frank's views.

Answer

Frank, a jurist who served on the United States Court of Appeals for the Second Circuit, was a self-styled 'fact-sceptic' and investigated the problem of certainty and uncertainty in trials in the American lower courts. His work was, essentially, a reaction against the 'rule sceptics' who had objected to the unreliability of 'paper rules' (ie, those formal legal rules expressed in the opinions of the courts) used as guidelines in the prediction of decisions. Behind the 'paper rules' they sought to discern 'real rules' which would reveal uniformities and regularities allowing more reliable predictions. Frank opposed the concept of 'decision-forecasting through the legal rules'; as a fact-sceptic he believed that the very elusiveness of the facts upon which decisions depend made reliable prediction almost impossible, and that attempts at increased 'legal certainty' were largely futile. The fallibility of witnesses, the prejudices (often unconscious) of judges and juries, made the accurate prediction of decisions very difficult. Certainty in forecasting was not possible.

Why, asked Frank, do we seek for an 'unrealisable certainty' in the law? Why is there a 'basic legal myth' that the law is defined and settled completely? Frank's answer utilises Freudian psychology. Because we have not given up 'the childish need for an authoritative father', we unconsciously seek in the law a substitute for the attribute of firmness and certainty ascribed in childhood to the father. Allen attacks Frank's explanation, pointing out that it is unnecessary to seek Freudian explanations for the simple fact that, in a precarious existence, men search for certainty, and those who are uncertain about their legal rights wish freedom from their doubts. For Frank, however, the situation is clear: the quest for certainty in the law derives from irrational desires.

Proof of the uncertainty of the fact-finding process in the lower courts emerges, according to Frank, from an investigation of the performance of juries and witnesses. Juries have the task of determining matters of fact, but they are partly conditioned by prejudices and unconscious beliefs. They may find difficulty in comprehending evidence, so that accurate prediction of their decisions is rarely possible. (An English trial in 1991 is instructive: defendants were accused of assisting in the escape from prison of a convicted spy, after they had written a book admitting their part in his escape and justifying their actions. In the event, the jury returned a verdict of not guilty.) Frank also points out that witnesses' reactions to past events may be coloured significantly by subjectivity. If, he notes, a trial court, by believing a perjured witness, decides 'that a deed is a mortgage', the court's legal rule may be sound, but the wrong litigant will be successful. Secret, unconscious and private norms applied by witnesses and juries to the fact-finding process are powerful contributory factors to 'legal uncertainty' in the lower courts.

The existence and exercise by judges of discretionary powers also bring uncertainties to the legal process. Discretion - the power which resides in a court to decide a question in circumstances where some latitude of judgement is allowed - ought to be exercised 'properly'. But, in practice, says Frank, judges demonstrate an 'amazing discretion' in finding the facts. 'Guessy choices' affect the exercise of discretion, making the outcome of a case impossible to predict.

May not certainty in prediction be assisted by reference to the judge's *written* opinion? Frank denies this emphatically. In his study, *What Courts Do In Fact* (1932), he suggests that the judge's opinion, set in the written form, gives merely an *appearance* of certainty, but this is largely an afterthought. It does not include many of the factors which induced the judge to decide as he did. His written opinion is often *ex post facto* and is no more than an eviscerated, censored exposition, a study of which cannot be a basis for a successful forecast of future decision.

It is in his analysis of the ways in which judges arrive at their decisions that Frank claims to find the key to the inevitability of uncertainty in the legal process. The background of the judge's decisions is the outcome of his *entire* life history: he cannot put to one side the effects of his upbringing, education, religious and political beliefs. Often the judge will be unaware of the significance, even the existence, of this set of factors. Concealed, highly-idiosyncratic biases cannot but contribute to uncertainty in forecasting judicial decisions.

A judge arrives at his decision, according to Frank, by a 'hunch' as to what is fair, wise and expedient. Allen describes the 'hunch' as 'a mere spasm, so to speak, of an incalculable intuitionism'. Frank seems to use the term to indicate a complex, but inspired, guess as a reaction to circumstances; it cannot be described in terms of legal rules and principles. He suggests a mathematical formula: let S be the stimuli in the given circumstances; let P be the judge's personality; and let D be the decision. Then $SP = D$. He stresses the looseness of these symbols and draws attention to the innumerable stimuli involved, and the complicated phenomena which make up the judge's personality. The formula emphasises Frank's belief in the ultimate uncertainty and, therefore, unpredictability, of judicial decisions.

Frank's view of the uncertain 'private hunch', leading to the unpredictable, personalised decision has been criticised. It is suggested that Frank is unduly magnifying personal and accidental factors and seeking to deny the relevance of certain significant determinants in the legal process. Law is not a mere mass of unrelated decisions, nor is it a product of 'judicial bellyaches'. Judges are trained in disciplined modes of thinking and conduct and they operate within a system in which precedent is potent and the importance of rules is obvious. Cohen has suggested that decisions cannot be interpreted validly as mere expressions of individual personality; they can be viewed as a function of *social forces*, that is, a product of social determinants and an index of social consequences. A judicial decision, says Cohen, is a 'social event', an 'intersection of social forces, which cannot be viewed in its true significance at the moment it is announced'. Further, if, as Frank suggests, reasonably certain predictions can *never* be made as to the outcome of legal proceedings, then so-called legal decisions are mere 'noises', signifying little save highly-individual reactions to particular data.

Other criticisms have been directed to Frank's 'cult of the single decision'. For Frank, the law consists of decisions: the single judgment in a given case *is* the law. Prior to that decision, the only law available rests, presumably, on the guesses of lawyers as to what, in the particular circumstances, the court might do. Frank stated his view in the following terms: law, concerning a given situation is either *actual law* (based on specific past decisions as to that situation) or *probable law* (a guess as to a particular future decision). In Cardozo's words: the law never *is*, but is always 'about to be'. When embodied in a decision, the law is 'realised' and, in being 'realised', it expires. Other jurists suggest that Frank's formulation ignores the significance of agreed rules, conventions, 'judicial protocol', in the administration of a law which has its basis in an accepted repertoire of responses within defined limits.

Frank summed up his views on 'legal uncertainty' in a group of propositions. Specific and enforceable decisions, such as judgments and decrees, in given cases, are the essential feature of the lawyer's work; anything else is subsidiary. Specific decisions in particular cases are the result of the judge's 'hunches'. So-called 'legal rules and principles' are among the many 'hunch-producers'. Whatever may be considered as the stimuli for the making of 'hunches', those stimuli operate through their effects on the judge's personality. It is not possible to state in terms of legal rules and principles phenomena such as 'background stimuli' or 'personality'. The failure to recognise the composite, complex nature of the judge's 'hunch', and the artificial separation within the judicial process of 'rules' and 'facts', explain, in part, the incorrect evaluations of the 'rules'. Legal formalists (ie, those who assert that judicial reasoning is based on logical deductions from appropriate rules applicable in given situations) are wrong because they tend to overlook the highly-subjective nature of some 'facts' in contested cases. The legal formalist neglects the influence of the jury in ascertaining the facts; the jury contributes its own uncertainties and subjectivities to this process.

General objections to Frank's perception of the significance of 'uncertainty in law' have been raised by jurists who doubt the accuracy of his methods of analysis. It seems that much of his 'evidence' for the role of the 'hunch' rests on anecdote. There is little empirical evidence to support his wider conclusions. His theory is an attempt to state a psychological principle and ought to be backed by the type of data expected from workers in this area of enquiry. If we assume, for example, that a judge makes a decision in a case turning on abortion, who is to say, and on what evidence may it be asserted positively or denied, that his religious beliefs have affected, or not affected, that decision?

To criticise Frank is not to deny that judges' 'hunches' *may* affect their decisions; but judges *do* have common standards by which facts and their significance are evaluated. Further, there are areas of law within which judges may not exercise discretion. Precedent and statute often provide clear rules which are intended to be followed. Hence, Frank's stark view that, fundamentally, there is no certainty in the law, save in a trivial sense, is not easy to accept without considerable qualification. Communal life in our society is based on the necessity for regularity and certainty in relation to the operations of the legal system. Commercial activity on a large scale, for example, presupposes relative certainties, such as are embodied within the law of contract. Judicial decisions - often conflicting - on matters of offer and acceptance have not undermined reliance on the 'near-certainties' of the Sale of Goods Act 1979. Lord Templeman's doubts as to the precise nature of leases and licences, expressed in the House of Lords, in *Street v Mountford* (1985), have not demolished the overall structure which supports our landlord-tenant law. The doubt which may lead to a less-than-absolute certainty cannot be eradicated from our forms of legal procedure.

The maintenance of complex social structures does demand from the law a general trend towards certainty: that is not to be denied. But this is a long way from Frank's assertion concerning the role of 'legal uncertainty'. It is to his credit that his theories continue to remind jurists of the multiplicity of those factors making the background within which the law operates. In Mill's words: 'Effects are commonly determined by a concurrence of causes'. The delineation and interpretation of these causes remain on the agenda for contemporary jurists who seek to discover the nature of law.

Notes

Among Frank's important works are *Law and the Modern Mind* (published in a UK edition in 1949) and 'What Courts Do in Fact' [1932] 26 Ill LR 645. There are discussions of Frank in Allen, ch 1, Riddall, ch 13, and Dias, ch 21. A useful commentary on Frank's approach to legal procedure is given by Cohen in 'Transcendental Nonsense and the Functional Approach' [1935] Col LR 809.

Question 37

Explain the concept of 'law jobs' in relation to Llewellyn's theory of law.

Answer plan

Llewellyn's contribution to American Realism was based on his insistence that rules had to be considered by examining the way in which they worked. Rules are, therefore, what they do. If society is to survive and progress, certain tasks ('jobs') must be carried out. Delineation of 'law jobs' and an examination of their implications for legal institutions constituted an important task for the jurist. The following skeleton plan is suggested:

Introduction -essence of rules in practice - basic functions of law seen as 'law jobs' - description of five 'law jobs' - style as an aspect of judicial reasoning - conclusion, general criticisms of Llewellyn's approach to law.

Answer

Llewellyn was a leading exponent of the principles of the American Realist movement - he was careful not to describe it as a 'school', using the word 'movement' to describe its thinking and investigation concerning law in society. Essentially a rule-sceptic, he argued that the rules of substantive law were less significant for the actual practice of law than had been suggested; the theory of 'rules deciding cases' had fooled even the judiciary. Rules were, in practice, little more than generalised predictions of what the courts will do. Realism, for Llewellyn, involves the acceptance of a law in flux and a society which changes faster than the law.

A basic premise of Llewellyn's concept of law is its interpretation as a means to social ends. The law may be considered as 'an engine', having certain purposes, but no values in itself. The social ends of law are in assisting the very survival of society and aiding the search for justice and a richer existence. Any part of the law should be examined, therefore, in terms of *purpose and effect*. Law is, fundamentally, a 'technology', or *an institution organised around the performance of necessary tasks*. The concepts of 'law as institution' and the vital nature of *law jobs* are at the centre of Llewellyn's analysis of law in society.

By 'institutions', Llewellyn had in mind a complex of organised activities centred on the performance of groups of tasks ('job clusters'). An institution, in his sense of that term, comprises techniques, precepts, rules and an ideology, all put to service in the great task of ensuring society's survival and its success in the quest for justice. A *major* institution is involved with fundamental tasks; *minor* institutions such as 'crafts' (which are considered below) relate essentially to skills, such as the practice of the law. The very concept of an institution provides 'points of orientation' allowing the monitoring of what is being achieved. An institution has defined jobs to perform and its function is to do this effectively. This, says Llewellyn, gives 'a pole and purpose and value to measure them by'. Additionally, the institution has 'results in life'; it must be tested by reference to those results. The real measure of an institution, in Llewellyn's sense, is an evaluation of 'how its results check in fact', ie, how it has performed its jobs. In practical terms, the day-to-day needs of the community will dictate the workings of 'law as institution', and open investigation will determine its success.

The basic functions of the law - the execution of law jobs - are related to social ends. If society is to survive, organisation of social matters must be effected and kept effective. Five fundamental law jobs have emerged, and they are considered by Llewellyn as universal and essential for most societies and groups. *First*, there is the disposition (ie, adjustment) of 'trouble cases' - possibly the most important of the law's tasks. *Second*, the 'preventing channelling of conduct and expectations' in order to avoid conflict and trouble. *Third*, the allocation and exercise of authority or jurisdiction within the group or society. *Fourth*, the provision of direction and incentive. *Fifth*, the provision of a juristic method.

The 'disposition of trouble cases', ie, wrongs, grievances, disputes, is of much importance. Llewellyn refers to it as 'garage repair work' (work of a basic nature which has to be done properly), with a continuous effect upon the existence and refashioning of society's structure. The performance of law jobs of this nature will provide new material for the doing of other jobs, and enough of this kind of activity must be carried out if society is to remain a coherent group. Jobs of this type will test which rules do prevail in reality, rather than in legal legend.

'Positive channelling' refers to areas of actual or potential conflict. The carrying out of this law job is intended to produce and maintain a 'going order' rather than a 'series of collisions and consequent disputes'. The allocation of authority and the arrangement of procedures which will legitimise action as being 'authoritative' are referred to by Llewellyn as 'arranging the say, and its saying'. He gives the example of a period of crisis in which there may occur conflict as to what to do and whose opinion is to guide action. Matters of this nature ought to be settled in advance of an actual crisis, procedures should have been worked out, powers decided and legitimised. The problems arising involve constitutions, the working of legislatures, modes of adjudication and the defining of limits on authority.

These three law jobs may be considered as defining the 'bare-bones' aspect of law: their major concern is with the maintaining of the life and cohesion of the group. From the operations associated with these jobs may emerge further tasks, related to the 'quest' for the true ends of society's legal endeavours - in Llewellyn's poetic phrase, 'the Whither of the net Totality'. Hence a fourth focus of law jobs concerns the total net effect of the previous three. The job of providing direction, incentive and social integration becomes essential for the organisation of society as an integrated, purposeful entity.

The fifth law job - ' juristic method' - involves 'law as technology', namely, 'the handling of legal tools'. The 'on-going upkeep and improvement of law matters' becomes important. It embraces the reform of legislation and the traditions and skills of 'the official craftsmen of the law'.

Llewellyn explains that around the performance of various clusters of law jobs will grow distinct activities from which it will become possible to discern and analyse 'the stuff of law'. When men begin to specialise in these activities it becomes possible to recognise 'the men of law'. Regularities in action are revealed and standards concerning the direction and manner of such action become clear. From the conjunction of men and activities in relation to law jobs there will emerge the craftsmen of the law and their crafts - 'Law's People'. The crafts of the law, which Llewellyn characterises as forming 'a minor institution', include advocacy, adjudication, law-making; these are essentially the specialities which, through education and example, are transmitted from one generation to another in the form of organised, methodical groups of skills.

One of the most important crafts of the law is, according to Llewellyn, 'judicial reasoning'. He provides a detailed study of two, polarised, aspects of judicial reasoning which he discusses under the general heading of 'period style'. Style may be discerned, in particular, in the performance of the law job concerned with the settling of disputes. In the common law jurisdictions may be perceived the 'grand style' and the 'formal style'; these titles refer to the courts' methods of thought and other activity, not merely to modes of legal writing, ie, they refer to the manner of *doing jobs*. It is important to note Llewellyn's attitude to 'words and deeds' in the law. *Before there were rules there were facts.* 'In the beginning was not a Word, but a Doing.' The words produced by a judge are merely a by-product of 'the doing'. Hence, when Llewellyn speaks of 'style', he has in mind much more than, say, a written decision handed down by an appellate court - the words comprising the decision are but one part of a whole set of activities.

The 'grand style' derives from the judge's appeal to *reason*. It attempts to minimise uncertainty and seeks to reduce any perceived conflict between the demands of justice and the commands of authorities; it produces, and improves on, rules which 'make sense on their face'. Precedent is not followed without good reason, and attention is paid to *principle* in evaluating the weight to be given to past, relevant decisions. Judges who adopt this style show what Llewellyn describes as 'situation sense' - they view a case in hand, not as a once-for-all matter, but as likely to involve a rule which may be used as a reference point for other, similar cases in the future. The 'grand style' seems to have been prevalent in American law during the early part of the nineteenth century - its 'creative phase'.

The 'formal style', which can be discerned in the execution of the law job related to the settling of disputes, owes much to reliance on rules of law rather than to any perception of the demands of 'policy' (which concern the legislature in particular). The style is one which is demanded by an orthodox ideology, speaking in stock, precise terms. 'Sense and the ways of men with words, the ways of business men in their dealings' are considered irrelevant or out-of-place. Adherence to this style often denotes 'a perverse drive for strong opinions'. Statutes which appear to be inconsistent with these strong opinions are regarded and dealt with as 'enemy invaders'. The 'formal style' is often characterised by the deductive form of reasoning and by expressions of what Llewellyn termed 'single line inevitability'. This style seems to have dominated the American courts during the second half of the nineteenth century. At the time of Llewellyn's publication of his theses (1960) he appeared to have detected a move by the American appellate courts in the direction of the 'grand tradition'. But, he warned, the influence of the formal style has not lost its grip; it continues to offer a standard style for the writing of judicial opinions, although its 'ancient aspect of a deep, unquestioned and powerful faith' is no longer as pervasive as it once was.

Llewellyn's approach to the law - novel, iconoclastic and couched in a strange style which owes much to his interest in anthropology and his poetry - produced a strong reaction among his fellow-jurists. His attitude to the significance of rules within the legal process has been rejected as based on an incorrect perception of the *function* of rules. Rules, say the critics, have to be studied, not as formal isolates, but in action. A judge who ignores rules as a guide to action may be substituting mere arbitrariness for certainty. The reality is that rules *are* studied, *are* observed and *are* rarely neglected. Indeed, the judge is himself a product of rules - his appointment stems from precisely-formulated rules and regulations (consider, in our system, the effect of the Courts and Legal Services Act 1990, s 71 and Schedule 10, upon the appointment to judicial office), his activities are hemmed about by a variety of specific rules and regulations, and the execution of his judgments will be in strict accordance with rules. It is one thing to criticise the *interpretation* of the place of rules within the legal process, but quite another to play down their strength in the process of adjudication and ensuring the growth of a legal order. (Some critics remind us that Llewellyn's feelings concerning the significance of rules did not prevent his producing a detailed, uniform commercial code which was adopted in several American States.)

Llewellyn's emphasis on the dichotomy of words and actions in the formulation of judicial decisions has been condemned as bizarre and unrealistic. We are asked to distinguish the judge's 'actions' from his 'real intentions and meanings', but how this is to be done is not clear. Fuller asks: just what do we *mean* by a judge's 'actions' as distinguished from intention and meaning? 'Is it a movement of the arms or jaw? Is it a movement at all, and if not, what is it?' Is it possible to describe a judge's actions without referring in that description to his reasoning?

Criticisms of Llewellyn tend increasingly to centre upon his confusion of 'actions' and 'intentions' as demonstrated in judicial reasoning. His concept of 'law jobs' remains of significance. The uncovering of the functions which the law sets out to perform in pursuit of social ends draws attention to law as *a means to an end* - an essential feature of the general interpretation of law favoured by American Realists.

Notes

Examples of Llewellyn's writings include: 'Some Realism about Realism' (1931) 44 Harv LR 1222; 'The Normative, The Legal, and the Law Jobs: The Problem of Juristic Method' (1940) 49 Yale LJ 1373, and *The Common Law Tradition*. Twining's *Karl*

Llewellyn and the Realist Movement is a valuable account of American Realism. Summaries of Llewellyn's thought appear in Lloyd, ch 8, Dias, ch 21, and Davies and Holdcroft, ch 15.

Question 38

'You see how the vague circumference of the notion of duty shrinks and at the same time grows more precise when we wash it with cynical acid and expel everything except the object of our study, the operations of the law': Holmes.

In what ways does this observation characterise Holmes' view of the 'path of the law'?

Answer plan

Holmes exerted very great influence as a jurist and a long-serving member of the Supreme Court. He inspired the American Realist movement with a jurisprudential theory based on the need to 'think things, not words'. The examination of facts must dominate legal investigation. The object of a study of the law is 'prediction', ie, 'the prediction of the incidence of the public force through the instrumentality of the courts'. The study of the law's operations demands that the law be kept in focus and that it be investigated in a methodical, realistic fashion. The following skeleton plan is used:

Introduction -Holmes' emphasis on objective investigation - importance of removing extraneous factors from an investigation - law as more than mere logic - operations of the courts - criticisms of Holmes' approach - conclusion, significance for Holmes of pragmatism.

Answer

Almost a century has passed since Holmes published *The Path of the Law* (1897), which assisted in the provision of a theoretical basis for American Realism. Holmes, whose long career included thirty years as a member of the Supreme Court (an experience which contributed to his declared views on the significance of the judiciary in the American legal process), stressed that the essence of the 'realist' contribution to jurisprudence was to be found in the careful *examination and verification of factual data*. Concepts incapable of verification (such as 'the vague notion of duty') had to be scrapped. The jurist should be guided by what a contemporary of Holmes referred to as 'the humility of the experimental scientist' who wastes no time in worrying about the absence of 'ultimates'. In Holmes' early writings, such as *The Path of the Law*, there is emphasis on the need to identify problems and to investigate them by keeping one's observations uncontaminated by irrelevancies. The application of 'cynical acid' should remove extraneous factors, allowing the true form and proportions of problems to emerge. By studying the real operations of law one would discover the facts which constituted 'the law'.

This quasi-scientific approach involved a deliberate exclusion from the pattern of study of 'every word of moral significance'. This was not to suggest that society's moral standards were of no consequence. They were, however, rarely significant for an analysis of *operational* matters. Indeed, Holmes suggested, it might be advantageous for the jurist if he were to use only words which could carry legal ideas uncoloured by matters outside the law.

Holmes illustrated the importance of 'dissolving' extraneous irrelevance, by reference to the notion of 'legal duty'. We have filled the word 'duty' with a content drawn from morality. But when we wash away from the phrase 'legal duty' its moral overtones we are left with 'duty' viewed in terms of the *consequences* for those who break the law. It is what the law *does* (as seen in sanctions, for example) that gives 'duty' its real meaning and significance. The law of contract provides further examples of confusion engendered by the use of 'moral phraseology'. The concept of 'irrefragable undertakings', with its high-sounding overtones of moral purpose, should be washed away from any study of the principles of contract as known to business men. Remove the irrelevancies and discover the realities of the contractual relationship: this is the guidance to be given to those who seek to discover the meaning of the law.

Holmes considers it necessary to expose as a fallacy, which has affected investigation of the law, the notion that 'the only force at work in the development of the law is logic'. On the contrary, *the life of the law has been, not logic, but experience.* In a very broad sense, he argues, it may be true that the law is partly the result of some kind of logical development, but the danger is in a confusion among jurists relating to the *logical format* of a judicial decision and the inarticulate, unconscious attitudes of judges as to the relative worth and significance of competing claims. The language of logic, which may be used to provide the 'wrappings' of a decision may mask 'the very root and nerve' of unconscious determinants of legal judgments. To understand the precise reasons behind a judgment requires, in Holmes' colourful language, the 'acid' of an investigation which will 'eat away' expressive formalities and the confusion of logic with legal principle, exposing at the heart of the problem a shifting array of preferences and values - often unacknowledged.

In *The Common Law* (1923) Holmes repeats and elaborates his injunction to jurists to discount the part supposedly played by logical reasoning in the courts' processes of adjudication. The rules by which men should be governed may owe something to formal modes of logical expression (such as the syllogism), but this must not be exaggerated. The role played by the perceived 'necessities of the time', prevalent political ideologies, intuitions concerning public policy, shared prejudices, cannot be over-emphasised in considering the basis of the law. Indeed, law may be seen as the embodiment of a nation's long development; it cannot be interpreted in terms of mere logic. Hence it is important that lawyers and judges be well-acquainted with the historical and social contexts of the law they administer. To be a master of the law, one must master the branches of knowledge that lie next to it. Anthropology, history, should not be neglected by the jurist.

Holmes stated clearly what he understood by 'the law'. In his celebrated epigrammatic definition, which became one of the starting points of American 'functional' jurisprudence, he notes: *'The prophecies of what the courts will do in fact, and nothing more pretentious, are what I mean by the law'.* This is an application of the doctrine of 'washing away with cynical acid' the so-called 'logical certainties', the 'moral essence', of the law. Concentrate upon the law in action; the data produced will lend themselves to an interpretation of law as reality.

It has been objected repeatedly that Holmes' observation is, simply, incorrect. Cohen, in his analysis of 'definition in law' suggests that the real test of a definition is whether it is useful or useless. The words of a definition carry their own problems of ambiguity. 'What courts do' is a phrase heavy with a variety of meanings. Does it have equal application to *all* types of court? The magistrates' courts as well as the House of Lords? Is there a significant distinction between what courts *do* and what they *say*, given the fact that many jurists and lawyers tend to perceive most 'judicial behaviour' as verbal? It may be that the real value of Holmes' definition is in its drawing attention to operations, to the functioning, of the courts. It is arguable, however, whether or not the definition advances our understanding of the *basis* of law. Goodhart criticised Holmes' formulation by suggesting that 'Law is what the courts do' can be no more satisfactory to the jurist than the statement, 'Medicine is what the doctor gives you'.

In an interesting extension of his argument concerning the perception of the essential features of law, Holmes suggested that if one wants to know the 'real law', and nothing else, one ought to consider it from the point of view of 'the bad man' who cares only for the material consequences which such knowledge enables him to predict. Do not, he urged, take into account the point of view of 'the good man', who may find reasons for his conduct in 'the vaguer sanctions of conscience'. The 'bad man' cares nothing for axioms or deductions; he wants to know what 'the Massachusetts or the English courts' are likely to do *in fact*. 'I am much of his mind', declares Holmes. It is the *consequence* of the mode of operations of the courts which is of importance; this constitutes, in reality, 'the law'. The events which follow on, say, failure to register a registrable land charge, under the Land Charges Act 1972, or the pickpocket's placing his hand into an empty pocket, intending to steal, as interpreted under the Criminal Attempts Act 1981, constitute parts of 'the law'.

Although Holmes draws attention to the importance of consequences of the courts' decisions, he is emphatic in his belief that the making of laws is the business, not of the courts, but of the legislative bodies within communities. He proclaims the urgency of recognising the principle that the people have the right to make, through their elected representatives, whatever legislation they feel to be necessary, given the needs of the community. Further, he reminds judges of their important duty of 'weighing considerations of social advantage'. The training of lawyers ought to lead them, and judges, 'habitually to consider more definitely and explicitly' the advantages to society of the rules they lay down. The workings of the legislature and the courts should not be seen in isolation from the societies from which they spring and from which alone they derive their significance.

To view the law in its true relationships, clearly, and free from linguistic and moral overtones which distort the picture, forms the basis of the advice which Holmes offers to jurists who seek to understand the reality of the legal process. In investigating the work of the courts one must keep in mind William James' insistence that adherence to the philosophy of Pragmatism involved 'looking towards last things, fruits, consequences'. Factual analysis of data from which 'cynical acid' has taken away layers of prejudice and invisible preconceptions is the key to the methodology required by jurists in their attempts to understand the path of the law.

It would be a mistake, however, to imagine that Holmes rejected the need for legal theory. The philosophy of Pragmatism, to which he adhered, is itself the product of a complicated process of applying principles to an interpretation of data. Holmes believed that 'we have too little theory in the law, rather than too much ... Read the works of the great German jurists and see how much more the world is governed today by Kant than by Bonaparte'. The 'path of the law' demands from those who seek to explore it a knowledge of legal theory and an understanding of the observed operations of the law in action.

Notes

Holmes' *The Path of the Law* appears in several anthologies of jurisprudential texts; see, for example, *Philosophy of Law*, ed Feinberg and Gross. *The Collected Legal Papers of Holmes*, edited by Laski, is a valuable anthology of Holmes' views on the essence of Realism. Lerner's *The Mind and Faith of Justice Holmes* provides an interesting picture of 'the Great Dissenter', as Holmes was called (particularly in view of his celebrated dissenting opinions in the Supreme Court).

Question 39

Consider the effects of jurisprudence on the claimed 'scientific prediction' of judicial behaviour, and the science of jurimetrics.

Answer plan

One of the 'scientific' developments of American Realism occurred during the final years of the Second World War and the succeeding decade. Information storage and retrieval, computer technology and the growth of the science of cybernetics pointed the way to the harnessing of technology in the interests of legal science. The promise of the 1950s has not come to fruition, but the work of jurists such as Schubert and Loevinger remains as an indication of a direction which might be taken by legal thought based upon the rigorous premises of behavioural science and information control. The following skeleton plan has been used:

Introduction -the essence of technology in the service of behavioural science - Schubert's work - cybernetics and the legal system - Loevinger's use of computerised techniques - jurimetrics - conclusion, little has been added by the new technology to our understanding of jurisprudence.

Answer

An offshoot of American Realism which burgeoned with great promise in the post-Second World War era was the movement based upon the scientific investigation of jurisprudential problems, utilising methodologies and technologies which had grown during the 1950s. Advances in behavioural research, ie, the study of observable behaviour, rather than the investigation of 'mental phenomena', the growth of computer technology, cybernetics, and new techniques for the formulation and resolution of problems associated with probability, seemed to promise a novel and fruitful approach to problems of legal theory. In the event, comparatively little has emerged of any consequence to jurisprudence.

Behavioural scientists, such as Schubert, took as their theme Holmes' view of law as 'the prophecies of what the courts will do in fact'. Believing that the framework of a 'science of forecasting judicial behaviour' could be constructed, and that the essence of the validity of any science rests on its capacity to predict successfully on the basis of its data, Schubert concentrated his attention on the *judicial behaviour* of a sample of American judges, with a view to outlining a method of attempting to forecast their decisions. The knowledge to be obtained from this investigation might evolve from mere empirical data into a *theoretical understanding* which could characterise a novel, behaviourist approach to realist jurisprudence.

Schubert had been impressed with the work of the jurist, Haines, who, in the 1920s had attempted an analysis of factors 'likely to influence judicial behaviour'. These factors were classified as: *remote and indirect* (education, family associations, wealth, social position), and *direct* (legal and political experiences, political opinions and affiliations, intellectual and temperamental traits). Schubert expanded the analysis by the construction of elaborate models, ie, theoretical mappings of behaviour variables, from which the effects of change might be deduced. The decision-making processes of judges were considered in terms of 'game theory' which claimed to assist in the prediction of some types of outcome, given highly-specific conditions.

Schubert analysed the decisions of the American appeal courts in terms of *conversion structure*, a process which seeks to recognise the essence of group interactions and the interpretation of the 'values' of individual judges who constitute an appeal court. The attitudes of judges (based on their experience) and their attitudinal orientations (political and economic) were noted. A 'bloc analysis' was made of the 'concurrences and conflict of decisions' among members of the appeal court, followed by a 'scalogram analysis', which seeks to record the value-attitudes of judges towards issues related to that which is the subject of the current appeal. 'Multivariate analysis', ie, the statistical analysis of data involving several types of measurement and observation, is then used to establish whether there exists a significant degree of concurrence of variables with certain types of decisions, not to be explained by mere chance, and whether that concurrence is likely to be repeated in future decisions. In the event, Rodell was able to forecast correctly a Supreme Court decision, using this methodology of investigation (*Baker v Carr* (1962)) and Lawler was able to forecast correctly an important civil rights decision (*Gideon v Wainwright* (1963)).

Critics have stressed the importance of the highly-variable, seemingly random element of *choice* which enters into judicial decision-making, rendering reliable forecasting virtually impossible. The behaviouralists reply that the laws of choice mimic the laws of chance, which are now well-understood, so that correct forecasting is not entirely impossible of achievement. Other critics of 'scientific prediction' suggest that the attempted quantification of the 'unquantifiable', such as individual attitudes, provides approximations only which have added little to legal theory.

The theory of cybernetics (defined by its founder, Norbert Wiener, in 1964 as 'the study of control and communication in man and machine) became the basis for some investigations of the workings of the courts in terms of systems analysis. A court was considered for analysis as a unified, purposeful system composed of interrelated parts. Judge, jury, counsel, defendant, court environment, are seen as a complex of interdependencies revealing discernible regularities of relationship. The essence of a 'system' is that each constituent part affects, and is affected by, all other parts. This type of analysis requires use of the concept of 'feedback' - an essential characteristic of a goal-seeking system (such as a court of law), allowing control by awareness of the results of activities. The American jurist and lawyer, D'Amato, has analysed, in cybernetic modelling terms, jurisprudential concepts such as positivism and the naturalist view of law. He illustrates in cybernetical-type diagrams, the *relationships* which constitute certain types of legal concept, but little is added to our knowledge of the reasoning behind the formation of the concepts.

Jurimetrics, which appeared in the early 1960s, offered a new methodology of legal enquiry. The new science was described by Loevinger, as a study concerned with matters such as the quantitative analysis of judicial behaviour, the use of mathematical logic in law, the application of communication theory to legal experience and the formulation of a calculus of legal probability. Jurimetrics, said Loevinger, utilises scientific method and provides conclusions which are testable, in contrast to traditional jurisprudence which can provide conclusions which are merely debatable.

Loevinger's 'new methodology' requires the use of computers for its operational techniques. The use of the computer for 'mechanical' tasks, such as information retrieval and indexing of legal material is now well-known. Jurimetrics has in mind other, more exciting, uses. It was suggested that some relatively simple, 'mechanical', legal procedures seemed to lend themselves well to the use of computerised techniques. The conveyancing of registered land, the search of land charges registers, and some matters concerning the making of wills seemed obvious examples. The more schematic and formalised a type of legislation (particularly in the case of rules and regulations), the more amenable to computerised techniques its application ought to be.

Later, Loevinger and others suggested experiments in 'computerised adjudication'. Those who proposed this advance claimed that, given an appropriate level of computer technology, it might be possible to program a machine so that it could make *qualitative judgments*, eg, not only that A was *larger* than B, but that A was superior to, or *better* than, B. The possibility of constructing an appropriate computer program so that it could decide, on the basis of data presented to it, between plaintiff and defendant, was canvassed. Program the appropriate facts, relevant cases, precedents, arguments of the parties, and a decision would emerge 'free from prejudices, conscious or unconscious'.

Experiments of this type were thought to be appropriate for areas in which factual data predominated. Small claims adjudication, the alleged breach of minor traffic regulations, taxation claims, seemed to provide likely areas for experimentation. It was hoped that success in these areas might be followed by computerised adjudication in more complex cases. Hopes were raised by the publicity given to advances in the search for an artificial intelligence. (It was accepted that the adoption of techniques of this nature would require a revolution in the thinking of lawyers, judges, legislators and members of the public.) In the event, however, these proposals were not pursued. The slow progress of scientists in the creation of an artificial intelligence and the publicity given to the nature of the obstacles in the path of a movement towards the programming of a machine which might give an impression of rudimentary 'thought', contributed to the abandonment of those lines of enquiry which were to lead to adjudication by computer.

Some jurists have queried the *role* of the computer as set out in the claims of jurimetrics and scientific prediction. Few seek to deny the value of the computer as a tool in the retrieval and classification of legal data. But there is much scepticism as to the possibility of the utilisation of computerised techniques in the solution of qualitative legal problems. The instructions given to a computer (its 'program') may reflect the programmer's individual predilections, thus introducing subjective elements into a procedure claimed to be highly-objective. Further, the vast task of extracting a *ratio decidendi* from each case to be fed into the computer store of data is daunting. Stone has raised social and philosophical objections. Does the spread of computer units promise an intensification of centralised and technocratic power over the legal system? Would control of data banks in which legal data might be stored give an unacceptable measure of control to those who programmed the data? Would the growth of computer usage involve an abdication by the lawyer of his skills? Does the precise terminology required by the computer programmer vitiate the 'semantic fertility' of legal vocabulary? Above all, does the promised advance towards the use of programs said to be capable of solving qualitative problems reflect a philosophy irreconcilably alien to the law and its traditions? Weizenbaum, a computer technologist, notes that 'since we do not have any ways of making computers wise, we ought not now to give computers tasks that demand wisdom'.

In general, little of substance seems to have been added to jurisprudential theory by the studies under the headings of 'scientific prediction of judicial behaviour' and 'jurimetrics'. There has been interesting, but inconclusive, speculation on the nature of the *systems* underlying legal institutions, and there has emerged some useful investigation of the problems of legal terminology, undertaken for the purpose of constructing a legal thesaurus (Statsky has produced such a text intended for the legal computer-researcher). D'Amato's analysis of the systems-basis of some jurisprudential concepts promised much but, together with the general cybernetical principles upon which it was based, seems to have run into the sands. The expected modifications of jurisprudential thought which were confidently expected from a scientific investigation of the nature of the legal process have not taken place. Yet it would be surprising, and altogether exceptional, were the techniques which have revolutionised our understanding of human genetics and the working of the brain not to be found capable of contributing to an understanding of those aspects of thought which emerge in legal theory. But the necessary techniques would appear, at the moment, to lie, in Celan's phrase, 'North of the future'.

Notes

Law and Contemporary Problems (1963), vol 28, contains the following important articles: 'Judicial Analysis and Voting Behaviour' by Schubert, and 'Jurimetrics, the Methodology of Legal Inquiry' by Loevinger. *Cybernetics* by Wiener, and *Jurisprudence - a Descriptive and Normative Analysis of Law* by D'Amato, include accounts of the fundamentals of information control. D'Amato's diagrammatic analysis of jurisprudential concepts is of great interest. Lloyd, ch 8, and Dias, ch 21, offer accounts of jurimetrics. Tapper's work on computers (see, eg, *Computers and the Law*) is very informative. A general picture of computer models of mental processes is given in Johnson-Laird's *The Computer and The Mind*.

Contemporary American Jurisprudence

Introduction

The questions in this chapter concern jurists who typify certain strands of thought in contemporary American jurisprudence. Those selected are Rawls (b 1921), his pupil, Nozick (b 1938), Dworkin (b 1931), and those writers whose work is considered under the heading of American Critical Legal Studies. These jurists share no common platform: Rawls and Nozick have diametrically opposite views on matters such as the distribution of wealth; Dworkin is a lone figure, rooted in the doctrines of no particular movement, but owing some patterns of analysis to the early Realist school; the representatives of the Critical Legal Studies movement appear to be mavericks, restating the doctrines of the ultra-left in novel fashion.

Checklist

Ensure that you are acquainted with the following topics:

- Rawls' 'original position' concept
- Rawls' two principles of justice
- primary social goods

- Nozick's 'minimal state'
- Dworkin's 'right thesis'
- hard cases

- American Critical Legal Studies

Question 40

'Rawls' theory of justice is a credible, radical alternative to the conception of justice based on classical utilitarianism.'

Is it?

Answer plan

Rawls is a contemporary philosopher who is interested particularly in questions of social justice. His theory is based on the necessity of perceiving questions of justice as more important than questions of happiness: what is *right* is a matter of priority, whereas what is *good* is a secondary matter. The theory of justice associated with Rawls is, therefore, in contrast to the utilitarian concept. Essentials of the theory are based on a set of limitations which must be explained in an answer to the question. The following skeleton plan is used:

Introduction -essence of Rawls' approach - the well-ordered society - justice viewed in rational terms - social contract - 'original position' and the 'veil of ignorance' - primary social goods - principles of justice - priority of justice and liberty - credibility of the theory - conclusion, Rawls' theory as an alternative to utilitarianism.

Answer

The problem of what ought to be the principles of justice - basic to ethics and jurisprudence - was subjected to a detailed analysis by Rawls in *A Theory of Justice* (1971). An elaborate, systematic argument emerged in which Rawls provided an alternative to earlier doctrines of justice as conceived by utilitarians such as Bentham, for whom a 'just system' required legal institutions directed at the creation of 'the greatest happiness for the greatest number'. Rawls' approach is epitomised in the statement: 'Justice is fairness'. His theory is, without doubt, a radical alternative to utilitarian justice; whether it is credible is less certain.

The society which Rawls seeks to analyse is a more or less self-sufficient association of individuals who stand in a relationship one to the other which is characterised by recognition of the binding nature of certain rules of conduct which are generally acted upon. Rawls assumes that this society wishes to decide a set of principles upon which to construct 'social justice'. The principles are to be used in assigning rights and duties and in defining the distribution of burdens and benefits considered appropriate for social cooperation. A well-ordered society is one which is designed to advance the good of its members and is regulated by 'a public conception of justice'. Each individual accepts the principles of justice and is aware of their general acceptance. Society's basic institutions seek to satisfy these principles. Essentially, a public conception of justice constitutes the 'fundamental charter' of society. Here is a concept at variance with the doctrine of classical utilitarianism

Rawls is concerned to show that the 'principles of justice' required for such a society would be precisely those that would be chosen by 'rational persons'. The circumstances in which the choice is made give Rawls' theory a highly-unusual basis. He utilises the theory of 'the social contract' to suggest that principles of justice rest on a compact made by society's members. The principles constitute the very *object*, the very *reason*, of the compact. We are to imagine, says Rawls, a hypothetical situation in which those who have entered the compact are deciding a fundamental charter for their society. The people involved are rational and free, and desirous of furthering their own interests. The initial position is one based on equality - *'the original position'*.

If the principles of justice to be decided upon are to be objective and fair, then, says Rawls, those in the 'original position' must accept *limitations* and must step behind a 'veil of ignorance'. None of the participants knows (and, therefore, acts as though he does not know) any of his special circumstances. The veil eliminates any prejudices. One's place in society, class, position, intelligence, are 'unknowns'. Since all participants in the enquiry accept this limitation, none will fashion principles deliberately so as to suit his condition. The principles of justice which emerge will be the result of a 'fair' agreement. Rawls assumes, however, that those in the 'original position' will be capable of maintaining a 'sense of justice'. They will, apparently, without question, see justice as 'fairness'.

Rawls assumes, further, that those in the 'original position' will have no information as to the particular circumstances of their society, ie, they are not aware of its level of culture and civilisation. Nor do they know the generation to which they belong, so that they must derive principles with which *they* are prepared to live. It is assumed, however, that they know the general facts about society and that they understand the basic principles of economics, politics and psychology. 'The veil' will ensure that they are not prejudiced by 'arbitrary contingencies'.

Because the participants intend to evolve their charter of justice on the basis of rationality, Rawls suggests that the communal structure which will be evolved will be concerned with *the rational distribution of 'primary social goods'*. These are things which every rational person is presumed to want; they have a use whatever a person's rational life-plan may be. The 'primary social goods' are rights and liberties, opportunities and powers, income and wealth. For every person, 'the good' is the satisfaction of rational desire; whatever one's ends, the primary goods are, in rational terms, the necessary means. (At a later stage, Rawls added 'the most important of the primary goods - self-respect.')

From Rawls' perception of the overall 'good' and his view of 'primary goods', comes his belief that there will emerge from the deliberations of those in the 'original position', *two vital principles of justice. The first principle will be a resounding affirmation of equality and fairness as basic to justice.* Each individual must have an equal right to the most extensive total system of equal, basic liberties compatible with a similar system of liberty for all. This involves a maximisation of liberty deliberately intended to furnish maximum freedom of speech and conscience. 'Liberty for all' may have to be restricted but *only for the sake of liberty itself,* as where, for example, freedom of speech requires a system of public order regulations (see the Public Order Act 1986, for example). The maintenance of public order must be accepted as a necessary condition for each person to achieve his ends. Further, less-than-equal liberty may be justified but only where it is acceptable by those who have the lesser liberty; resulting inequalities in one liberty must be shown to have the effect of a greater overall protection of other liberties as a direct result of a restriction (the Road Traffic Act 1988 provides an example).

The *second principle of justice* (as amended by Rawls after publication of his book in 1971) is as follows: *social and economic inequalities are to be arranged so that they will be to the greatest benefit of the least advantaged persons, consistent with a 'just savings principle', and are attached to offices and positions open to all under conditions of fairness and equality of opportunity.* Rawls recognises that those in the 'original position' will be aware of the facts of inequality and differences among individuals and will wish to ensure that these differences do not result in injustice. There is no suggestion that wealth and income ought to be divided equally; but any unequal division will be justifiable only if *all* persons are better off as a result, ie, the unequal division is to result to everyone's advantage. The 'just savings principle' involves justice operating not only among the members of society represented in the 'original position', but among those of succeeding generations also; savings involve a recognition of the responsibilities of one generation to the next.

Rawls is aware that there may be conflicts of principle. A resolution of such conflict may be effected, he suggests, by the application of 'principles of priority'. This concept is referred to as 'lexical', that is, the first principle must be satisfied totally before any consideration can be given to the second. The first priority rule is *the absolute priority of liberty*: one may restrict liberty *only* for the sake of liberty. The second priority rule is that *justice shall prevail over efficiency and welfare*. In a conflict of principles of liberty and social need, liberty has an unalterable priority. Concerns derived from 'maximisation of utility' must give way to the overriding necessity for liberty. To depart from the principle of equal liberty cannot be justified, therefore, by the promise of greater economic and social advantage.

The credibility of Rawls' theory of justice has been questioned persistently. The 'original position' seems so hypothetical, so artificial, and so very difficult to visualise, that it is perceived by some jurists as weakening the basis of the theory. Is it possible to imagine persons from whom individual histories, environmental links, and values have been removed? Is what remains sufficient to constitute a 'rational person' from whom reasoning can be expected? Those in the 'original position' are not in possession of data appropriate to the task of working out principles of justice, say the critics. And if, as Rawls suggests, those 'behind the veil' must be presumed to know the principles of psychology, they will be aware of the results of speculating *in vacuo*.

It is not at all certain, continue the critics, that those in the 'original position' would come to the 'liberal-democratic' conclusions suggested by Rawls. Why would they necessarily prefer liberty to equality? Why would they not invoke a 'winner-takes-all' philosophy? Suppose that some of those in the 'original position' concluded, on the strength of their 'allowed knowledge', that there can be no true liberty save on the basis of economic sufficiency, or that material goods are of relatively small worth.

There is doubt, too, as to whether pure ratiocination 'behind the veil' would produce anything like Rawls' principles of justice. Has Rawls confused 'liberty' and 'liberties'? Is it that the logic of 'liberty as indivisible' has been overlooked? And would rational thought produce, inevitably, Rawls' catalogue of 'primary social goods'?

There is no doubt that Rawls has produced a radical alternative to the rigidities of utilitarianism. The exponents of that philosophy were prepared to accept inequalities if the result would be the maximisation of the happiness of the greatest number. Rawls' principles constitute a rejection of this view. He sees liberty as a means to the promotion of society's good, but, unlike the utilitarians, he is not prepared to put it aside so as to 'increase' that good. Liberty, for Rawls, is a good in itself and may not be limited save in the few circumstances he mentions. This is indeed a radical alternative to the simplistic views of utilitarianism; whether it is 'credible', given the hypothetical circumstances postulated by Rawls as necessary for the emergence of principles of justice, must remain arguable.

Notes

Lloyd, ch 6, Dias, ch 22, Riddall, ch 12, and Harris, ch 20, contain outlines of Rawls' theory. A useful introduction to the fundamentals of Rawls' views is given in *Reading Rawls*, edited by Daniels. *John Rawls' Theory of Justice* by Blocker and Smith is a complete exposition of the theory. Wolff analyses the theory in *Understanding Rawls: A Reconstruction and Critique of A Theory of Justice*. Davies and Holdcroft, ch 9, explore Rawls' theory in detail.

Question 41

Give a critical account of the theory of civil disobedience enunciated by Rawls in *A Theory of Justice*.

Answer plan

Rawls' theory of disobedience arises directly from his response to specific conditions in the USA which were characterised by widespread civil disobedience and violence. He examines the place of civil disobedience in a 'nearly-just society' and calls for the toleration of carefully-defined types of protest. The question calls for a 'critical account', so that an answer ought to contain an examination of the essence of the theory and a consideration of objections to it. The following skeleton plan is used:

Introduction -Rawls' theory as a reaction to events in the USA - essence of civil disobedience - a definition - constituent features of civil disobedience in action - conscientious refusal - justification of civil disobedience - risks in civil disobedience - conclusion, Rawls' theory is, perhaps, over-optimistic.

Answer

A Theory of Justice, which Rawls published in 1971, one year after the intervention of the American National Guard in university anti-war demonstrations, includes a consideration of the circumstances in which civil disobedience (carefully and restrictively defined) might be justified. For many Americans, the role of civil disobedience in a democratic community was under discussion and Rawls' contribution was, essentially, a measured response to the apparent paradox of members of a democratic State engaged in activities which seemed to deny their belief in the values generally attributed to the process of decision-making within that State.

Rawls emphasises that the design of his theory is appropriate for the 'special case' of a 'nearly-just society', characterised by a legitimately-established democracy, the members of which recognise the validity of its constitutional basis. Critics have noted that societies of this nature are generally mature, confident and able to tolerate the expression of dissent; the real problems arise in those immature societies in which dissent is often equated with sedition and treason. Civil disobedience provides for Rawls a test-case of the ability of a democracy to discuss the very circumstances in which one's duty to comply with the law is called into question. It is necessary, therefore, to provide a theory which will define civil disobedience in terms which separate it from other forms of opposition to democratic authority, which will set out the grounds upon which it might be justified, and which will explain its role in a constitutional system. Precise, overall principles cannot, however, be stated; each case must be judged separately.

Critics suggest that much more argument is needed *initially* as to the 'acceptability' of overtly illegal activity within a free society for any purposes whatsoever. Rawls' definition of civil disobedience is disarming: he sees it as a *public, non-violent, conscientious political act, contrary to law, usually with the aim of effecting a change in law or government policy*. It is this type of disobedience which, Rawls argues, should be acceptable to a democratic community. Rawls does not provide, however, examples of what a community might consider as 'acceptable forms' of civil disobedience.

Rawls stresses civil disobedience as a political, public act, ie, comprising events which are visible 'in the public forum'. It must, therefore, be non-violent, since one person's violence is an interference with the civil liberty of others. Its character must be such that it 'warns and admonishes'; it is not perceived as a threat. Indeed, it has to be viewed as a non-violent expression of disagreement couched within the limits of overall fidelity to the law and as a bond of the participants' sincerity. Civil disobedience differs fundamentally from mere 'militant action' and organised *forcible* resistance to government policy. The militant attacks policy as an expression of his profound opposition to the legal order, whereas civil disobedience, by its nature, threatens no one. The problem here is that much depends on how civil disobedience is viewed *in practice* by the public and the authorities. Thus, the continued presence of a well-behaved group of non-violent protesters outside a foreign embassy may be construed as a threat to law and order. The polite refusal of the leaders of a procession, protesting against taxation policy, to remove their banners, might be construed by public and police as a threat. Rawls' thesis implies a sophisticated awareness of political ideologies and activities which is not as widespread within democracies as it ought to be.

Rawls is at pains to distinguish civil disobedience from 'conscientious refusal'. He interprets the latter phenomenon as non-compliance with legal injunctions or administrative orders, and exemplifies it by the refusal of a religious group to salute the

American flag. The differences between the two activities are, he suggests: conscientious refusal is not always an event in 'the public forum'; it may be based on no expectation of changing the law; and it is not always based on political principle (it may have a religious basis). Rawls does acknowledge that in practice it may be impossible to draw distinctions. It is extremely difficult to separate, for example, the motives of those who participate in a show of opposition to the brutal policies of a foreign state - they may be largely political, or religious, or a combination of the two.

Rawls discussed conscientious refusal in terms of opposition to undertaking military service. Conscription is, he argues, 'permissible' *only* if demanded for the defence of liberty itself - a highly-arguable proposition, couched in terms which are inescapably controversial. He advocates a 'discriminating conscientious refusal' to carry out military service and suggests that a refusal to participate in war under *any* circumstances is an 'unworldly' stance. Yet for many conscientious objectors it is precisely the 'unworldly' nature of their principles upon which they rest their case.

The justification of civil disobedience necessitates, according to Rawls, an examination of the kinds of wrong which are appropriate objects of that action. Policies which affect the principle of equal liberty (seen by Rawls as a prerequisite of justice) fall clearly within that category. Where normal appeals to the political majority have failed to right a perceived wrong, resulting in the violation of liberties in deliberate fashion over a considerable period of time, and where past activities of a government, and community support, indicate an 'immovable majority', then civil disobedience may be justified. Those who adopt this stance must ensure that it has become necessary as a last resort, that it will be embarked upon rationally, that it will be exercised in terms understood by the wider community and that it takes into account the possibility of an undesirable escalation which might lead to a breakdown in respect for law and the constitution.

The problem is in the fact (which Rawls tends to underplay) that the events consequent on a display of civil disobedience may not remain under the effective control of the participants. What begins as a disciplined manifestation of principled dissent may move swiftly out of control, particularly in the face of public reaction to events perceived as undesirable and illegal. It is often not possible, in practice, to recognise the fundamentally rational, peaceful nature of those who participate in acts of civil disobedience. This may mark a point at which anger replaces passivity and moves into civil strife.

Rawls views civil disobedience in somewhat paradoxical terms by suggesting that it may act as a 'stabilising device' within a constitutional, democratic system and that it is, therefore, a part of the mechanism of free government. The basis of this argument is an assumption that within the 'nearly-just society' the principles of justice will be recognised, for the most part, in terms of free cooperation among members of that society. Civil disobedience may be seen as the serving of notice on the majority (who do accept the place of justice within the community) that the conditions of free cooperation are being violated. Notice of this nature should, according to Rawls, inhibit further departures from justice and ought to lead to the correction of faults. In this way, civil disobedience may assist in the stabilisation of a constitutional system. A difficulty is that although a majority may view justice as all-important, they may not see the phenomenon of civil disobedience as a 'desirable corrective'; they may, indeed, perceive it as extra-constitutional activity which threatens the consensus basis of a mature democracy in which fundamental disputes are settled in the courts or, in the final analysis, the voting booths, rather than in the streets.

Rawls appeals to the doctrine of 'the community based on contract': the implied contract which binds us as members of society emphasises cooperation among equals, so that to deny justice is to consider some persons as unequal. It becomes the objective of civil disobedience to expose 'contractual breaches' and to restore liberties. Critics retort that the doctrine of society as based on contract is unproven, and, in any event, not accepted by the majority within society. Further, even if people were motivated by a sense of justice they might not recognise a particular source of complaint within the community as derived from an 'injustice'. Rawls believes, however, that the community's sense of justice is strong enough 'to be invoked to significant effect' when properly addressed and that it can play a decisive role in correcting abuses uncovered by those who are engaged in civil disobedience.

The risks attendant on a resort to civil disobedience are obvious to Rawls. In particular there is the difficulty which arises when citizens are invited to participate in an activity which they know to be contrary to the law. Who takes the decision as to when an illegal action becomes 'necessary'? Is there not an invitation to anarchy in the statement that *all* must decide for themselves? Rawls does not agree. Within the 'nearly-just society' each individual must make his own decisions. Members of such a society cannot divest themselves of their responsibilities and transfer the burden of decisions (and blame) to others. If, after a consideration of all the risks involved, a person decides on a course of action involving civil disobedience, he has acted conscientiously (although, perhaps, mistakenly). He has not done as he may have wished to do; he has, however, elevated his conscience to a point at which his general desires become subsidiary to his duty. In the terms of the natural law, he has discerned what must be done, and has proceeded to do it.

Writing in 1971, Rawls was able to say, with optimism, that after each person has taken counsel with himself, then 'with reasonableness, comity and good fortune, it often works out well enough'. Given the short history of Western society since that date, one wonders whether Rawls' optimism was warranted. The same degree of optimism characterises Rawls' concluding remarks: there is, he believes, no danger of anarchy so long as there exists a 'working agreement' between citizens on the basis of their conception of justice, *and* the conditions for a resort to civil disobedience are respected. Again there emerges the problem of the *perception* by citizens of the character and potentiality of non-violent activities. At what stage should tolerance be withdrawn? Should the citizens of the 'nearly-just society' view with equanimity a campaign, based on civil disobedience, which aims overtly at the creation of a new society based on intolerance and injustice? How, and at what stage, does society protect its existence in the face of non-violent campaigns of disobedience aimed at its overthrow? In America, and elsewhere in the Western world, communities remain awake to the necessity of drawing a clear line between what can be

tolerated and what is unacceptable. It cannot be said that Rawls
has provided a clear guide to those who have to provide
leadership on matters involving the distinction between the
tolerable and the intolerable.

Notes

Rawls' 'Theory of Civil Disobedience', extracted from *A Theory of
Justice*, has been reprinted in *The Philosophy of Law*, edited by
Dworkin, and *Philosophy of Law*, edited by Feinberg and Gross.
Dias, ch 15, and Riddall, ch 15, discuss the essentials of Rawls'
view on this topic. Greenawalt's *Conflict of Law and Morality*
examines the implications of Rawls' stance. Smith's essay, 'Is
there a Prima Facie Obligation to Obey the Law?', in Yale LJ 82
(1973) and Wasserstrom's discussion of 'The Obligation to Obey
the Law' in *Essays in Legal Philosophy*, edited by Summers, will be
found extremely helpful.

Question 42

'Nozick's theory of justice is really a political manifesto in the
guise of jurisprudential fables.'

Outline the theory and comment on the criticism.

Answer plan

Nozick was a pupil of Rawls and rejected his teacher's insistence
on the need for governmental intervention so as to achieve a
redistribution of wealth. The concepts of individual libertarianism
formed the basis of Nozick's view of society. Man's rights are of
great importance, but their protection requires no more than the
exercise by a 'minimal State' of 'night watchman functions'.
Liberty and equality are not to be confused, and the right to
property is inseparable from liberty. Nozick's appeal to
politicians on the right of the political spectrum cannot be denied.
An answer to the question involves an explanation of the
'minimal State' and a discussion of the 'fable' of its development.
Nozick's attitudes to property and its distribution require
comment. The following skeleton plan is suggested:

Introduction -Nozick's principal theses - right to acquisition and possession of property - creation of the 'minimal State' - distributive justice - Nozick's appeal to the political right wing - criticism of Nozick's 'poetic fantasies' - his 'taxation and forced labour equivalence' - conclusion, criticism of Nozick's 'parable of individuality'.

Answer

A 'just society', according to Nozick, is one based on *individualism*. The natural rights of the individual are inviolable, and each person may enjoy those rights subject only to certain moral 'side restraints' concerning the rights of others. The only type of State which is acceptable is that which functions in a *minimal mode*; attempts by the State to redistribute wealth are generally unjustifiable and it is very doubtful whether liberty and equality are compatible. These are the theses elaborated by Nozick in *Anarchy, State and Utopia* (1974). Ideas of this type have been used to underpin some political ideologies that have emerged in Western societies in recent years, but it is doubtful whether Nozick intended to produce a political manifesto as such. It is the *basis* of his ideas which has produced criticism from jurists and others.

Nozick assumes for purposes of his theory that persons exist as 'distinct entities'. Adopting and adapting Locke's fable of the 'state of freedom' which accompanied the 'state of nature' in which man originally existed, he draws attention to the 'law of nature' which allowed no individual to act in ways which brought harm to another's life, liberty or possessions. We have our 'natural rights' - freedom from violence against the person, freedom to hold property and freedom to enforce our rights against those who violate these basic freedoms. The freedom to hold property is based on 'legitimate acquisition': *just initial acquisition*, by which an individual acquires the ownership of that which was previously unowned; *legitimate transfer*, eg, by gift, exchange; and *rectification of former unjust distribution*, as where a person has obtained property unjustly and it has been returned to its proper owner. 'Justice in holdings' (in acquisition, transfer and rectification) constitutes the individual's natural right to possessions.

None of these rights may be interfered with in the absence of the individual's consent. A person's 'distinctiveness' ensures that he may not be treated as a means to an end; hence the concept of one person's natural abilities being available for exploitation merely for the benefit of, say, those within society who lack some advantage, is unacceptable. There can be no justice where social 'goals' or 'end state' demand that one person may claim rights in another. No individual has a right to something whose realisation requires the use of things, and activities, involving other individuals' rights and entitlements. We may have a right to life (ie, the right not to be deprived of it by others), but not to the means needed to sustain life.

If goal-based societies are to be rejected, what principle ought to be favoured in the search for justice? Nozick suggests the principle of 'historical entitlement'. In order to test the presence of justice within a society it is necessary to ask whether that society emerged in 'just fashion', whether its workings infringe rights and whether property is acquired and held there on the basis of 'justice in holdings'. The touchstones are, according to Nozick, total respect for individual rights and the existence of moral 'side constraints', forbidding any actions which negate individual rights. The right to liberty, the right to property, are interdependent: take away one, and the other is rendered meaningless. (It is interesting to note that in 1830 Bentham had argued that property and law 'are born and must die together'.) An important expression of the individual's right to liberty is to be found in his right to acquire and keep property; indeed, says Nozick, an extension of private property may be interpreted as a growth of freedom.

What of the State in Nozick's theory? He approves only of the 'minimal State' which, he suggests, best realises the aspirations of many visionaries. He sees the 'minimal State' as expressing an 'invisible hand process' (the phraseology is that of Adam Smith, who used it to personify 'beneficent Providence'), which allows development of society without the violation of individual rights. Nozick uses his 'state of nature' fable to show how the 'minimal State' emerges. Initially, groups formed for themselves 'mutual protection associations' in which each member acted so as to defend all other members of the association. Eventually there emerged 'protection agencies', paid for their services, acting as 'protection associations', and dealing with complaints by association members against one another. Conflicts among protection associations began, and one association emerged as the strongest and, therefore, dominant. Outside the protection associations were, of course, 'independents' who chose initially not to join. Finally, the dominant protection association agency took over control of all persons within its area of operations; the 'independents' received compensation for their loss of independence by being allowed to join the dominant association. The State was born. It has since developed in spontaneous fashion, its growth mirroring the self-interest of individuals and the workings of an 'invisible hand process'.

The 'minimal State' is, in effect, no more than a 'night-watchman State': it operates only on a range of minimal activities. It will protect from force, fraud and theft; it will enforce contracts; it enjoys a monopoly of force. It has come into existence by morally permissible means and without violation of anyone's rights; it must operate so as to keep those rights inviolate. Nozick rejects any growth of the State beyond these narrow confines. That there ought to be a State is unquestioned, and to argue otherwise is to plunge into the errors of anarchy; but that there ought to be a 'supra-minimal State' is unacceptable.

Nozick's rejection of any State other than that of the 'night-watchman' type emerges in his attitude to 'distributive justice', ie, where poorer, weaker citizens are assisted through the fruits of taxation and redistribution of resources. This is unacceptable to Nozick. The 'difference principle', advocated by Rawls, which allows an arrangement of economic and other advantages so as to assist those who are less well-off, is an unwarranted interference with the norms of distribution and a violation of individual liberties. Indeed, a State which acted in this way so as to effect a 'patterned distribution of wealth' is to be regarded as intrinsically immoral. The task is not to redistribute resources, but rather to protect persons' rights to what they already possess. If an individual has obtained his property by 'just initial acquisition', he is entitled to keep it and it may not be utilised through a process of redistribution, save by his agreement. Where each person's holdings are just, then the total set of holdings is just.

The 'fair redistribution of resources' is, in Nozick's eyes, a mask for the violation of liberty.

In a celebrated aphorism, Nozick states that taxation of earnings of labour is on a par with forced labour. To take the earnings of, say, x hours of labour is like taking x hours from the person; it is like forcing that person to work x hours for the purposes of another. The fact that others may intentionally intervene to threaten force to ensure that taxes are paid makes the tax system equivalent to forced labour. Those who create wealth have inviolable rights over its possession and utilisation. Redistribution on grounds of 'social justice', 'difference principles', 'welfare claims', is essentially unjust. Justice does not exist where processes involving redistribution without consent are common.

Nozick's thesis, appearing at a period in American history during which legal, political and ethical argument seemed to be moving ineluctably in favour of an increased degree of State intervention, was unpopular among many jurists. On the agenda of public discussion were topics such as socialised medicine, free legal aid, improved welfare benefits and positive 'reverse discrimination' in favour of disadvantaged ethnic communities, all of which pointed to the need for intensified government intervention and a redistribution of social resources. Nozick's parable of the 'minimal State' and its social and legal consequences were unpopular. It was suggested by one lawyer that a subtitle for Nozick's book might be 'Forward to the 1770s', referring, presumably, to the period which saw the publication of Adam Smith's *Wealth of Nations*, with its emphasis on economic libertarianism. But it is not easy to accept the view that Nozick's writings constitute a political manifesto for the right wing. The fact that they may have given ideological comfort to those who espouse the politics of non-interventionism is no more proof of the 'political manifesto' charge than the purloining by the Nazis of extracts from the writing of Savigny is proof that he would have approved their political creed.

Objection has been taken to Nozick's theses on the ground of lack of supporting data; his views on the emergence of the State have been dismissed as 'little more than poetic fantasy'. There is little direct proof of the State's *evolution* as envisaged by Nozick. It may sound convincing, and it has a ring of authenticity, particularly in its insistence on 'survival' as being the aim of earlier societies. But there is little direct evidence in favour of the 'protective association' thesis. Further, Nozick does not explain in convincing fashion the *derivation* of fundamental rights. Where and how did they originate? And why does his enumeration of fundamental rights exclude, say, the right to work, education, shelter? Why does he provide no catalogue of fundamental duties? Given the reciprocity and relationships without which our type of society would be doomed, would it not have been useful to postulate the duties arising 'naturally' from the right to have one's liberties respected?

Additionally, is it possible to keep a State in its 'minimal' form? Is it not mere wishful thinking to suggest that a 'night-watchman State' will not seek to grow as its tasks increase in scope and complexity? How will the 'minimal State' cope with problems of internal and external security save by a significant extension of its activities? Just as the State emerged, in Nozick's terms, by imposing restraints on the 'independents' outside the original 'protective associations', how will it be possible for a State to carry out its basic functions of 'night watchman' without infringing the rights of some individuals? Above all, how can the 'minimal State' be *controlled* by those on whose behalf it operates?

Nozick's discovery of an equivalence of taxation and forced labour has been dismissed as a delusion. Thus, taxation can be avoided by a person's freely choosing not to undertake taxed employment; 'forced labour' arises from no free choice. Taxation may be viewed legitimately as a contribution to the welfare of others; forced labour is in no sense a contribution of this nature. Taxation is not an undignified violation of human rights; forced labour robs the individual of dignity and rights. Similarly, Nozick's claim that an extension of ownership of private property increases liberty may exemplify the error, pointed out by many contemporary jurists, of assuming that the conditions of freedom for *single* individuals can be defined *before* considering conditions of freedom for *all* individuals within a community. What is the nature of the 'freedom' enjoyed by a minority of individuals within a community which deprives the majority of its citizens of dignity?

It may be that Nozick's 'parable of individuality' rests on his failure to accept that 'no man is an island entire of itself'. His concept of 'inviolable, individual rights' seems to ignore the social setting which is required to give substance to those rights. The relationship of rights and duties is indeed fundamental to our type of society. A perception of redistribution of social resources as invariably 'unjust' acts, it has been said, as a justification of a society without charity, philanthropy and compassion. Nozick's elevation of individualism guided by the 'minimal State' is probably of limited value for an understanding of the complex web of rights, duties, relationships and reciprocity which we term 'society'.

Notes

Lloyd, ch 6, and Riddall, ch 12, discuss the concept of the 'minimal State'. Paul has edited a collection of essays entitled *Reading Nozick. Courts and Administrators: A Study in Jurisprudence*, by Detmold, contains criticisms of Nozick's theory of justice.

Question 43

It has been said that Dworkin occupies an intermediate position between natural law and positivism.

Do you agree?

Answer plan

Dworkin, an American lawyer who has occupied the chairs of jurisprudence at Yale and Oxford, has evolved a thesis of rights which gives absolute priority to individual rights even over programmes and policies aimed at the promotion of society's welfare. His search for a basis of rights has involved him in an examination, and rejection, of the doctrines of natural law and legal positivism. Neither doctrine throws light on the central question: what is the law? An answer to the question necessitates an exposition of Dworkin's attitudes to natural law and positivism and an examination, in particular, of his view of the phenomena of 'rules' and 'judicial discretion'. The following skeleton plan is suggested:

Introduction -Dworkin's rejection of natural law and positivism - opposition to the essence of natural law - rejection of key principles of positivism - hard cases - rules - law and morality - judge-made law - judicial discretion - Dworkin's general position - conclusion, Dworkin's principles seen by some as constituting a 'third theory of law'.

Answer

Dworkin's view of law is set out in his text, *Taking Rights Seriously* (1977), the essence of which is reiterated, with some modifications, in *Law's Empire* (1986). Both texts present a legal theory which involves a total rejection of natural law and the positivism associated, in particular, with Hart. Whether Dworkin's position is of an 'intermediate' nature is arguable, and some jurists suggest that he has evolved a 'third theory of law' which deserves study in its own right and is entirely distinct from the traditional natural law and positivist schools of thought.

The concept of natural law which, in Blackstone's words, 'is binding over the whole globe, in all countries and at all times' and which suggests that a judge, basing his decisions on a 'rational knowledge' of that law, may rightly overrule the fixed law of his country, is not acceptable to Dworkin. For him, the validity of a law must be examined solely in relation to the legal system of which it is a part; any investigation of law must involve empirical study in which the *a priori reasoning* which categorises natural law thinking has no place. The natural law view of law and justice as identical, making it impossible to speak of an 'unjust proposition of law' is, he says, implausible. Lawyers may believe that progressive income tax is 'unjust', but none of them entertains doubts that English and American laws include measures which impose this tax. Further, the claim of natural law that morality is relevant to the truth of propositions of law, and that where a statute is open to different interpretations, the more accurate statement of the law is that which is 'morally superior', is arguable.

Dworkin's attitude to legal positivism is one of principled opposition. He examines and rejects three of its key principles: that the law is composed of rules only; that a line must be drawn so as to separate law and morality; and that judges make the law. In his examination of positivism, Dworkin refers repeatedly to the concept of 'hard cases'. This phrase does not refer to difficult or complicated cases, but rather to cases in which *there is a larger than usual degree of uncertainty as to their eventual outcome*. 'Hard cases' involve difficulty in discovering existing *rules* appropriate to the facts in issue; even when appropriate rules are discovered, their application to the case in hand may not produce a satisfactory result.

Dworkin accepts rules as a significant part of the law; relatively simple cases are decided by the mere application of appropriate rules. But the law includes rules *and principles*. 'Principles' mean, for Dworkin, standards to be observed in the interests of justice, fairness 'or some other dimension of morality'. Principles may be contrasted with 'policies', which generally involve social goals. A judge, faced with a 'hard case', will be guided by appropriate rules *and* standards (which involve principles and policies). Dworkin discusses the American case of *Riggs v Palmer* (1899) in which the court took into account not only an appropriate rule allowing a person to inherit under a valid will, but also the principle that no person may profit from his own fraud. *Law is an amalgam of rules and principles*, and the positivist contention that rules alone are significant is an inadequate explanation of reality.

The so-called dividing line between law and morality, which features prominently in positivist jurisprudence, is rejected by Dworkin. The process of adjudication often demands substantive moral judgments. Indeed, when a judge weighs matters of principle and policy, he is reflecting to an appreciable extent the community's morality. The judge will discover that morality by keeping in mind the variety of abstract rights which the community accepts as highly-important and which appear to be embodied in the life of a society and its institutional policies. He must ask what sets of answers to certain problems would be acceptable, given the community's views on abstract rights, such as equality and liberty. Thus, a judge faced with a 'hard case' involving the possibility of a decision which might be interpreted as a clear denial of human dignity by a community which was dedicated to the preservation of that dignity, will recognise this in coming to a decision. Morality has then passed into decision-making in the name of the law. The positivist separation of law and morality ignores the reality of the process of adjudication.

A third bastion of positivism, which Dworkin attacks headlong, is embodied in the observation that 'much law is judge-made'. The argument that judges merely 'declare the law as it is' has been rejected by positivists from Bentham and Austin onwards. Contemporary positivists will point, for example, to decisions of the House of Lords in cases such as *R v Shivpuri* (1986) for confirmation of the principle of 'judicial legislation'. Dworkin will have none of this: judges do *not* make the law. In an advanced legal system, such as that of the UK or the USA, where a question arises as to what *is* the law relating to a given case, *there is always a right answer*. It can be 'hunted by reason and imagination', and the judge has a duty to discover it. In legal proceedings, one of the parties always has a right to a decision in his favour. Either X's allegation of a breach of contract is right or it is not; there is no half-way house. Either Y's plea that Z trespassed on his land is accepted or it is not; there is no 'middle-ground' answer. Dworkin admits the possibility, in theory, of a 'dead heat' between competing principles after every relevant factor seems to have been considered. But, he claims, this will be so improbable that one may ignore the chances of its happening. The judge is discovering, in principle, the 'right answer'; he is *not* utilising legal reasoning so as to 'make law where there was none before'.

Dworkin insists that although judges in 'hard cases' may have a 'discretion', this term must be interpreted in a 'weak sense' only. They are obliged to exercise judgment and must not apply standards mechanically, and they are not provided with any routine 'discretion procedures'. They do *not* have a 'discretion' in the 'strong sense', which would exclude their duty to decide a case one way or the other. There can be no 'hard cases' in which 'the reasons run out', so that a judge declares himself unable to decide either for plaintiff or defendant, and then substitutes his own preferences. This would be to rob the law of any certainty of principle. In reality, a judge is never placed in a position in which he needs to act ('even surreptitiously') as a legislator.

It is clear that Dworkin is far-removed from the position of the legal positivists. In *Taking Rights Seriously*, he states openly his intention 'to make a general attack on positivism'. In relation to *natural law*, his objections to the methodology and basic principles of that type of jurisprudential thought preclude his adopting a stance which might place him near that position. Yet some critics have discerned a strain of idealism within his general approach which, they suggest, moves him towards the philosophy of the natural law. Thus, *Between Positivism and Idealism* suggests that Dworkin's jurisprudence reveals a 'ghostly background presence of idealism'. His approach to the problem of individual rights seems, to some critics, 'idealistic' in the popular sense: it seems to comprehend the notion of law in terms of a highly-abstract vision of 'equality and liberty'. Law, for Dworkin, is not to be understood in mere instrumental terms; its essence is in its 'fulfilment of the ideal' - a terminology which would be acceptable to many jurists of the natural law school.

It is in *Law's Empire* that some critics see Dworkin's 'idealism' expressed in more obvious terms. He refers repeatedly to 'the moral dimensions' of law and to the significance of the concept of 'law as integrity'. By 'integrity' he has in mind 'justice and fairness' - concepts which have provided a basis for much jurisprudence associated with idealism. He insists that 'justice' and 'fairness' are not synonymous; fair institutions sometimes produce unjust decisions, and unfair institutions may produce just ones. 'Fairness' necessitates the treatment of individuals on the basis of the community's moral code (which he assumes will be founded on respect for life and recognition of the significance of human dignity, liberty and equality). Justice will emerge, says Dworkin, *when judges act on behalf of the community in pursuance of its declared ends*. He concludes *Law's Empire* with phrases which distance him, without doubt, from traditional positivism and the dogma of a universal, immutable natural law. 'Law is, finally, a fraternal attitude, an expression of how we are united in community though divided in project, interest and conviction. That is, anyway, what law is for us: for the people we want to be and the community we aim to have'. This expression of Dworkin's perception of law cannot be said to place him in an 'intermediate position' between natural law and positivism. Some critics see in it an expression of sentiments which may be read into the philosophy of natural law jurists such as Maritain; others view it as an expression of the general humanistic principles which are shared by jurists of all persuasions. It would be more precise, perhaps, to suggest that Dworkin's stance points to a 'third theory of law', quite separate from the opposing schools of natural law and positivism.

Notes

Davies and Holdcroft, ch 4, Harris, ch 14, and Riddall, ch 9, include expositions of Dworkin's 'rights thesis' and his general approach to law. *Ronald Dworkin and Contemporary Jurisprudence*, by Cohen is a detailed examination of Dworkin's legal thought. 'Between Positivism and Idealism' by Simonds, which appears in the Cambridge Law Journal, July 1991, is of particular interest. Mackie's 'The Third Theory of Law' is a detailed analysis and criticism of Dworkin; it is reprinted in *Philosophy of Law*, edited by Feinberg and Gross.

Question 44

'Save in its self-conscious leftist posture and its particular choice of other disciplines to celebrate, critical legal studies resembles the older movement of American legal realism ...': Dworkin (*Law's Empire*).

Discuss.

Answer plan

The American Critical Legal Studies movement, which originated in the 1970s, has aroused much interest, possibly because of the uncompromising nature of its radical attack on current legal thought. It calls for an abandonment of patterns of jurisprudential analysis which fail to recognise the function of law in an essentially-flawed society. Dworkin's strictures are seen by some jurists as based on a misunderstanding of the dimensions of the gulf which now separates CLS from the early American realists. The following skeleton plan is suggested:

Introduction -essence of CLS - its anti-liberal stance - principles of CLS - absence of a programme arising from CLS theory - distance of CLS from earlier American legal realism - belief of CLS that law is politics - conclusion, gulf between early realism and CLS may be wider than imagined by Dworkin.

Answer

The American Critical Legal Studies movement (CLS) grew rapidly in influence following the first annual meeting of the Conference on CLS in 1977, which was intended to bring together scholars who are 'pursuing a critical approach towards the study of law in society'. It remains a loose federation of jurists, such as Unger, Kennedy, Horwitz and Klare, united by radical 'sceptical realism' and committed to a 'frontal ideological assault' against traditional legal doctrine. Although many of its adherents are avowedly anti-Marxist and hostile to the legal theories which were prevalent in the Communist States, much of the writing produced by members of the CLS movement is difficult to comprehend save in the ideological context of neo-Marxist jurisprudence. Methodology, choice of 'targets', style of analysis and vocabulary of discourse associated with CLS have close affinities with the Marxism of Gramsci and Althusser. In some ways, as Dworkin implies, CLS can be considered as a direct descendant of American realism, but the movement is now pursuing a path which could not have been envisaged by the early realists such as Holmes and Llewellyn.

In essence, the CLS movement is characterised by a basic anti-liberal stance. The term 'liberal' was used by the earlier realists in a positive sense as referring to a legal system based on widely-accepted principles of freedom, tolerance, etc. For CLS writers it has a pejorative significance: 'liberalism' and its values are equated with a reactionary retrogression. Specifically, CLS rejects the liberal concern with 'rights'. 'Rights-talk' paralyses the will to action and induces a false sense of security which produces hallucination and passivity. Further, a concern with the struggle for rights 'exalts individual autonomy over communal needs'. In Kennedy's words: 'Exactly what people do not need is their *rights* ... It may be necessary to use the rights argument in the course of the political struggle in order to make gains. But the thing to be understood is the extent to which it is enervating to use it', In similar fashion, CLS rejects the desirability, even the possibility, of the rule of law. Horwitz suggests that it 'legitimates an adversarial and atomistic conception of human relations'. Critics such as Sparer have condemned this line of thought as being 'blind to the significance of legal protection for certain fundamental human rights' and as leading 'to a nihilistic perspective which can encourage repression and tyranny'.

CLS writers are highly critical of the 'liberal consensus view' of law. The early legal realists who favoured it are denounced by Unger for their failure to consider the 'basic terms of social life'. By extension, CLS questions the liberal reasoning which sees judges as neutral officials who adjudicate on the basis of compliance with a prescribed body of rules. The truth is, according to CLS, that the law, its theoretical spokesmen and judges, actively promote the interests of the dominant economic and social class. This instrumental view of the legal system is based almost precisely upon the writings of earlier Marxist jurists. A further objection to the liberal tradition in law is its reliance on social science. CLS writers emphasise that because social science is itself based on a justification of a particular kind of society, its influence upon legal doctrine is far from neutral. On several grounds, therefore, 'liberal jurisprudence' stands condemned: at best it is muddled, at worst it is a cloak for class interests.

It is possible, although not always easy, to discern within CLS writings a number of specific principles. It is argued that there is no 'comprehensive system' of legal doctrine which will cover every possible legal situation. So-called 'legal reasoning' which is claimed to be able to provide correct answers to legal problems is no more than 'the manipulation of abstract categories'. A second principle is 'contradiction'. It involves the rejection of 'a single, coherent view of human relations' and is an assertion of legal doctrine as mirroring a number of different views, none of which is dominant. The principle appears to be based on the Hegelian metaphysical doctrine which perceives in all phenomena a 'unity of opposites'. A contract, for example, is based, at one and the same time, on a recognition of the freedom to negotiate terms, and an acceptance of restrictions on the kind of terms which may be utilised. Freedom of contract is based, therefore, on the recognition of the necessity to limit that freedom. Dworkin speaks, in scathing terms, of the attempt of CLS to grasp a culture 'through the infertile metric of contradiction'.

The principle of 'opposition to formalism' is seen in the rejection of the alleged neutrality of legal reasoning. 'Conceptual formalism' is said, by some CLS writers, to stultify any serious attempt to understand the real basis of law because of its adoption of the view of law as 'standing above' political and social struggle. Law is objectively non-neutral and, therefore, legal institutions are non-neutral. CLS also supports arguments that law does not exert a decisive influence on social behaviour; at best it is a marginal factor only.

CLS appears to favour some of the teachings of the Italian Marxist, Gramsci, who had argued that one of the functions of the legal system in a capitalist society is to propagate an ideology which gives legitimacy to the activities of the ruling class. (Exploitation is presented as 'technological advance', and repression of minority views is sanctified as being 'in the interests of the majority'.) CLS historians, such as Horwitz, have interpreted the economic history of America in these terms, so that the advance of the doctrine of corporate personality is presented as a mask for the intensification of exploitation by bankers and industrialists. Formal jurisprudence which teaches acceptance of the status quo is condemned as aiding and abetting the process of 'legitimisation'.

It is not easy to outline any positive programme advocated by the CLS movement. Its writers eschew traditional politics, and 'practical objectives' of the movement are not made clear. The matter of social goals is hazy and vague. Thus, Singer speaks, in very general terms, of alleviating misery and changing the social conditions which produce loneliness. Frug advocates the granting of extensive powers to citizens enabling them to make rules for society. Kennedy argues for social and economic egalitarianism, suggesting equality of salaries, regardless of educational qualifications or difficulty of job. Unger is more specific: he calls for 'emancipation from background plans of social division or hierarchy', and outlines proposals for an institutional structure of a 'self-revising nature' that will give opportunities 'to disrupt any fixed structure of power and co-ordination in social life'. He urges the replacement of private control of property by 'market rights', allowing every individual the right to a share of 'social capital'. The means to these ends are not easy to discover in CLS writings.

It would seem, therefore, that the resemblance of CLS doctrine to that of earlier American legal realism, as mentioned by Dworkin, is slight. The realism of CLS is now moving in deliberate fashion away from the liberal-democratic jurisprudence formulated in earlier times. Some few points of similarity do remain, however. Scepticism characterises both schools of thought. CLS and American legal realism sought to demystify the law. Both show a concern to reveal the law as it really is - in action.

But the differences between CLS and its early progenitors are profound. The pragmatic concern of the legal realists in relation to law in action, ie, the work of the legislature and the courts, is of no interest to CLS. For CLS, what the courts do in practice is not to be analysed by reference to observation of judicial behaviour. A correct analysis requires an understanding of the underlying class structures and conflicts which emerge in the legal process of adjudication. Further, CLS stresses, in a way which the legal realists would have found unacceptable, the very close links between law and politics. In CLS terminology, *law is politics*. Hence the 'neutrality of the law', envisaged by the legal realists as a desirable goal for society and its legal institutions, is dismissed as a worthless (if not dangerous) illusion by the new realists. The sustained polemic against 'liberalism' which is a hallmark of CLS scholarship would have been incomprehensible to the earlier legal realists for whom the communal benefits of the 1930s New Deal and the later successful civil rights campaigns were vindications of the liberal-democratic outlook and its jurisprudence.

The methodology of the CLS movement, indebted in part to Hegelian and Marxist philosophies, epitomises the extent of the gulf between CLS and American legal realism. CLS is concerned to provide a theory which recognises the equivalence of law and politics and which will provide a mode of interpretation of legal phenomena so as to reveal class structural influences. This objective has marked off CLS jurisprudence from that of American legal realism. The social thought of Gramsci and the techniques of 'deconstruction' associated with Derrida, which seek to expose paradoxes and irreconcilable contradictions within legal thought, are a world away from the positive, investigative approach favoured by the legal realists. Relatively simple empiricism has given way to a complex analysis which results in what Dworkin describes as a 'leftist posture', and which owes much to a singular interpretation of, and borrowings from, disciplines such as semiotics and political science.

Altman praises the advances made by CLS analysts in their efforts to discover the conflicting doctrines which infuse contemporary legal thought. He praises them for having exposed doctrinal inconsistencies and incoherent beliefs by showing 'how debates in the political area are replicated in unsuspected corners of private law doctrine'. That the CLS movement has undermined the central ideas of contemporary jurisprudence, as has been claimed, and replaced the main principles of our legal thinking, is doubtful. That it has stimulated some contemporary jurists to a re-examination of their assumptions, is likely. That, as a result of its advances, it is ceasing to resemble the older school of American legal realism, particularly in the development of its modes of criticism and its analytical tools, is certain.

Notes

Kelman's *Guide to CLS* and Kramer's *Political Theory and Deconstruction* are valuable guides to the principles of the movement. Lloyd, ch 7, and Davies and Holdcroft, ch 16, consider CLS theory. Price makes an outstanding analysis of the CLS movement in 'Taking Rights Cynically: a Review of CLS' (1989) Cambridge LJ 271. Writings by members of the CLS movement include *Law in Modern Society*, by Unger, *The Transformation of American Law*, by Horwitz, and *Legal Education and the Reproduction of Hierarchy*, by Kennedy. An article by Altman, 'Legal Realism, Critical Legal Studies and Dworkin', which gives support to the CLS movement, is reprinted in *Philosophy of Law*, edited by Feinberg and Gross.

Rights

Introduction

In this chapter the questions concern problems arising from the concept of 'rights'. Some jurists have referred to jurisprudence as 'the science of rights', seeking to stress, presumably, the significance of human rights in any legal system and in any analysis of the purposes and functions of the law. The questions relate to Hohfeld (1879-1917), an American jurist who attempted to 'isolate' fundamental legal concepts so as to present them in a specific, unambiguous terminology, the contentious area of 'human rights', the basis of so-called 'natural justice', and the circumstances in which the overriding of individual rights might be justified.

Checklist

Ensure that you are acquainted with the following topics:

- jural relations
- opposites and correlatives
- basic, inalienable rights
- European Convention on Human Rights 1950

- natural justice
- *nemo judex in causa sua*
- *audi alteram partem*
- the overriding of rights

Question 45

'In any closely-reasoned problem, whether legal or non-legal, chameleon-hued words are a peril both to clear thought and lucid expression': Hohfeld.

How does Hohfeld's analysis of rights attempt to deal with this difficulty?

Answer plan

Hohfeld believed that the assumption that all legal relations may be reduced to 'rights' and 'duties' was a hindrance to an understanding of the law. Other basic relations (the 'fundamental jural relations') existed and required discussion and elucidation. Simple diagrams will assist in an answer to the question. The 'fundamental unity and harmony in the law', with which Hohfeld was concerned, would emerge, he claimed, from an examination of the relations between basic concepts. The following skeleton plan is used:

Introduction -Hohfeld's concern for precision in the description of functions and relations - the four rights - jural relations - opposites and correlatives - diagrams - criticism of Hohfeld - conclusion, Pound's reminder as to the importance of Hohfeld's analysis.

Answer

The question of 'rights' is fundamental to jurisprudence: attempts to answer the question: 'What *is* a right?' fall within *analytical* jurisprudence; the question of what rights people possess or *ought* to possess is a matter for *normative* jurisprudence. Hohfeld was concerned essentially with the analysis of rights. In his *Fundamental Legal Conceptions as Applied in Judicial Reasoning* (1919) he sought to deal with the inadequate assumption that all legal relations can be reduced to 'rights' and 'duties' and he attempted to free the discussion of rights from verbal ambiguities.

Hohfeld sought clarification of phrases, such as, 'X has a right'. The use of 'right' in the following examples is instructive. X, who loaned money to Y, has a *right* to be repaid. X, in his capacity as mortgagee, has a *right* of sale of the mortgaged property under the Law of Property Act 1925, s 101(1). X, accused of an offence, has a *right* to be presumed innocent until found guilty. Here the term 'right' takes on a colour (rather like a chameleon) which may change according to context. Hohfeld attempts to split up the concepts embodied in the term 'right' (in its wider sense) and to give them precise meanings by grouping them into 'jural opposites' and 'jural correlatives'.

Hohfeld analyses, in terms of *functions and relationships*, the terms he refers to as 'the lowest common denominators of the law'. These are right, duty, power, liability, privilege and immunity. A consideration of their relationships will help in lessening the effect of their ambiguities. Thus, the term 'right' involves four 'strictly fundamental legal relations' - 'right (or claim)', 'privilege', 'power' and 'immunity'. These terms are used by Hohfeld in a specialised sense that is at variance with popular usage - as in expressions such as, 'He has a *right* to his point of view', 'It is a *privilege* to be taught by X', 'They seized *power* in 1917', 'This drug gives *immunity* against ...'.

By 'right', Hohfeld has in mind 'a claim': everyone is under a duty to allow A to perform some action, and A has a *claim* to enforce his right of performance. B has a 'claim right' in his capacity as landlord to receive a stipulated rent from C; he may enforce that right against those who seek to prevent its exercise. By 'privilege' is meant E's freedom to do, or refrain from doing, some act (E 'may' perform an act, if he so desires). F, in his capacity as landlord, may - but need not - grant leases; in general, no one has a claim on him should he decide to exercise, or not to exercise, his privilege. By 'power', Hohfeld means that G has freedom to perform some act which may alter his and others' legal rights and duties, whether or not G has a claim or privilege. An example is G's power to sell his property. By 'immunity', Hohfeld refers to the relation of H to I when I has no legal power to affect one or more of the existing legal relations of H.

Hohfeld proceeds to construct and analyse a scheme of 'jural relations' based on 'opposites' and 'correlatives'. The term 'jural opposites' may be illustrated by 'right and no-right', or 'immunity and liability'. In Hohfeld's scheme, no pair of opposites can co-exist in the same person: thus, if P has a privilege in relation to the sale of his house, he cannot have a duty in relation to the same subject-matter at the same time. The 'jural opposites' are designated as 'right and no-right', 'privilege and duty', 'power and disability' and 'immunity and liability'.

The 'jural opposites' may be explained further. Should X have an enforceable claim to performance (action or forbearance) by Y, ie, a right, he is precluded from having a non-right in relation to Y concerning the same matter. Hohfeld speaks of non-right as a legal relationship involving a person on whose behalf society is not commanding some particular conduct or other. Where X has a privilege, eg, the right to sell or not to sell his property, that cannot co-exist with a duty (an act the opposite of which would constitute a legal wrong) to sell. Should X enjoy a power, ie, the freedom to alter legal relationships, he cannot be under a simultaneous disability which, in effect, forbids him to effect the alteration. Should X have an immunity as against Y, he cannot have a liability in relation to Y on the same matter at the same time. Hohfeld refers to 'disability' as the relationship of X to Y when, by no voluntary act of his own, can X extinguish one or more of the existing legal relations of Y. 'Liability' means, in his terms, 'the relation of X to Y where X may be brought into new legal relations by the voluntary act of Y'.

'Jural correlatives' may be illustrated by X's right against Y, whereby Y shall stay off X's land. The correlative of X's right is Y's duty not to enter. The correlative of X's privilege of entry is Y's 'no-right' that X shall not enter. Where X enjoys a power, the correlative is a liability. Where X possesses an immunity, the correlative is a disability. Each 'pair' of correlatives must exist as a related unity; hence, if X has one of the pair, some other person (eg, Y) must have the other. The 'pair' is an expression of the relation of X to Y and of Y to X.

Jural opposites and correlatives may be summarised thus:

Opposites	right	privilege	power	immunity
	no-right	duty	disability	liability
Correlatives	right	privilege	power	immunity
	duty	no-right	liability	disability

Jural relations may be illustrated by the following diagrams. Jural correlatives are connected by *vertical* arrows; opposites are connected by *diagonal* arrows; contradictories are connected by *horizontal* arrows. In the case of the correlatives, the diagram may be interpreted as indicating, eg, that a privilege in X implies the presence in Y of a no-right. In the case of the opposites, the diagram may be interpreted as showing, eg, that a duty in X implies the absence in X of a privilege.

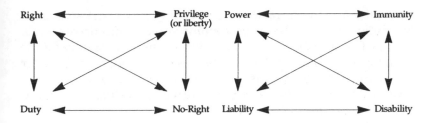

Hohfeld's aim of analysing rights so as to negate the influence of words that take colour from their context was generally applauded, but the resulting scheme did not meet with universal approval. Pound, for example, noting that Hohfeld's teacher was a celebrated exponent of Hegelian logic (which builds on 'opposites'), emphasises that the 'jural opposites' were often not 'opposites', but merely 'contrasts'. Hohfeld merely *contrasts* a power with the absence of a power, for example. He presupposes that there can be only *one* opposite and only *one* correlative and that there must exist an opposite and a correlative; but there may be several contrasts and sometimes *more than one* correlative. Further, says Pound, Hohfeld's scheme involves the discovery of opposites and correlatives whether or not they possess any legal significance; but, for example, a 'no-right' is not a legal concept of consequence.

Raz suggests that Hohfeld may have been in error in some matters. First, he appears to have considered all rights as sets of any number of the four elementary rights (right-claim, privilege, power, immunity). In fact, this is not so. To possess 'one right' may mean the possession of *other* rights, as where X possesses the fee simple in Blackacre, which gives him the right of possession, the right of alienation, the right to grant leases, etc. Ownership is, in practice, a 'bundle of rights'. Secondly, Raz comments on Hohfeld's apparent view of a right as involving a relationship between two persons, and no more. Yet this is incompatible with possession of a right *in rem* (against 'the world'). Nor, as Hohfeld appears to assume in his analysis, do all rights relate to persons only: X's right may be against a corporate body.

Criticism has arisen, too, from the attempted application of Hohfeld's analysis to the criminal law, where there are many examples of *duties* being imposed upon X, while no other specific individual has the correlative *right* relating to X's performance of his duties. Thus, a driver of a motor vehicle who drives while disqualified is in breach of a duty. But to whom is the duty owed? In whom is a correlative right vested? A general answer suggesting that the duty is owed to every person who may be a potential victim of the disqualified driver's conduct does not fit easily into Hohfeld's categories.

On another level, Hohfeld's analysis of rights has been criticised as no more than a mechanical exercise in logical analysis, involving an unusual terminology which has not found favour with jurists or practitioners. Hohfeld's expressed desire that judges and lawyers might be brought to a *use* of the terminology of his scheme has not come to pass. It may be that the very difficulty against which he warned - the chameleon-like quality of the vocabulary associated with 'rights' - clings to the terminology he has chosen to employ.

The positive features of Hohfeld's analysis should not be overlooked. His scheme has advanced our knowledge of concepts of 'rights' and 'duties', particularly through his specific comparisons. He has drawn attention to the legal circumstances which may flow from the existence or absence of defined rights, liabilities, etc. The practical effect of the analysis may be seen, for example, in the American Restatement of the Law of Property (1936), in which 'right', 'privilege', 'power', and 'immunity' are defined in Hohfeld's terms. Pound, in an article which is generally critical of Hohfeld, refers to the 'great service' he performed in bringing home to teachers, practitioners and judges the necessity to use caution in the employment of the conventional terms used in discussion concerning rights, and to realise that whatever we choose to call basic conceptions, they must be understood clearly. This is, to a large extent, what Hohfeld had in mind as the purpose of his analysis of rights in terms which would reduce significantly the deleterious effect of chameleon-hued words.

Notes

Hohfeld's analysis is reprinted in *Philosophy of Law*, edited by Feinberg and Gross. Lloyd, ch 6, Dias, ch 2, Harris, ch 7, contain accounts of the principles of the analysis. Radin's 'A Restatement of Hohfeld' appears in 51 Harv LR (1938). Criticisms of Hohfeld are made in Pound's 'Fifty Years of Jurisprudence' 50 Harv LR 557 (1937) and Raz's *The Concept of a Legal System*.

Question 46

'We hold these truths to be self-evident, that all men are created equal, that they are endowed by their Creator with certain inalienable rights, that among these are life, liberty, and the pursuit of happiness': The American Declaration of Independence, 1776.

What do you consider to be the basis of human rights?

Answer plan

The temptation to present a long catalogue of 'human rights' in answer to the question ought to be resisted. Attention should be given to the significance of the word 'basis' in the question. Reference ought to be made to examples of constitutional documents which seek to enshrine the recognition of human rights. A brief discussion of the European Convention would be valuable. The following skeleton plan is suggested:

Introduction -persistence of demands for certain fundamental rights - examples of 'essential freedoms and rights' - man's entitlement to rights - State recognition of human rights - ECHR - Canadian Charter of Rights - conclusion, enduring power of the call for human rights.

Answer

The concept of human rights has been enunciated throughout history in a wide variety of forms. In its essence, a demand for human rights is often capable of interpretation as a statement about human dignity, the basic freedoms needed so as to realise that dignity and the legal forms and practices considered necessary for the maintenance of those freedoms. A review of some of the many documents and law reports relating to human rights shows that certain freedoms - 'natural, fundamental entitlements' - are referred to repeatedly as characterising the prerequisites for human dignity. Rights of life, liberty of the person, freedom of expression, of conscience and creed are examples. In our time these rights have been assailed often, and the validity of their basis challenged repeatedly. The significance of the basis of human rights emerges in jurisprudential theory as resting largely on their being perceived as the foundations for human development.

In early articulations of the 'natural law', God's plan for humanity was often interpreted as giving rise to basic rights. The duties of the Decalogue ('Thou shalt not ...') in relation, for example, to abstaining from killing and stealing were held to imply rights to life and property. Respect for these rights became the basis for moral (and later, legal) duties. Locke, writing in the seventeenth century, saw man's 'natural state' as governed by a 'law of nature' which, if obeyed, would bring peace and preservation of mankind. That law bestowed rights to life, health, liberty and property. In the following century Rousseau wrote of man who was born free but was everywhere in chains. In 1791, the National Assembly of France declared that men are born free and equal in respect of their 'natural and imprescriptible rights' of liberty, property and security. In statements of this nature the basis of human rights is viewed in relation to a desirable state of liberty and individual development.

In 1776 the Constitution of Virginia made reference to certain 'inherent rights possessed by all people, because by nature they are equally free and independent'. Life, liberty, the means of acquiring and possessing property were among these rights, and men might not, by any compact, deprive their posterity of them. A century later, the judgment delivered in the American case, *Savings and Loan Association v Topeka* (1875), referred to rights 'beyond the control of the State', and noted that a government which did not recognise such rights was, in truth, a despotism. President Roosevelt, in 1941, in a statement which was echoed later in the Declaration of Rights adopted by the United Nations, referred to 'essential freedoms of speech, religion, and freedom from fear and want' as 'fundamental human rights'. In these and similar documents human rights are perceived as a means to desirable ends, and their basis appears to be their relevance for human freedom.

Stated more precisely, concepts of human rights often suggest that *man as man* is entitled *by his very nature* to certain inviolable rights, respect for which is a duty. Humanity is man's essence, or nature, and it is that nature which determines the quality of his basic rights. His race, religion, citizenship are generally matters of accident; they may determine the nature of his *social rights*. But his human nature, it is argued, is not accidental; it is this which vests in him *inalienable rights*. Couched in these wide terms, the entire concept of 'basic rights' has been criticised by jurists and others. It is argued, for example, that use of the word 'entitlement' begs the question. What is the *basis* of the 'entitlement', if that word is understood in its primary sense as suggesting the bestowing of rights? Which rights are to be considered as 'basic'? Why is the right to privacy, the right to a minimum standard of shelter, not always included in lists of basic rights? May one consider the right to life and liberty as inalienable in the face of demands by a government which has the 'inalienable duty' to protect its own citizens against internal and external threat?

There is the allied argument that rights of all types result only from decisions of the State, acting on behalf of the community, and aimed at the recognition and protection of certain types of interest. Interests will be converted into rights when the community and State recognise their vital significance. This may not be perceived immediately. Only when certain social and political conditions are appropriate will a community recognise, for example, the 'right to freedom of expression'. Further, a community may be committed to a general recognition of human rights, including, say, freedom of expression, but may feel the need to restrict rights in the interests of what is perceived as a more significant freedom. States have not yet resolved the apparent contradiction between proclaiming human rights and taking action against minorities who may seek to subvert authority in pursuance of their perception of legitimate demands. (Thus, in *Davis v Commonwealth of Australia* (1988), Brennan J recognised that 'it is of the essence of a free and mature nation that minorities are entitled to equality in the enjoyment of human rights'.) The argument that the call for 'inviolable human rights' is a demand for absolute freedom and, therefore, unrealistic, becomes, in some cases, an argument that the law itself must delineate the boundaries beyond which exercise of certain 'rights' may, in given circumstances, become intolerable. The concept of the inviolability of human rights, which presupposes the recognition of 'absolutes', must fade in the light of social necessities.

And yet modern social and legal development seems to proceed on the basis of the desirability of the maintenance and extension of freedom, seen in terms of human rights, as a prerequisite of overall human development. It seems to be recognised in growing measure that there are rights to which all human beings are entitled independently of their social and political relationships. The Charter of the United Nations (1945) affirmed faith in 'fundamental human rights, in the dignity and worth of the human person, in the equality of men and women and of nations large and small'. The Universal Declaration of Human Rights (1948) attempts a summation of the vital, traditional rights considered necessary for a civilised society: equality before the law, freedom of thought and religion, freedom of peaceful assembly, protection from arbitrary arrest, etc. The Constitution of the Federal Republic of Germany (1949), (drafted after consultation with jurists of many countries), begins with an article concerning the inviolability of certain 'inalienable human rights' and the inviolability of man's dignity, as the basis of peace and justice. 'Basic human rights' recognised by this Constitution include the right to liberty, freedom of faith, equality before the law.

The following cases, decided in recent years, are of particular interest in the context of human rights. *Roe v Wade* (1973), heard by the US Supreme Court, relating to the right to procure an abortion, produced a judgment which spoke of circumstances in which some 'fundamental rights' might be limited. The Court stated that the limitation of such rights may be justified *only* by 'a compelling State interest'. In *Firma Nold v EEC Commission* (1974), the Court of Justice of EC declared that fundamental rights form an integral part of the principles of law which the Court will enforce. But, the Court noted, the rights of individuals may be limited, although such limitations would have to be exercised with great care. The *substance of human rights* must not be impaired as a result of such limitations.

The European Convention on Human Rights (1950) (ECHR), to which the UK is a party, marks an important advance in the recognition of a category of basic human rights. It is of interest to note the pattern of these rights alongside the American Declaration of 1776. ECHR commences with a declaration of intention by the contracting parties that they will secure to everyone within their jurisdictions specified rights and freedoms. The right to life is protected, as is liberty and individual security. Torture, slavery and other degrading treatments of persons are outlawed. Freedom of religion and conscience is assured, as is the freedom of peaceful assembly. Discrimination on grounds of sex, race, colour, language, religion, is banned. The Fourth Protocol (1963) states that no person shall be deprived of his liberty merely on grounds of inability to fulfil a contractual obligation. The Sixth Protocol (1983), to which the UK is not a party, abolished the death penalty. Discussions leading to the ECHR included far-ranging examinations of what was meant by 'basic human rights'. There was general agreement on the need to recognise certain traditional rights as representing a *sine qua non* for a civilised society.

Yet another significant step in the direction of recognising and implementing 'basic human rights' is evident in the Canadian Charter of Rights and Freedoms, embodied within the Canada Act 1982. It commences with an intention to guarantee certain rights and freedoms, subject only to such reasonable limits prescribed by law 'as can be demonstrably justified in a free and democratic society'. Fundamental freedoms are listed as freedom of conscience, religion, thought, belief, opinion, and peaceful assembly. The right to life, liberty and security of the person and the right not to be deprived thereof except in accordance with the principles of fundamental justice, are recognised. The provisions of the Charter have resulted in some Canadian enactments being declared invalid. Thus, the Alberta Court of Appeal has ruled that the Lord's Day Act 1970, involving the observance of Sunday as a religious holy day, is invalid as infringing the guarantee of freedom of conscience and religion.

It may be that the concept of human rights is, according to some jurists, little more than a jurisprudential fiction. But the call for these rights has an enduring power. In Britain, the Parliamentary debates which preceded the enactment of the Race Relations Act 1965 and the Public Order Act 1986 testified to deep belief in, and a growing concern for, fundamental freedoms. Criticisms of the 'unverifiable nature of human rights' are indeed powerful, and the contradictory nature of some governmental actions when public order and freedom appear to be in peril has to be noted. But this does not reduce to nonsense the widely-held belief that in a free society individuals should be able to think and express their thoughts freely, to live their lives free from the fear of arbitrary arrest, and to garner and dispose freely of the produce of their labour. In Macdonald's words, 'It is by the observance of such conditions, I suggest, that human societies are distinguished from ant hills and beehives'. Current jurisprudential thought, and legislation, are marked increasingly by a concern for the basic human rights which exist in our type of society.

Notes

Bodenheimer, ch 3, and Lloyd, ch 3, discuss aspects of human rights. 'Natural Rights' by Macdonald, in *Philosophy, Politics and Society*, edited by Laslett, is a useful summary of problems concerning the interpretation of human rights. *The Rights of Peoples*, edited by Crawford, provides background material to the problems of rights.

Question 47

'The phrase "the requirements of natural justice" seems to be mesmerising people at the moment. This must, I think, be due to the apposition of the words "natural" and "justice". It has been pointed out many times that the word "natural" adds nothing except perhaps a hint of nostalgia for the good old days when nasty things did not happen': *per* Ormrod LJ in *Norwest Holt Ltd v Department of Trade* (1978).

Comment.

Answer plan

Lord Justice Ormrod is not alone in condemning what he sees as an empty phrase. Lord Shaw, in *LGB v Arlidge* (1915), considered the phrase to be 'high-sounding but harmless'. Lord Justice Scrutton, in *Holt v Markham* (1923), suggested that use of the phrase indicated 'well-meaning sloppiness of thought'. The continued use of the concept of natural justice, particularly in administrative law, has resulted in the phrase acquiring a clearly-understood content and significance. Relevant case law ought to be referred to in the answer and attention paid to the two maxims which have become fundamental to the interpretation of natural justice and the rights which it seeks to protect. The following skeleton plan is used:

> Introduction -concept of natural law in legal literature and cases - principles of right and wrong - concept and minimum standards in decision-making - administrative law and principles of *nemo judex* and *audi alteram partem* - procedural propriety - conclusion, significance of the phrase.

Answer

The comments of Ormrod LJ typify an important line of criticism of the doctrine of so-called natural justice. It has been rejected as 'mere verbiage', 'yet another synonym for natural law', 'a jurisprudential fiction' and 'a popular misnomer for proper dealing'. The phrase has appeared in the literature of the law including, the law reports, for centuries past. Thus, in *Thornborough v Baker* (1675), Lord Nottingham considered the mortgagee's interest in relation to 'natural justice and equity'. The doctrine of *actus non facit reum* was said, in *Fowler v Padget* (1798), to be 'a principle of natural justice'. Lord Blackburn, in *Dalton v Angus* (1881), held that prescription was not a law 'derived from natural justice'. The right to tack (in relation to mortgages) was held in *Union Bank of Scotland v National Bank of Scotland* (1886) to rest upon 'principles of natural justice'. *Valentini v Canali* (1889) involved the rejection of a minor's claim which, had it been allowed, would have been a 'violation of natural justice'.

In more recent times the phrase has taken on a more precise meaning related to its embodiment of rights. Tucker LJ referred in *Russell v Duke of Norfolk* (1949) to the 'requirements of natural justice' as dependent on the nature of the case and the rights being considered. Cooke J referred in *R v Gravesend Justices ex p Doodney* (1971) to the 'requirements of natural justice', suggesting that they were best considered on the basis of facts in individual cases. *Calvin v Carr* (1979) discussed an alleged failure to observe natural justice in proceedings before stewards of a racing club. *R v Parole Board ex p Wilson* (1992) considered natural justice in relation to the rights of a prisoner.

The term 'natural justice' seems to be used so as to reflect the concern of the courts with principles of 'right' and 'wrong'. There is an implication in the phrase, not of the immutable categories of the natural law, but rather, in a more prosaic sense, of the breaching of fundamental values which underpin concepts involving rights, eg, as in the case of mortgages, contracts, etc. Although the basic meaning of the term seems not to have been defined, its context generally suggests an indication of questions related to 'fair play', 'even-handedness' and 'individual rights'.

During this century the concept of natural justice seems to have been refined by the courts in the consideration of problems of administrative law in particular. The term is now employed not merely as a synonym for 'equitable dealings' but in contexts which suggest 'reasonableness', 'impartiality'. Fundamental to modern interpretations of the term is a general belief that natural justice suggests *minimum standards of rational and fair decision-making* which are expected from those who are under a duty to act judicially. The old view that these standards were expected from the courts only has disappeared, so that observation of the principles of natural justice is now demanded from *all* bodies and individuals who take decisions involving the rights of others in circumstances where procedures are subject to rules.

Some modern criticism of the use of the phrase has stemmed from the belief that the adjective 'natural' is misleading. It seeks to invest the phrase 'according to natural justice' with the solemnity and grandeur which attaches to the concept of 'natural law' - so runs one criticism. It affects to interpret justice as a manifestation of nature itself. Yet, as has been pointed out repeatedly, the nearer one moves to nature 'in the raw', the more one is made aware of the lack of anything which could be interpreted correctly as indicating the presence of 'justice'. Maugham J, in *Green v Blake* (1948), pointed out that use of the phrase 'natural justice' must not be taken to mean that there is any justice 'natural among men'; among savage peoples, there is rarely justice in our sense of that word. Indeed, modern field studies carried out by anthropologists do not support the poetic concept of 'the just savage'.

Modern administrative law has given 'natural justice' the status of a precise and powerful principle. A long series of cases has established that observance of the principles of natural justice, in relation to individual rights, involves a recognised standard of behaviour based upon two fundamental principles - *nemo judex in causa sua*, and *audi alteram partem*. It is now taken for granted that natural justice demands the presence of a thoroughly impartial judge, and that it necessitates parties to a hearing being allowed to present their point of view.

Nemo judex in causa sua is a shortened version of the maxim that a person ought not to be judge in his own cause. Originally this was interpreted as prohibiting a person from judging a case in which he was involved personally, but its significance has been extended so that it now refers to the necessity for a judge to be disinterested and totally impartial. Any suggestion of bias, actual or likely, of a general or specific nature, will suffice, if established, to cast doubt upon the validity of his judgment. In recent years the rule has been held to apply to *any* party, such as a departmental Minister, or his representative, who hears a case in which the Ministry is involved directly.

The rule is exemplified by *Metropolitan Properties v Lannon* (1969), where the chairman of a rent assessment committee belonged to a firm of solicitors which was negotiating rents with one of the parties to the proceedings; the committee's decision was set aside. Similarly, in *R v Altrincham Justices ex p Pennington* (1975), bias was established when a magistrate who was a member of an education committee heard the case concerning persons charged with delivering a short measure of goods to a local school. In general it seems to have been established that if a judge has, say, a pecuniary interest in the case he is barred from hearing it. If he has a non-pecuniary interest, such as a business connection, or a family relationship with one of the parties, he is disqualified from hearing the case. A real likelihood of bias, or even a reasonable suspicion of bias, will suffice. In the absence of such a rule there could be no guarantee that the rights of the parties to the hearing would be protected.

Audi alteram partem (hear the other side) is interpreted as a demand of natural justice that no person shall be condemned unheard. 'If the right to be heard is a real right which is worth anything, it must carry with it a right in the accused man to know the case which is made against him': *Kanda v Government of Malaya* (1962). Each party must be given an opportunity to state his view of the facts in issue. This applies irrespective of status, so that a prisoner, accused of participating in a prison riot, must be allowed to present his own case in subsequent disciplinary hearings. Thus, in *Ridge v Baldwin* (1964), the appellant, a chief constable, had been dismissed by the Watch Committee in pursuance of its statutory powers, but he was not given an opportunity of being heard in his own defence. The House of Lords held that the Watch Committee was in breach of the principles of natural justice. In *Malloch v Aberdeen Corporation* (1971), it was held that a schoolteacher 'dismissible at pleasure' had to be given a full opportunity to present his case before he was formally dismissed. In *R v Thames Magistrates ex p Polemis* (1974), it was held that the unreasonable refusal of an adjournment to enable defendant to prepare his case may amount to a denial of natural justice.

Natural justice appears, in the context of today's cases, to be virtually synonymous with *procedural propriety*. Where procedural requirements imposed by statute or common law are ignored, doubt may arise as to the validity of judgements. Case law seems to indicate that, in particular, judicial bias will invalidate a decision, as will failure to allow either party to have an opportunity 'of either defending or palliating his conduct'.

In *Council of Civil Service Unions v Minister for the Civil Service* (1985), Lord Roskill suggested that the phrase 'natural justice' be allowed to find a permanent resting place and be better replaced by speaking of a duty to act 'fairly'. This may be read as indicating that the ambiguities and misunderstandings attached to the phrase ought not to be allowed to continue. It may be that the phrase is so imprecise as to be misleading. It is unlikely, however, that the principles which are now seen as embodying 'natural justice' will lose their significance. Continued use of the phrase testifies, perhaps, to a deeply-rooted belief that a legal system which seeks to protect rights will fail in its purpose unless based upon the acceptance of the principle of even-handedness. As Lord Diplock pointed out, in *Maharaj v A-G of Trinidad and Tobago* (1978): 'The fundamental human right is not to a legal system that is infallible but to one that is fair'.

Notes

Natural Justice, by Jackson, discusses the issues involved in the concept. *The Lawful Rights of Mankind*, by Sieghart, deals with codes of human rights. *Law and Modern Society*, by Atiyah, and *Liberty, Law and Justice*, by Anderson, are of interest. Issues of natural justice in relation to administrative law are discussed by Bradley in *Constitutional and Administrative Law*.

Question 48

Consider the circumstances in which the overriding of individual rights might be justifiable.

Answer plan

Arguments concerning 'inviolable rights' generally turn upon the belief that they are of an *absolute nature*, a belief which presupposes that there are no circumstances whatsoever in which an interference with those rights may be justified. Natural law jurists may suggest that a God-given right, by its very nature, is not subject to any violation. Other jurists take the view that circumstances are bound to arise in which it becomes necessary to override rights, and this necessity is the basis for justification of the action. The answer should consider some of the circumstances in which legislators, judges and others might seek to justify an interference with human rights. The following skeleton answer is used:

Introduction -inviolability of rights - substantial and
procedural rights - restriction of rights in war and peace -
competing rights - other conflict situations - attitude of
Critical Legal Studies movement, and Rawls, to rights -
ECHR 1950 - conclusion, problem of absolute rights.

Answer

The argument examined below rests on the assumption that there
are circumstances in which it might be justifiable to override an
individual's rights. The circumstances generally refer expressly or
by implication to the existence of 'greater rights' to which
individual rights have to be subordinated. There are arguments
suggesting that there are *never* such circumstances, that
individual rights have a sanctity, a significance, a value-in-
themselves which render them inviolable and that if one ignores
the force of this argument, then the way is open to the wholesale
disregard and destruction of those rights. To accept this argument
is to close the debate before it begins. Thus, Finnis' enunciation of
'the right to life' as 'inviolable', which forms the basis of his
contribution to the discussion on abortion, weakens the
significance of that discussion. To pose the absolute nature of a
matter under discussion is to render controversy difficult.

A right may be described, in Allen's phrase, as 'the legally
guaranteed power to realise an interest'. Existence of the power is
recognised under the law and its exercise is based on a guarantee
by the law as to the acceptability of consequences. The rights of a
human being may be *substantial* (right to life, liberty) or merely
procedural (the right, in defined cases, to trial by jury, to silence,
resulting from exercise of the privilege against self-incrimination).
Because rights are underpinned in practice by a guarantee
bestowed by the law, it may be argued that, no matter what their
nature (substantial or procedural), they can be negated if the
guarantee ceases to apply. The repeal of a statute allowing certain
rights to be exercised effectively ends those rights.

Possibly the most significant of the circumstances in which
rights may be suspended or withdrawn arises during a period in
which the security, or even the continued existence, of the
community is perceived as under threat, as in time of war.

Legislation such as the Emergency Powers (Defence) Acts 1939-40, and the subsequent Defence Regulations, restricted some rights and imposed conditions considered appropriate for the defence of the realm. The power of a government to detain individuals, with its clear effect upon rights is not easily controlled by the courts. *Liversidge v Anderson* (1942) (which concerned the detention of an individual believed to be 'of hostile origin or association') emphasises that '... The liberty of the subject is a liberty controlled by law, whether common law or statute. It is, in Burke's words, a regulated freedom. It is not an abstract or absolute freedom ... In the constitution of this country there are no guaranteed or absolute rights'.

Where the government believes that, in time of peace, the untrammelled exercise of certain rights would be disadvantageous to internal security, those rights may be limited or removed. Thus, the Official Secrets Acts 1911-89 limit the rights of certain classes of persons to freedom of speech. *Council of Civil Service Unions v Minister for the Civil Service* (1985) justified a restriction upon the right to join a trade union of one's choice when the interests of national security could be interpreted as requiring this. Emergencies in time of peace, such as those arising in Northern Ireland, have produced restrictive legislation, ie, the Northern Ireland (Emergency Provisions) Act 1991, intended 'to make further provision for the preservation of the peace and the maintenance of order'. The Diplock Courts, which remove the right to jury trial in some cases in Northern Ireland, and limitations upon the right of free expression, as evidenced by the decision of the House of Lords in *Brind v Secretary of State for the Home Department* (1991), exemplify the circumstances in which the overriding of a right is considered justifiable.

Where individual rights are perceived as being in conflict with general 'communal rights', there may be little hesitation on the part of the government in overriding them. Some claims of the environment, for example, are held to be of greater significance than certain rights exercised by individuals. Thus, the Environmental Protection Act 1990 seeks to create an integrated system of pollution control which will restrict in considerable measure the rights of individuals engaged in the processes of production. Similarly, legislation aimed at restricting the right to sell tobacco in certain specified circumstances involves the overriding of some rights in the interests of other rights perceived as having wider communal significance.

In some cases the courts will not hesitate to override the rights of one individual where they are weighed against the competing rights of another and found wanting. 'Judging the superiority of rights' may be seen clearly in the determination of some kinds of dispute relating to real property, as where X claims a right of way over B's land, or C sues to enforce a covenant entered into by D. The so-called 'right of the adverse possessor', which arises from the general law of limitation of actions (see the Limitation Act 1980), may be considered by the court as overriding the claims of those who have 'slept on their rights'. The importance of land as a productive resource may be held to be of greater significance than the preservation of the rights of the 'paper owner'.

There are other 'conflict situations' - actual and potential - in which individual rights will bend before the overriding force of other rights. Thus, the Public Order Act 1986, s 4(1), interferes with the exercise of freedom of speech which results in threatening, abusive or insulting words causing individuals to fear that violence may be used against them. Indeed, the 'right to freedom of speech', if exercised by one person in a manner which robs another of his deserved reputation, may result in a tort. Bans on certain types of procession, on picketing a place of work under specified circumstances, exemplify the overriding of rights. The power of magistrates to bind over persons to keep the peace provides a further example of the suspension of some rights in the interests of a wider, communal right.

Statute and common law have created restrictions of the right to express one's views by the written word where questions of morality are thought to be involved. The Obscene Publications Acts 1959 and 1964, and the common law offence of blasphemy (see *R v Lemon* (1979)), have fettered the right of expression. It is in the vexed area of 'law and morality' that calls for an extension of the overriding of rights continue to be made. Some jurists have interpreted Lord Devlin's contribution to the debate on the Wolfenden Report (1957) as suggesting that, in the wider interests of that community (its 'moral health', and indeed, its continued existence as a group united by a common standard of morality), some types of sexual behaviour ought not to be tolerated. Devlin seems to have challenged the notion of an individual right being tolerated when, by its very nature, it is destructive of the individual and of the 'seamless web' of morality necessary for communal existence.

In recent years there has emerged in the USA a group of jurists who appear to be particularly concerned with the character and maintenance of individual rights. The Critical Legal Studies movement has engendered discussion on a variety of issues related to the question of the very existence of individual rights. The neo-Marxist wing of the movement stresses 'the good of society' as an overriding principle which must outweigh the calls for 'individual rights'. Within the society which seems to be the desired objective of the movement's jurists, communal welfare will be the ultimate goal, and that can exist only when the rights of the individual are seen as subservient to his duties. ('Man has no rights, only duties', as proclaimed by jurists, such as Duguit, in the last century.) Outside that movement, the American jurist, Rawls, calls for a redistribution of wealth in the interests of society as a whole, which means that individual property rights may have to give way to the overriding interest of ridding society of economic and social inequalities.

Dworkin has argued that individual rights are 'political trumps' held by individuals. They arise 'when a collective goal is *not* a sufficient justification for denying them what they desire as individuals, to have or to do, or not a sufficient justification for imposing a loss or injury on them'. He would allow the restriction of rights in two cases only: first, to protect another and more important right, and, secondly, to prevent a state of affairs which might spell disaster for the community's general interests. The significance of Dworkin's view may be in his belief that rights are *not* inviolable and that the community's overriding of these rights can be justified in the light of the importance of overall communal goals.

It is of interest to observe that the European Convention on Human Rights (1950) appears to recognise the difficulties inherent in postulating absolute rights. Thus, it states: 'No one shall be required to perform forced or compulsory labour'. But this is stated to have no reference to 'any service exacted in case of an emergency or calamity threatening the life or well-being of the community'. The 'right to manifest one's religion or beliefs' is subject to 'the limitations prescribed by law' which 'are necessary in a democratic society in the interests of public safety ... or for the protection of the rights and freedoms of others'. From the content of the Convention one may presume that the signatories accept that some rights (not to be subjected to torture, for example) are of an inviolable nature, but that others may be set aside in specified circumstances. The Constitution of Japan, promulgated in 1946, and drawn up with the assistance of Western jurists, states: 'These fundamental rights guaranteed to the people by this Constitution shall be conferred upon the people of this and future generations as eternal and inviolate rights ... The right of the people to life, liberty and the pursuit of happiness shall, to the extent that it does not interfere with the public welfare, be the supreme consideration in legislation and in other governmental affairs'. Here, again, is the statement of inviolability followed by qualification.

Individual rights recognised by governments as absolute, ie, inviolable in all circumstances, seem, in practice, to be very rare - and this in spite of the movement in jurisprudence against relativism and in favour of the supreme importance of 'basic rights'. Radbruch, for example, has argued forcefully against the denial of human rights in arbitrary fashion and, at a later period in his life, against the denial in any circumstances of certain individual rights. Finnis stresses the validity of the claim to some rights for *all* persons in *all* circumstances. There remains, nevertheless, an abiding question as to the *purposes*, if any, for which a government may interfere justifiably with individual liberties. This question, fundamental to political science, is of much importance for legal theory also, because our legal institutions provide the means by which restrictions on rights are imposed. It is likely, therefore, that jurists will continue to investigate the legal aspects of the tensions which must arise from attempts to balance the recognition and protection of individual interests against some demands of the State.

Notes

Dworkin's *Taking Rights Seriously* is a valuable exposition of individual and communal rights. *Human Rights*, edited by

Kamenka, discusses problems of the inviolability of rights. 'Freedom of Expression and Its Limits', by Feinberg, in *Philosophy of Law*, edited by Feinberg and Gross, considers the problem of the right to free expression. Part Five of De Smith's *Constitutional and Administrative Law* outlines the nature of civil rights and freedoms. *Civil Liberties: Cases and Materials*, edited by Bailey, includes useful source material relating to rights.

Law and Morality

Introduction

In this final chapter attention is drawn to the age-old question of the links between law and morality. Ought the law to reflect morality? Ought it to change as social morality changes? Ought the institutions of the law to be viewed as guardians of morality? The Wolfenden Report of 1957 precipitated an intensive debate on the law and sexual morality in which Hart and Devlin appeared as advocates of different attitudes to this problem. The moral implications of obeying a law which, because of its barbaric nature, may have forfeited the right to be described as 'law' were discussed in a debate between Hart and Fuller in relation to the Nazi legal regime. These matters form the basis of the two questions set out in this chapter.

Checklist

Ensure that you are acquainted with the following topics:

- the Wolfenden Report
- the 'seamless web of morality'
- the 'right-thinking man'
- governance of rules
- inner morality of the law

Question 49

In the discussion which followed the publication of the Wolfenden Report (1957) Devlin posed as a fundamental question: 'What is the connection between crime and sin and to what extent, if at all, should the criminal law of England concern itself with the enforcement of morals and punish sin or morality as such?'

How did Devlin answer this question, and what reactions did his answer elicit from Hart?

Answer plan

In the controversy which followed publication of the Wolfenden Report (1957), Devlin spoke for those who rejected its findings. His personal ground of opposition was the failure of the Report to justify the philosophy upon which it appeared to be based. In support of his opposition he raised the old problem of the relationship of crime, morality and the law. Hart sought to support the recommendations of the Report and in so doing attempted to expose some of Devlin's arguments as fallacious. The answer ought to concentrate on the essential features of Devlin's three questions and his answers, together with an outline of Hart's stand on the law-morality link as he perceives it to be. The following skeleton plan is used:

Introduction -background to the controversy - Devlin's interrogatories and answers - Hart's counter-arguments - summary of the debate - conclusion, the unresolved questions concerning the social significance of morality.

Answer

The Wolfenden Report on Homosexual Offences and Prostitution (1957) suggested the decriminalisation of specific homosexual acts between consenting adults in private, and stressed the significance of two particular principles. First: that the function of the criminal law, in the area with which the Report had been concerned, was to preserve public order and decency, to protect the public from that which was injurious or offensive and to safeguard the vulnerable against corruption and exploitation. Secondly: that there must remain a realm of private morality which is not the law's business (but to say this was not to condone in any way private immorality). Devlin criticised the thinking behind the Report; Hart supported the general proposals of the Report and sought to attack the principles upon which Devlin argued.

There are, said Devlin, certain moral principles which our society does require to be observed; their breach can be considered as an offence against society as a whole. The law does not punish *all* immorality; it does not condone *any* immorality. It becomes necessary to investigate the links between sin and the tasks of the criminal law. Devlin put three questions. The first asked whether a society had the right to pass judgment at all on matters of morals, and whether there ought to be a public morality, or whether morals should always be a matter for private judgment. The second question asked whether, if society has a right to pass a judgment, it may use the law to enforce it. The third question asked whether the weapon of the law should be used in all cases or only in some, and, if only in some, what principles should be kept in mind.

Devlin answered the first question with a resounding 'Yes'. The Report took for granted the existence of a public morality. If the bonds of that morality are relaxed too far, then members of society will drift apart. These bonds are a part of the 'price of society' and, because mankind has a need of society, the price must be paid.

The second question produced an uncompromising answer. A society *is* entitled to use the law in order to preserve its morality in precisely the same way that it uses the law to safeguard anything else considered essential to its existence. It is not possible, says Devlin, to set any theoretical limits to the government's power to legislate against immorality. A society has an undeniable right to legislate against internal and external dangers - the law of treason provides an example. The loosening of communal bonds may be a preliminary to total social disintegration and, therefore, a society should take steps to preserve its moral code.

The third question involves the circumstances in which a government ought to act in the event of a threatened disintegration of its moral basis. How may the moral judgments of society be ascertained? Devlin suggests that reference be made to the judgment of 'the right-minded man' (not to be confused with 'the reasonable man'). He may be thought of as 'the man in the jury box'. Let *his* judgment prevail and, for the purposes of the law, let immorality be thought of as what 'every right-minded man' considers to be immoral.

At this stage of his argument, Devlin refers to certain 'elastic principles' to be kept in mind by a legislature. First, there ought to be toleration of the maximum individual freedom consistent with society's integrity. Second, only that which lies 'beyond the limits of tolerance' ought to be punished; these limits will be reached when an activity creates disgust among 'right-minded persons'. Not everything can be tolerated, and disgust marks the point at which tolerance must be questioned. It should be remembered, too, that the limits of tolerance may shift from generation to generation. Third, privacy must be respected and this needs to be balanced against the need to enforce the law. Finally, the law is concerned with minima, not maxima; society should set its standards above those of the law.

Hart reacted by questioning the basis of Devlin's axioms. He was concerned, in particular with Devlin's implicit 'legal moralism' - the attempted prevention of conduct because it is perceived as immoral, even though it harms no person. Hart objected to Devlin's stress on 'intolerance, indignation and disgust' as marking the boundaries for tolerance. Hart reminds legislators that the popular limits of tolerance shift; they are not static for long periods of time. Devlin's concept of morality as a 'seamless web' which will collapse unless the community's vetoes are enforced by law is not accepted by Hart. He denies that breaches of morality will necessarily affect the integrity of society as a whole. Devlin's analogy which was drawn between the suppression of treason and the suppression of sexual immorality was 'quite absurd'. It was 'grotesque' to suggest that homosexual activity could lead to the destruction of society. To offend against one aspect of society's moral code is not necessarily to jeopardise its entire structure. Devlin ignores, according to Hart, the fact that there cannot be, logically, a sphere of 'private treason', but there is, undoubtedly, a sphere of 'private morality and immorality'.

Hart is moved to argue, further, that legal punishment which may follow on sexual misdemeanour may provide disproportionate personal misery. This must not be disregarded. Indeed, he claims, blackmail and other evil consequences of criminal punishment may outweigh the harm caused by the practices classified as sexual offences.

Hart's argument continues with a caution to legislators. Devlin's criterion for the 'immorality' of a sexual practice is, apparently, the disgust it produces in the mind of 'the right-thinking man'. Given this criterion, the legislator must ask himself certain questions. What is the *nature* of the general morality embraced by 'the right-thinking man'? Is it based in any way on ignorance, superstition or misunderstanding? Does that morality engender the misconception that deviants from its code are in some other ways dangerous to society? Is the weight of the misery attendant on punishment for homosexual offences well-understood? Hart concludes with a warning against 'populism' as an arbiter of how we should live. There is, he suggests, a danger of 'populism' in Devlin's reliance on the feelings of 'the right-minded man'; it should be resisted.

To summarise: Devlin sees the preservation of morality as vital to society's well-being; morality is very much more than mere integument, it expresses essential aspects of the bonds which serve to unify society; the law has an important, inescapable, role to fulfil in safeguarding society from attempts to shatter its shared morality. Hart does not accept Devlin's fundamental assumption that morality in its entirety forms a unique 'seamless web'; deviants from a conventional sexual morality are not necessarily antagonistic in other ways to society as a whole and its demands; there is always the danger of entrenching irrational and harmful prejudices in the guise of a legal stance designed to safeguard 'basic patterns' of morality. Devlin turns attention on society as a whole; Hart, on the individual. Devlin accentuates, therefore, the significance of a shared public morality and its maintenance; Hart underlines (as did the Wolfenden Report) the important distinction between public and private behaviour, public and private areas of morality, and reminds legislators that there is a private area which ought not to be the concern of the law.

The debate has not ended. Its preoccupations are revived particularly on those occasions upon which legislators make proposals relating to basic changes in the law in areas concerned with sexual behaviour. The debate which preceded the passing of the Sexual Offences Act 1967 (the provisions of which reflected the recommendations of the Wolfenden Report) was a reminder of the intensity of feeling which surrounds this area of the criminal law. Devlin's supporters continue to insist that 'the suppression of vice is as much the law's business as the suppression of subversive activities'. They are reminded by their opponents of Spinoza's warning, some three centuries ago, that: 'He who tries to fix and determine everything by law will inflame rather than correct the vices of the world'. Hart's supporters repeat his view that: 'To use coercion to maintain the moral *status quo* at any given point in history would be artificially to arrest the process which gives social institutions their value'. They are warned by opponents of the reminder of Holmes that a sound body of law must correspond with the community's actual feelings and demands. They are urged to remember that legal and moral rules 'are in a symbiotic relationship - people learn what is moral by observing what other people tend to enforce'.

Essentially, the debate turned on the *social significance of morality* and, in particular, on the importance for society of private reactions to a generally-accepted code of moral behaviour. But some jurists saw the debate as drawing attention to a deeper question for general jurisprudence, namely, how far legality ought to be considered simply in terms of *restraint*. Is it to be 'the whip of the animal trainer or the voice of conscience'? The path from the authoritarian 'must' to the autonomous 'ought' is tortuous. It is suggested that the principal value of the debate might reside in its insistent reminder that the concept of law as a means to an end demands continuous examination of that end.

Notes

The key texts in this area are Devlin's *The Enforcement of Morals*, Hart's *Immorality and Treason*, and *Law, Liberty and Morality*. The Wolfenden Report (Cmnd 1957) contains the precise recommendations which were discussed in the subsequent debate on law and morality. Riddall, ch 14, summarises the debate on enforcement of morality. Mitchell's *Law, Morality and Religion in a Secular Society* treats in detail some of the questions posed by Hart and Devlin. Lee's *Law and Morals* is a useful summary of the fundamental questions; it contains a bibliography relating to the problems.

Question 50

What was the occasion for, and the nature of, the Hart-Fuller debate?

Answer plan

What have the positivists and advocates of natural law to say to the suggestion that 'lawless law' must yield to justice? Or that there are circumstances in which law may be so debased that it cannot be dignified with the name 'law' and ought not to be obeyed? Or that there is an 'inner morality' which law ought to possess if it is to be respected? Hart and Fuller considered these questions in their debate. Their answers ought to be outlined, and attention should be given to the unusual circumstances from which the debate arose. The following skeleton plan is used:

Introduction -essence of the debate - Radbruch's point of view - The German case of the 'wife-informer' - Hart's reaction - Fuller's reply - further arguments - conclusion, unresolved issues.

Answer

The Hart-Fuller debate concerned the fundamental relationship between law and morality which emerges in a legal system. Such a system, if it is to work 'in just fashion', requires, according to Fuller, *a moral foundation.* Positivists, such as Hart, deny this. Hart insists that concepts of legal validity and moral values must remain discrete and disjunctive. Hart believes that a law does not shed its legal character merely because it is perceived as immoral; Fuller would deny the title 'law' to a legal system based on terror and the denial of human rights. The debate between Hart and Fuller was occasioned by Hart's interpretation of certain events in Germany during the immediate post-war period.

The debate received its initial impetus from an article by Hart in 1958 in which he commented on two legal matters which he saw as connected: the first concerned the 'conversion' of the German jurist, Radbruch, from 'legal relativism' to a doctrine close to natural law; the second concerned the trial of a war-time informer.

Radbruch had been a prominent advocate of 'legal relativism' - a doctrine which concentrated on the importance of 'legal certainty' in matters of dispute. The excesses of the Nazi regime convinced Radbruch of the need to stress the fact that some principles of law were stronger than *any* statutes, so that a law which conflicts with those principles should be considered as devoid of validity. A 'law' which denied individual freedom was 'absolutely false law', which must yield to 'justice'.

Radbruch's 'new' views found favour with the post-1945 German courts, anxious to remove the taint of the former regime. Hart saw the influence of these views in a remarkable trial in 1949, before a West German court, of a woman charged with having deprived a person illegally of his freedom. She had denounced her husband to the authorities during the war because of 'disloyal remarks' he had made, with the result that he was punished. Her defence was based on the 'legality' of her action, since her husband's behaviour had contravened a 1934 law which was valid at the time of the denunciation. She was found guilty, the court declaring that the particular law was contrary to the sense of justice of decent human beings.

Hart interpreted the decision as a blow against positivism and a triumph for natural law doctrine. He took issue with Radbruch's attitudes and their implications. Hart sympathised, of course, with the efforts of the German courts to remove all remnants of the former law, but he saw a dangerous confusion in Radbruch's new stance. For Hart, *the law is the law* and it remains the law even though it may not meet the demands of external moral criteria. A law may be so evil that it ought not to be obeyed, but that is a separate, though worthy and related, issue. It is, therefore, confusing to say of a law that, because it rests on immoral theories and results in vileness, it is not, therefore, the law. This is to obscure the real and difficult nature of the problem.

Fuller's response was swift and emphatic. The German courts had acted correctly. Law must have certain characteristics, the most important of which was an 'inner morality', which had to command respect. Remove that morality and there is no true legal system. The 'tinsel of legal form' which the Nazis used to disguise their brutalities had to be seen for what it was. Fuller stressed the total indifference to human rights characterised by the Nazi regime and said that this destroyed any claim by that legal system to respect. Fuller suggested that Hart had failed to recognise that under the Nazis *nothing* persisted that deserved the title of 'law'. Positivists, including Hart, seemed unable to give any coherent meaning to the moral obligation of 'fidelity to the law'.

Hart initiated the second round of the debate in 1961, with the publication of *The Concept of Law* in which he re-affirmed his position. It may be that a legal system ought to show some conformity with justice or morality, but it does not follow that the various criteria of legal validity must include, expressly or by implication, any references as such to justice or morality. *Law and morality are not interchangeable terms.* A rule of law may be morally iniquitous, but it is still the law; its validity may not be impugned on this ground alone. The important question of whether or not to obey an immoral law raises a different, but 'delicate and complex', moral issue.

In 1963, Fuller published *The Morality of Law* in which his opposition to Hart was expanded and intensified. He gave a more detailed exposition of the 'morality' which must characterise an acceptable legal system. Such a system will be concerned with subjecting human conduct to 'the governance of rules'. The 'external morality' of such a system will reflect ideals and aspirations, in particular the 'aspiration to legality'. The 'internal morality' of the law is effectively a 'procedural version' of natural law. It demands, first, that a system's rules of law be expressed in comprehensible fashion and that they be free from contradiction. They should be stated in terms of general applicability and, save on rare occasion, should be applied only prospectively. Impossible standards should not be enunciated and the rules should hold over a long period of time. Finally, the law must be, and must be seen to be, efficacious - there must be a visible consistency between its prescribed norms and the actions of those agencies committed to its enforcement.

Any significant departure from these principles of the law's 'inner morality' is, according to Fuller, an affront to the dignity of the human being as a responsible agent. How, then, ought we to react to a regime, such as the Nazis installed, which deliberately and overtly ignored the precepts of 'inner morality' when it chose to legislate? How ought individuals to behave when the legal system under which they live operates so as to debase and finally abandon all civilised forms of social order? What is to be done by members of a society in which large numbers are systematically robbed of their dignity, their citizenship and even their lives, under laws which are passed with formality?

Fuller's answer is simple, but its implications are far-reaching and highly-controversial. Law predicated on a fundamentally 'unjust' theory which results in obvious and widespread injustice is *no law at all*. The regime in question has forfeited the right to expect allegiance from its people. Even though the law be promulgated in traditional form and articulated according to the terms of a constitution, its lack of any 'internal morality' deprives it of the nature of true law. Questions of law and morality are, for Fuller, totally integrated. They must not be separated, particularly for the reasons advocated by positivists such as Hart. Precisely because law is a purposeful enterprise it must reflect society's ideas of right and wrong; that involves, inevitably, a direct link between law, legal institutions and concepts of moral behaviour.

To recapitulate briefly: Hart and Fuller were united by an abhorrence of the regime in question and both saw the urgent need to eradicate its remaining influence on German law and administration. They were separated, however, by fundamental disagreement on the relationship of law and morality. Hart insists that the immorality of a law cannot be used as the basis of a denial that it is, and will remain, law until repealed. Fuller will have none of this: where a law is clearly evil it loses the right to be called law. In particular where its theory and practice are founded on a denial of the premises of the 'inner morality of the law', which Fuller sets out, it is entitled to no respect since it is little more than evil masked by the traditional forms associated with a rational law.

Critics have drawn attention to what they perceived as an unsatisfactory debate. Terms were not agreed upon at the outset. Both parties ought, it has been suggested, to have agreed on the meanings to be attached to terms such as 'law', 'justice', 'morality'. This might have shortened the debate, but it would have clarified some essential matters of dispute. Are Hart and Fuller talking about the same concepts? It has been suggested, too, that there was almost no 'give or take' on either side and that the deep issues were not pursued. One critic stated that the discussion reminded him of 'a courteous and ritual exchange of shot, followed by a return of both parties to entrenched positions'.

Other critics have drawn attention to the difficulty of eliciting with any degree of precision any rules of conduct to be derived from the prescriptive theories of Hart and Fuller. Given Hart's separation of law and morality, how is a judge in a democratic society to react in practice when faced in the courts with a fundamental contradiction between his personal moral tenets and an apparently immoral law? Given Fuller's attitude to 'unjust law' what ought we to expect from minorities within the community whose members feel that they are suffering from unwarranted discrimination? What ought to be the attitude of legislators and jurists to the collection of a tax which is considered by significant numbers of individuals to be based on unjust principles? Although the debate was commended by many as 'an overdue foray by jurists into the real world', it is not always easy to deduce practical modes of behaviour from the points of view set out by Hart or Fuller.

The uncertainties which prompted the debate remain with us. Societies continue to exist and flourish even though based upon legal systems which are unjust and harsh. Respect for human dignity and freedom is absent from a number of regimes which boast complex legal institutions. Law and morality remain, in many societies, far apart. It may be that the lasting value of the debate will be its significance for discussions which seek to raise questions relating to the very purpose of law in society.

Notes

Riddall, ch 7, outlines the content of the debate. Dias, ch 27, comments on the nature of the issues. Outlines of the positions taken by Hart and Fuller appear in *The Concept of Law* and *The Morality of Law*. Radbruch's changed legal philosophy is reprinted in *Philosophy of Law*, edited by Feinberg and Gross.

Index